Welcome to Window

It doesn't matter how clever you are, how experienced, or how much information you naturally keep in your brain: you'll never know everything. When it comes to Windows 7, that certainly applies to me. I've been using Microsoft's newest operating system for close to two years, from beta to Service Pack 1, and every now and then I have to reach for my now dog-eared Ultimate Guide to Windows 7 to remind myself of information lost or teach myself something new.

The good news for that bedraggled guide is it can now go into retirement. This new, expanded edition contains even more information to reflect an operating system that's reaching maturity. Quite aside from a guide on how to install Service Pack 1, and how to find out whether it's been automatically installed already (see p30), this edition goes into even more depth on the areas that matter.

THE ESSENTIALS Take entertainment, to which we dedicate the whole of chapter seven. The past two years have seen the BBC iPlayer move from niche tool for techies to a household name, while the speed and stability of most people's broadband, and their wireless networks, have been boosted to such an extent that it's now feasible to download and broadcast high-definition movies around your home. We're even starting to see hardware that can make the whole process simple (see p114).

Security has also been beefed up, with Microsoft now offering its own malware-fighting software as a free download. Discover how to install it and keep it up to date on p130, and the advantages commercial security software still has to offer on p132.

Nor is this the only piece of new and free Microsoft software to appear. Its free-to-download Live Essentials suite now offers a compelling set of tools, from Movie Maker to blogging software to a rather nifty photo-editing tool. And just to show we're broad-minded enough to look outside the Microsoft world, we round up 14 more fantastic pieces of free software from p82 to p85.

PRACTICAL ADVICE These are just the highlights. What made this book's predecessor the best-selling guide to Windows of its kind is still here: the practical, step-by-step advice. The tips and tricks to help you get that little bit more from Windows.

In short, it's the guide to Windows 7 that Microsoft could never have written. It's independent, authoritative and sometimes just a little controversial. Enjoy, and let me know if there's anything you'd like to see in the next edition by emailing tim_danton@dennis.co.uk.

Tim Danton
Editor, Ultimate Guide to Windows 7
tim_danton@dennis.co.uk

Contents

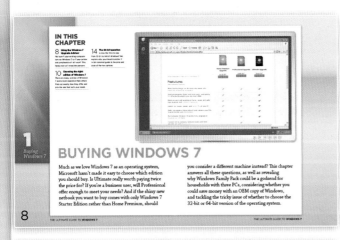

BUYING WINDOWS 7

Much as we love Windows 7 as an operating system, Microsoft hasn't made it easy to choose which edition you should buy. Is Ultimate really worth paying twice the price for? If you're a business user, will Professional offer enough to meet your needs? And if the shiny new netbook you want to buy comes with only Windows 7 Starter Edition rather than Home Premium, should you consider a different machine instead? This chapter answers all these questions, as well as revealing why Windows Family Pack could be a godsend for households with three PCs, considering whether you could save money with an OEM copy of Windows, and tackling the tricky issue of whether to choose the 32-bit or 64-bit version of the operating system.

INSTALLING WINDOWS 7

Windows 7's install process is a huge improvement on previous efforts. Gone are XP's ugly, intimidating text boxes and Vista's need for user input again and again throughout the process. Instead, Windows 7 asks you what you want up front, then goes away and takes care of everything itself. In this chapter, we guide you through the different install options available: either upgrade directly from Vista, replace your existing system with a clean install of Windows 7, or create a dual-boot setup in which you can continue to use your old Windows as well. Whichever you choose, it's easy to move the important files from your existing PC. Later, we'll also investigate the new option of installing Windows on a virtual disk: see page 60.

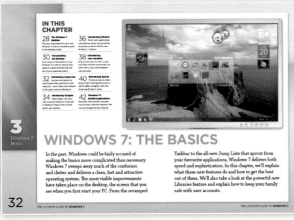

WINDOWS 7: THE BASICS

In the past, Windows could be fairly accused of making the basics more complicated than necessary. Windows 7 sweeps away much of the confusion and clutter and delivers a clean, fast and attractive operating system. The most visible improvements have taken place on the desktop, the screen that you see when you first start your PC. From the revamped Taskbar to the all-new Jump Lists that sprout from your favourite applications, Windows 7 delivers both speed and sophistication. In this chapter, we'll explain what these new features do and how to get the best out of them. We'll also take a look at the powerful new Libraries feature and explain how to keep your family safe with user accounts.

ADVANCED FEATURES

We've now covered the basics of Windows 7, but there's much more to it than a few tweaks. With just a little technical know-how, you can create virtual hard disks (and even install Windows 7 directly onto one), calibrate your monitor so that it displays colours more accurately, and speed up your day-to-day work in Windows with our pick of its keyboard shortcuts. We'll also reveal what the enhanced Aero interface has to offer, and it goes way beyond glossy effects – from shaking a window so that the others fall away, to instantly tiling windows and moving them between screens. And you'll discover exactly why so many people are getting excited about the new touchscreen technology built into Windows 7.

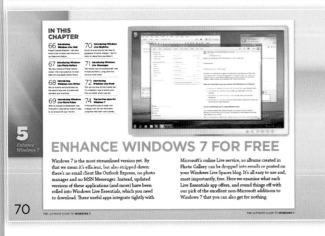

ENHANCE WINDOWS 7 FOR FREE

Windows 7 is the most streamlined version yet. By that we mean it's efficient, but also stripped-down: there's no email client like Outlook Express, no photo manager and no MSN Messenger. Instead, updated versions of these applications (and more) have been rolled into Windows Live Essentials, which you need to download. These useful apps integrate tightly with Microsoft's online Live service, so albums created in Photo Gallery can be dropped into emails or posted on your Windows Live Spaces blog. It's all easy to use and, most importantly, free. Here we examine what each Live Essentials app offers, and round things off with our pick of the excellent non-Microsoft additions to Windows 7 that you can also get for nothing.

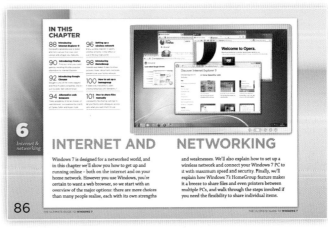

INTERNET AND NETWORKING

Windows 7 is designed for a networked world, and in this chapter we'll show you how to get up and running online – both on the internet and on your home network. However you use Windows, you're certain to want a web browser, so we start with an overview of the major options: there are more choices than many people realise, each with its own strengths and weaknesses. We'll also explain how to set up a wireless network and connect your Windows 7 PC to it with maximum speed and security. Finally, we'll explain how Windows 7's HomeGroup feature makes it a breeze to share files and even printers between multiple PCs, and walk through the steps involved if you need the flexibility to share individual items.

pct⚙⚙ls

Start your engines. Stop online threats.

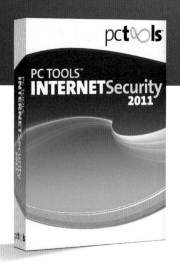

PC Tools™ Internet Security 2011 delivers our most advanced protection ever.

Win the race against cybercrime. PC Tools defends your online identity with multiple layers of hardworking protection. Plus, it's faster than traditional antivirus products, so it won't slow you down. That's why we're an official sponsor of World Series by Renault 2011, Europe's premier racing series. Pull in for a pit stop and you could WIN the ultimate race getaway. Learn more at **pctools.com/wsr**

Proud to be an official partner of the World Series by Renault 2011

built sharp. made simple.

Contents

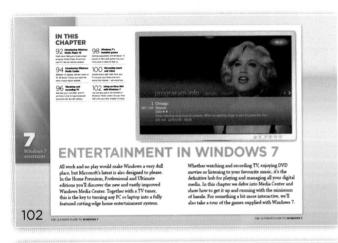

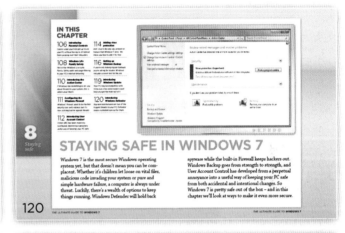

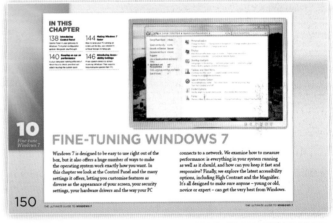

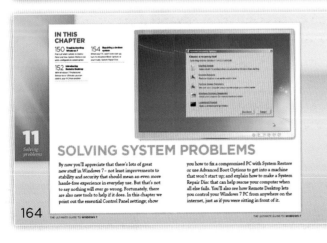

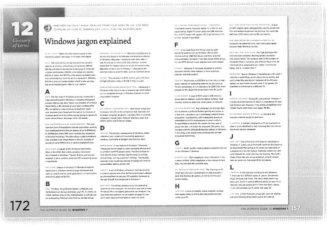

Seven reasons to up

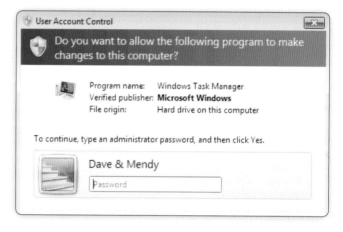

FAQ

Q: Is there any reason not to upgrade to Windows 7?

A: For most people there's no reason at all – the benefits over Windows XP are huge. Even if you're currently using Windows Vista, you'll find Windows 7 is slicker and more responsive. However, there are a few old programs and peripherals that will only work in Windows XP, so before you upgrade it's a good idea to run the Upgrade Advisor (see p10). If you do find something isn't compatible, all is not necessarily lost, however, as you may be able to use it in XP Mode – see p56.

to its design, which emphasises ease of use. Impressively, Windows 7 is actually more responsive than Windows Vista, its predecessor. When that version of Windows was released, some felt its new features caused the operating system to feel slow – but in Windows 7 those concerns are a thing of the past. So it's a great upgrade even if your PC isn't the most powerful computer in the world.

NEW TASKBAR Windows 7 brings plenty of new features that make it easier than ever to get at your programs and files – and the new taskbar is one you'll use every day. Gone are the endless tabs of older editions of Windows, replaced by an attractive and intuitive graphical display. You can launch applications with a single click, and see what's running at a glance. The new taskbar has some advanced tricks up its sleeve too, such as Aero Peek: hover over the icon of a running program and you'll see live previews of all of its open windows, making it easy to jump straight to the document you're looking for. Jump Lists let you control programs and open files directly from the taskbar. It's all designed to help you get things done more quickly and efficiently than ever. See chapter 3 for our guide to using the new Windows 7 interface.

PEAK PERFORMANCE Windows 7 is a sophisticated operating system, with an incredible wealth of features. Yet it still feels nimble and responsive, even when running on hardware that's a few years old. That's a testament

SOUND SECURITY Windows 7 is designed for the internet age, and that means keeping you safe. User Account Control, first seen in Windows Vista, has been improved so as to alert you before anything untoward happens on your PC – without constantly bugging you. The integrated Firewall keeps you safe from online attacks. Windows 7 also comes with access to a great selection of free applications: Microsoft Security Essentials is a fully-featured antivirus program that can prevent malicious software from messing with your system, while Windows Live Family Safety ensures your children aren't exposing themselves to inappropriate content on the web – nor exposing your computer to potentially dangerous websites. Familiar features such as System Restore are still here too, so you can easily rescue your system if disaster does strike. See chapter 8 for our guide to staying safe in Windows 7.

grade to Windows 7

WINDOWS YOUR WAY Windows 7 is not only powerful – it's flexible too. It's easy to customise almost every aspect of the operating system, from your desktop wallpaper and sounds to the way colours and text appear on your monitor and the way you connect to networks. Themes make it easy to apply a coherent look to your desktop, including high-quality photographic backgrounds and complementary colour schemes. You can also easily create separate user accounts for different people, so everyone can have their own personal Windows 7 experience. All through this MagBook, we'll show you ways to personalise Windows 7's many features to suit the way you work and play – but see chapters 3, 4 and 10 in particular for our guide to the numerous options at hand, and a guide to Windows 7's extensive Control Panel.

LIBRARIES Libraries are a new feature in Windows 7, but once you've tried them you'll wonder how we got by without them for so long. Simply put, Libraries collect all your files of various types together into one virtual folder – even if, in reality, they're spread across lots of different locations on your disks, or across a network. It's a great way to manage your files, and it also makes it easy to add extra storage to your PC in future: no longer do you have to mess around moving files back and forth. Simply add a new drive, add it to your library and go. Why can't everything be so simple?

THE LITTLE THINGS Windows 7 comes with lots of tiny touches that make everything just a little more enjoyable. The interface is filled with shortcuts and helpful features, so you rarely feel lost. Gadgets present information in a fun and attractive way. And the applications that accompany Windows 7 – whether preinstalled or bundled with the Windows Live Essentials pack – provide an easy way to work with pictures and video, keep in touch with your friends and more. See chapters 4 and 5 to see all the ways Windows 7 makes life a little nicer.

ENTERTAINMENT Windows has long been focused on entertainment, and Windows 7 brings a range of updates that make it ideal as a personal entertainment centre. The jewel in the crown is Windows Media Center, which can now act as a hub for Freeview and satellite services, even in high-definition. Windows Media Player has been upgraded too, with new streaming features so you don't need to keep your PC in the front room to enjoy your media on the big screen. In chapter 7 we'll show you all the reasons why Windows 7 is the most entertaining edition yet.

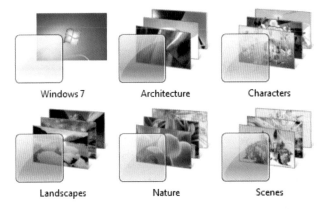

Windows 7   Architecture   Characters

Landscapes   Nature   Scenes

IN THIS CHAPTER

1
Buying Windows 7

BUYING WINDOW

Windows 7 is Microsoft's easiest-to-use operating system yet – but there are some important questions to consider before you take the plunge. If you're upgrading an existing computer, you need to be sure the hardware is compatible. Even if you're buying a new PC, you'll need to decide which edition of Windows 7 you want: Microsoft offers a whole range, from the netbook-

S 7

friendly Starter edition right up to the feature-laden Ultimate. In this chapter we show you how to make the right choice, and reveal some potential ways to save money on your Windows licence. We also explain the difference between 32-bit and 64-bit Windows, and show you how to connect your PC to the latest Windows Phone 7 smartphones.

HOW LONG?
Shouldn't take more than ten minutes, including the download.

HOW HARD?
This quick and simple process is just about the easiest thing to do in this book.

HOW TO...
USE UPGRADE ADVISOR

If you want to upgrade an existing PC to Windows 7, you'll need to check the hardware is compatible. Enter the free Windows 7 Upgrade Advisor tool.

Windows 7 runs snappily even on low-powered machines, so there's no reason why you shouldn't consider installing it on a PC that's currently running Windows Vista, or even Windows XP. But before shelling out for the upgrade, it's a good idea to double-check that your computer is powerful enough to provide a satisfactory Windows 7 experience. You should consider peripherals too: a ten-year-old laser printer might have drivers that work fine in XP, but will it cope with Windows 7? And how about your scanner or fax?

To answer those questions you could spend ages poring over manufacturers' websites, but there's a much easier solution: the Windows 7 Upgrade Advisor. This is a simple software tool that you can download for free from Microsoft's website. It analyses your system, looks for weaknesses and problems with incompatibility, and warns you about any potential issues before you take the plunge and purchase Windows 7. We'd advise you to run it now.

 DOWNLOAD THE ADVISOR The Microsoft website is a crowded place, and it may not be immediately apparent where to get the Advisor. The easiest way to find it is to search with Google or Bing: enter "windows 7 upgrade advisor" and you'll find the download page near the top of the results list. Double-check that the linked page is within the microsoft.com site before clicking it.

 INSTALL THE SOFTWARE Once you're on the right page, click the button labelled "Download the Windows 7 Upgrade Advisor", then click the "Download" button on the following page. Save the file to a convenient location on your hard disk – it's a small file, so even on a sluggish connection it shouldn't only take a few minutes to arrive. Once the file's downloaded, double-click on its icon to launch the installer, select "I accept the license terms" and click the "Install" button. The installation only takes a few seconds, and you'll be notified when it's complete.

③ **FIRE IT UP** There should now be an icon for the Upgrade Advisor on your desktop. You can also access it from the Start menu: in Vista, click the Start orb and select All Programs, and you'll find the Advisor has been added to your list of applications. In XP, you'll find it in a similar location: click Start, then Program Files, and again you'll find it in the main part of this directory.

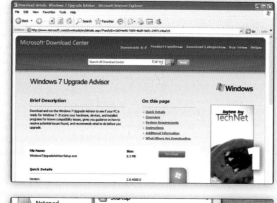

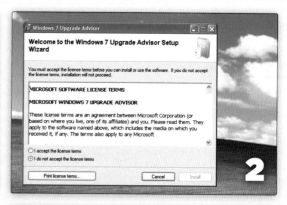

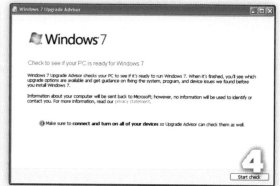

HOOK UP PERIPHERALS Before you launch the Windows Upgrade Advisor, make sure you've plugged in all of the peripherals you use on a regular basis. You want the utility to assess all of your hardware accessories, in addition to your computer's internal components, to check that they'll work in Windows 7. We're not just talking about printers and scanners here: it's best to hook up everything, including mobile phones, MP3 players, external hard disks, digital cameras, scanners, graphics tablets and so on.

 RUN THE ADVISOR When the application window appears, click the "Start check" button in the bottom right-hand corner. Upgrade Advisor will then go off and have a rummage around in your system to ensure it's up to the job of running the new operating system. The process will likely take a few minutes; the older your PC and the more accessories you have attached, the longer it will take, so be patient.

 UPGRADE INFORMATION The next screen presents a summary of potential issues with your PC and confirms which programs and devices are compatible with Windows 7. You'll probably have to scroll down to read it all. In our example we're using a Windows XP system, so the Advisor warns us that we'll need to perform a Custom installation of Windows 7. This isn't quite as straightforward as an upgrade, but it's still easy to do,

and you can keep your existing files and settings if you wish – we show you how on p24. The Advisor also warns us that Outlook Express, the Windows XP email program, isn't included in Windows 7. That's fine, because it's been replaced by the superior Windows Live Mail, as we discuss on p72. At the top of the report you'll see two tabs, labelled "32-bit report" and "64-bit report". Click between these to see what specific issues you might encounter with a 64-bit edition of Windows 7, rather than a 32-bit one – see p13 for our advice on choosing which to install.

 DETAILED REPORTS Scattered around the Advisor's report, you'll see various links in blue which you can click on for more detailed information about the programs and devices in your system. In our example we've clicked for more information about the hardware devices in our system. The Upgrade Advisor shows us all the devices it detected, and gives details of each one's compatibility with Windows 7.

 THE COMPATIBILITY CENTER If there's anything you're still not sure about, follow the Upgrade Advisor's link to the Windows 7 Compatibility Center. Here you can browse a huge database of programs and hardware devices new and old, and check their compatibility. It's a handy resource if there's a program or device you might need to use in the future – or if you simply forgot to plug something in while running the Advisor.

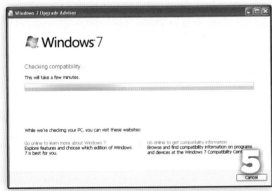

THE NUMEROUS VERSIONS OF WINDOWS 7 MAY SEEM CONFUSING, BUT A
LITTLE RESEARCH WILL REVEAL WHICH IS THE PERFECT EDITION FOR YOU.

Choosing the right edition

Back in the days of Windows XP there were only two editions of the operating system to choose between, namely XP Home and XP Professional. With Windows Vista, this number ballooned to take in seven different editions. Now, Windows 7 comes in six varieties: Starter, Home Basic, Home Premium, Professional, Enterprise and Ultimate, each offering a different combination of features and capabilities.

It's a confusing situation, but you don't have to wade through the pros and cons of all six editions to find the right OS for you. Windows 7 Home Basic can be discounted right away, as it isn't sold in the UK (it's only for emerging markets). The Enterprise edition is functionally the same as Ultimate, but it's restricted to businesses that sign up to a corporate licensing scheme.

That leaves four editions which you're likely to see on the market. Windows 7 Starter, the most cut-down edition, typically comes preinstalled on low-power netbooks, and isn't sold separately. The Home Premium, Professional and Ultimate editions are better suited to more powerful PCs and notebooks, and you can buy them either preinstalled on a new PC, or as standalone software packages to install yourself.

RETAIL OR UPGRADE? If you already own a PC running Windows XP or Vista, you can buy a Windows 7 upgrade pack for a lower price than the full retail version. That's the theory, at least – but since there's more demand for full retail packages, you may find retailers offering discounts that make it more cost effective to go via that route. It pays to shop around, because you can use the retail version to perform upgrades; you don't need the upgrade edition.

Equally, it's perfectly possible to perform a clean install of Windows 7 on your PC using the upgrade version. Both editions give you the full set of installation options, which we cover in chapter 2. The only difference is that when you install from an upgrade pack you'll be required to prove that your existing installation of Windows XP or Vista is genuine. That's easily done by booting into XP or Vista as usual, inserting the Windows 7 DVD and installing the new operating system from there.

GOING OEM All editions of Windows 7 are available in both retail and OEM packages. OEM stands for "original equipment manufacturer", and these packages are intended for sale to PC makers, for preinstallation on new machines.

FAQ

Q: I've seen Windows 7 on sale with a letter "N" after the name of the edition – what does this mean?

A: The "N" editions of Windows 7 exist to satisfy certain legal requirements. They don't include Windows Media Player, Media Center or DVD Maker, yet they cost the same as the regular editions. Whichever version of Windows 7 you choose, we suggest you avoid "N" packages and pick a fully-featured edition.

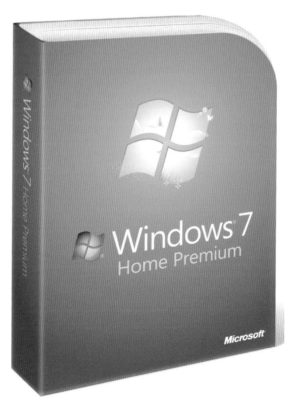

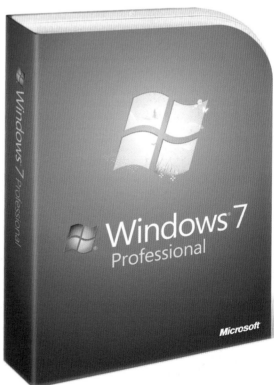

The Windows 7 Family Pack could save you a packet if you need to upgrade three different computers from earlier versions of Windows.

But there's nothing to stop you buying an OEM package for your personal use – many retailers sell OEM editions of Windows at low prices.

Going via this route has its drawbacks, though. OEM packages come with no manual or even any installation instructions, and if you run into difficulties down the line, you won't be entitled to technical support from Microsoft. What's more, OEM licences are only valid for the first PC they're installed on – so if you buy a new computer in a few months' time, you won't legally be able to transfer your OEM copy of Windows 7 onto it.

You'll also need to decide in advance whether you need the 32-bit or 64-bit version of Windows 7 (see box, below right). Windows 7 retail packages include both versions, but OEM packages contain only one or the other.

If you're confident with computers, going the OEM route can certainly save you money. But in many cases it could be a false economy.

FAMILY PACK For anyone upgrading multiple PCs at once, it's worth considering Microsoft's Family Pack for Windows 7. This is a deal that makes it cheap and easy for a whole household to get onto Windows 7 – an idea that makes a lot of sense when so many of the new features (such as HomeGroup, featured on p98) are aimed at homes with multiple PCs all running Windows 7.

The Family Pack only allows you to upgrade three PCs running previous editions of Windows to Windows 7 Home Premium. There's no support for other editions, or for different numbers of computers. But if it suits your needs, it's good value: the price of £150 is significantly less than you'd pay for three separate upgrade licences.

STARTER If you're shopping for a netbook, the odds are it will come with the stripped-down Windows 7 Starter edition. This edition will run all the same applications as the "mainstream" editions, but many of the multimedia features and cosmetic fripperies have been cut out.

For example, you can't run multiple monitors from a Windows 7 Starter PC; nor can you stream music from a Starter edition system to other computers on your network. There are no see-through windows (Aero Glass themes), no Taskbar preview feature, and you can't even change the desktop background. ▶

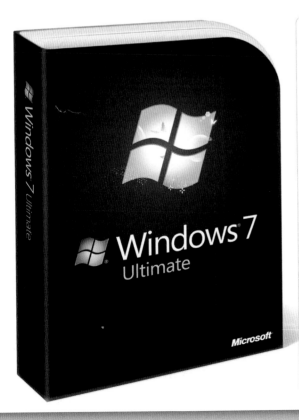

The 64-bit question

Every Windows 7 retail pack contains two discs: one to install a 32-bit version of Windows 7 and one for a 64-bit version. Each has its strengths and weaknesses, so the choice depends on your priorities and preferences. The 32-bit version will be more compatible with older software and hardware: practically every program of the past decade will work in 32-bit Windows 7, as will most peripherals. But 32-bit Windows can only use a maximum of 4GB of RAM, limiting your scope to upgrade your PC in the future.

64-bit editions let you install much more RAM (see table, over), and should also be slightly faster and more stable. For those reasons, most new PCs come preinstalled with the 64-bit edition – except for netbooks, as Windows 7 Starter is only offered in 32-bit flavour.

However, a small number of older programs, such as classic games, system tools and business applications, may not work on 64-bit Windows. And hardware compatibility is a consideration too. Some ageing computers don't have the advanced processor features required by 64-bit Windows, and older peripherals (such as sound cards and scanners) may lack 64-bit drivers, meaning they'll only work in 32-bit versions of the operating system. Before installing, we suggest you use the Windows 7 Upgrade Advisor to analyse your hardware (see p10), and check manufacturers' websites for 64-bit driver updates.

You should also note that you can't perform an "in-place" upgrade to 64-bit Windows 7 – not unless you already have a 64-bit version of XP or Vista installed on your PC, which isn't usual. You'll probably have to perform a clean install instead, but this needn't be painful (as we explain on p24) and you won't lose your personal documents and data.

1

Buying Windows 7

Considering how attractive and versatile the other editions of Windows 7 are, Starter is a little disappointing. If you have the choice of which edition of Windows comes preinstalled on your new notebook, we suggest you opt for Home Premium instead. If you don't have that option, you can always buy the machine with Starter, then use the Anytime Upgrade system (see box, below) to perform an "in-place" upgrade from Starter to Home Premium.

HOME PREMIUM Home Premium is the version of Windows 7 that's best suited to home users. It contains new tools and options that will appeal to anyone who uses their PC for entertainment. The star of the show is the latest version of Windows Media Center (see p108). This can turn your PC into a full-screen entertainment system, complete with video on demand and TV recording capabilities if your computer's equipped with a TV tuner. The whole thing can be controlled with a remote from the comfort of your sofa, or connected to a Media Center Extender, such as the Xbox 360, so your PC can be your home's entertainment hub.

Media Player, now in version 12, is much improved too. It's a superb way to control a large music and video collection, thanks to an intuitive interface and media-streaming abilities: see p104 for our in-depth review.

The Windows Aero interface, only partially supported in Windows 7 Starter, is fully installed in Home Premium – and it doesn't just look pretty but makes your computer more intuitive. As we'll show you in chapters 3 and 4, it's packed with little touches for managing windows and applications. If you're fortunate enough to have a touchscreen PC, you can also make use of a full roster of multitouch features, adding a new dimension to Windows' usability.

Home Premium will suit most users perfectly, but it lacks some of Windows 7's most advanced features. There's no BitLocker disk encryption (see p148), no Remote Desktop (p168) and no Windows XP Mode (p56). The Backup and Restore Center is also restricted to local hard disk or DVD backups, rather than offering the full versatility available with more advanced editions. So power users, professionals and tweakers should consider paying the extra for Windows 7 Professional or Ultimate.

PROFESSIONAL As its name suggests, Windows 7 Professional is primarily targeted at businesses, but its powerful new features will also appeal to advanced users looking for more versatility than Home Premium offers.

For a start, it comes with an enhanced version of Backup and Restore Center that allows you to back up both personal and system files and to schedule backups (the version included in Home Premium only allows for manual backup of

Windows Anytime Upgrade

What can you do if you want Home Premium, but your chosen system is offered only with Windows 7 Starter? Or, what if you've bought a Professional laptop but need a feature that's only in Ultimate? The answer is a scheme called Windows Anytime Upgrade, which allows you to switch between versions of Windows 7 easily and with minimal disruption – for a fee.

To start the process, type "anytime upgrade" into the Windows 7 search box. Click the Windows Anytime Upgrade icon and you'll be taken to the window below. The advisor will guide you through the various editions of the operating system, and you'll then be able to buy a new product key to unlock the features of your chosen version.

Many of the new features may already be installed on your computer, but locked away, so the whole process can be completed in as little as ten minutes – though it's likely to take longer on slower systems – and all your existing programs, files and settings will be kept intact.

HOW MUCH IS THAT UPGRADE IN THE WINDOW?*

Starter to Home Premium	£70
Starter to Professional	£120
Starter to Ultimate	£140
Home Premium to Professional	£120
Home Premium to Ultimate	£125
Professional to Ultimate	£85

*RRP as of April 2011

Windows Anytime Upgrade — Your computer is currently running Windows 7 Home Premium

Do even more with your PC

In as few as 10 minutes, you can add new features to Windows 7 and do more with your PC. It's easy, quick, and you'll keep your programs, files, and settings. The upgrade might take longer depending on your particular PC and whether online updates are needed.

How do you want to begin?

Go online to choose the edition of Windows 7 that's best for you
After your purchase, Windows will upgrade automatically.

Enter an upgrade key
If you already have a Windows Anytime Upgrade key, begin the process here.

Microsoft's Anytime Upgrade system makes it remarkably easy to swap your edition of Windows 7 for a higher version, so if you outgrow the one you buy initially (or get preinstalled on a PC) it isn't the end of the world.

Tip

Windows Anytime Upgrade is a nice option to have, but it's an expensive way to get an upgrade. For example, the price difference between the Home Premium and Ultimate retail packages is £80 – but if you buy Home Premium and then upgrade to Ultimate, you'll pay a whopping £125. Clearly, if you want the features of Professional or Ultimate, it's best to buy that edition in the first place, rather than upgrading later.

personal files). The Encrypting File System adds a layer of protection to your hard disk, using new algorithms that are effectively impossible to hack – good for peace of mind if you're worried about your notebook being lost or stolen.

Perhaps the most interesting addition in Windows 7 Professional is Windows XP Mode. The vast majority of older applications will work in Windows 7 without any problems, but in a few cases a recalcitrant application might refuse to run in the newer OS. Clearly this is unacceptable for companies that rely on bespoke software for their business. So Windows 7 Professional includes built-in support for a virtual machine, using Microsoft's Virtual PC virtualisation host, running a real copy of Windows XP inside Windows 7. This enables absolutely any program to run just as it did before.

There are several other features aimed at business use too. Presentation Mode can reset your desktop wallpaper to a default image, specify a preset volume level and prevent your screensaver from appearing – an instant way to set up your PC for use in the boardroom. Unlike Windows 7 Starter and Home Premium systems, Windows 7 Professional PCs can also join network domains (a necessary feature if your computer is centrally managed by an IT department using a domain).

Windows 7 Professional also includes every feature of 7 Home Premium, including Aero, multitouch functionality for touchscreen displays, Media Player 12 and (though it may seem surplus to business requirements) Windows Media Center. Couple this with a raft of technical, security and networking enhancements and it's clear that, if work is on your mind, Windows 7 Professional edition is probably the way to go.

Unless, that is, you need the additional features offered by the similarly priced Windows 7 Ultimate.

ULTIMATE As the name suggests, the Ultimate edition contains absolutely everything that's new in Windows 7 – every feature from Home Premium and Professional, plus a few extra features that appear only in this edition. Two such features of particular interest are AppLocker, which restricts which applications can run on a network, and BitLocker, which offers full-disk encryption to ensure no-one can get their hands on your sensitive data. BitLocker to Go (see p148) also allows encryption to be used on USB sticks and other portable devices, ensuring your data stays confidential if a drive is accidentally misplaced.

There are other technical improvements, too. The DirectAccess tool enables seamless connections between mobile users and their office network. And it's possible to switch your operating system between 35 different languages, which isn't available in either the Home Premium or Professional editions. Support for booting from Virtual Hard Disks – the benefits of which we describe in detail on p64 – is also reserved for Ultimate users.

In short, if you're looking for unparalleled power and every feature on the block, Windows 7 Ultimate will suit you perfectly, and it's hardly any more expensive than the Professional edition.

EDITIONS COMPARED

	Starter	Home Premium	Professional	Ultimate
Official price	—	£150	£220	£230
Street price*	—	£115	£175	£175
Official upgrade price	—	£100	£190	£200
Upgrade street price*	—	£75	£150	£160
Family Pack price	—	£150	—	—
USER INTERFACE				
Aero Glass	·	●	●	●
Aero Peek	·	●	●	●
Aero Shake	·	●	●	●
Aero Snap	●	●	●	●
Instant Search	●	●	●	●
Live Preview	·	●	●	●
Windows Flip 3D	·	●	●	●
Multitouch	·	●	●	●
BUNDLED APPLICATIONS AND SERVICES				
Windows Live Essentials (free download)	●	●	●	●
Windows Fax and Scan	●	●	●	●
Gadgets	●	●	●	●
Paint, Calculator and WordPad	●	●	●	●
Windows Media Player	●	●	●	●
Remote Media Experience	·	●	●	●
HomeGroup	●†	●	●	●
Device Stage	●	●	●	●
ENTERTAINMENT				
Basic Games	●	●	●	●
Premium Games	·	●	●	●
Media Center Extender support	·	●	●	●
Windows Media Center	·	●	●	●
SECURITY AND BACKUP				
BitLocker	·	·	·	●
AppLocker	·	·	·	●
Backup scheduling	●	●	●	●
Backup to network	·	·	●	●
Encrypting File System	·	·	●	●
Windows Complete PC Backup and Restore	·	·	●	●
Windows Defender	●	●	●	●
Windows Firewall	●	●	●	●
Biometric support	·	●	●	●
ADVANCED FEATURES				
64-bit processor support	·	●	●	●
Maximum RAM supported (32-bit)	4GB	4GB	4GB	4GB
Maximum RAM supported (64-bit)	—	16GB	192GB	192GB
DirectX 11	●	●	●	●
Dual processor support	·	●	●	●
Windows XP Mode	·	·	●	●
Mobility Center	·	●	●	●
Presentation Mode	·	·	●	●
Virtual Hard Disk booting	·	·	·	●
NETWORKING				
Offline Files & Folders	·	·	●	●
Remote Desktop (ability to join)	●	●	●	●
Remote Desktop (ability to organise)	·	·	●	●
Windows Server Domain (join)	·	·	●	●
Multilingual User Interface language packs	·	·	·	●
DirectAccess	·	·	·	●

*Street prices correct in April 2011 †Can join but not create a homegroup

WINDOWS 7'S MOBILE COUSIN MAKES THE WINDOWS EXPERIENCE EVEN BETTER, PUTTING YOUR FILES AND MEDIA RIGHT IN YOUR POCKET.

Connect with Windows Phone 7

Windows 7 is great on desktop PCs, laptops, netbooks and even tablets. But smartphones need a different approach – one tailored to getting things done on the move. Enter Windows Phone 7, Microsoft's mobile version of Windows that's available on a range of sophisticated handsets.

Despite the name, Windows Phone 7 can't run normal Windows 7 programs; only Windows Phone 7-specific applications will work. But the two systems are designed to work together seamlessly. It's easy to share files between your phone and PC, either via Microsoft's SkyDrive service (see p78), or by synchronising files directly – see opposite. For anyone who's already using Windows 7, a Windows Phone 7 device could be the perfect complement.

TILES IN STYLE Windows Phone 7 doesn't use the familiar system of icons and menus. Instead, it uses tiles – touch-sensitive panels that appear on the home screen of your phone. You can choose which tiles appear here, so you can have your favourite games and services at your fingertips, as well as useful tools such as text messaging and web browsing. Tiles don't just act as buttons: they also display live information, so you can see at a glance whether you've missed a phone call or have unread email to attend to. They can also give your phone the personal touch: the Pictures tile, for example, displays images from your photo library.

A HUBBUB OF HUBS To access Windows Phone 7's full set of features, you simply visit one of its "hubs" – a page that brings together a set of related actions. In the People hub, for example, you can browse your contacts, or send them messages. In the Music + Video hub you can enjoy your media files. Hubs use a grid-type arrangement: scroll left and right to browse the types of task you can do, then scroll up and down to see different options within a task.

PORTABLE PROGRAMS Windows Phone 7 comes with some useful built-in applications. One familiar name is the mobile version of Internet Explorer. It doesn't have all the advanced features of Internet Explorer 9 (see p88) but it's a slick way to browse the web on your phone.

There's also a Microsoft Office suite, including mobile editions of Outlook, Word, Excel, PowerPoint and OneNote. Again, they're not as fully featured as their desktop counterparts, but they're perfect if you need to quickly refer to a document or make a change on the move. Files can be effortlessly moved back and forth between your phone and PC using either SkyDrive or SharePoint services.

If you hanker after more applications, visit the Marketplace hub. From here you can download any number of additional applications, both free and paid-for. The only limit is the amount of space on your phone!

Tip

Windows 7 works with all smartphone operating systems, not just Windows Phone 7. If you prefer an Apple iPhone, or an Android phone, that's no problem. Whichever handset you choose, you'll still be able to download apps, surf the web, check your email and enjoy your music and videos. Be aware, though, that the mobile Office suite is only available for Windows Phone 7. If you need that feature, you'll have to stick with Microsoft.

The Windows Phone 7 home screen (far left) shows a selection of tiles, giving information at a glance and direct access to commonly used tasks. The full set of options is arranged into "hubs". The People hub (left) opens with a list of contacts: scroll sideways and you'll see different options such as sending messages or checking friends' activities on social networking services.

HOW TO...
SYNC WITH WINDOWS PHONE 7

① SYNC YOUR CONTACTS If you've previously used Windows Mobile PDAs or phones then you might expect to be able to synchronise your contacts, your email and calendar items by plugging your Windows 7 Phone straight into your PC. But it doesn't work like that anymore; instead, Windows 7 Phone downloads contacts direct from the internet (or Microsoft Exchange). For instance, if you have a Google Mail account, you first need to set that up on your phone. It will then download all your contacts and calendar details at the same time as checking for email. For details on setting up email accounts on a Windows 7 Phone, visit www.pcpro.co.uk/links/win7email.

② DOWNLOAD ZUNE The key to synchronising multimedia to your Windows 7 Phone device – think podcasts, music, videos and pictures – is a free piece of Microsoft software called Zune. This doesn't come bundled with Windows 7 and instead needs to be downloaded from www.pcpro.co.uk/links/win7zune.

③ FIRST SYNC When you first launch Zune it will search through your PC to find your multimedia collection, which may take some time. Once complete, click Collection. This will reveal all the music, videos, photos and podcasts Zune has discovered. If you haven't already connected your phone to your PC, do

so now. Note the pink writing in the bottom-left corner of the window that says "Drag and drop things here to sync with your phone", complete with an arrow to a thumbnail photo of your phone. As it says, syncing media is as simple as clicking on it and dragging it. However, by default Zune may attempt to add all your music, videos and pictures, and that will cause a problem if your music collection, for example, is bigger than the amount of storage on your phone (which is quite likely, because many Windows 7 Phone devices only come with 8GB of memory and with no way to expand the memory).

TWEAK AWAY Running out of storage space is just one of the reasons why you might need to tweak the settings from their defaults. To do so, click on SETTINGS at the top of the Zune software window. The key setting is SYNC OPTIONS.

④ Click this, and then click PHONE (found at the top-left of the Zune window). You can then take more control over your music, video, picture and podcast settings. The choices are self-explanatory but basic. We recommend you also click on SOFTWARE (top left) and then the various menus down the left-hand side, to ensure these are as you wish them to be; for example, you may want to keep more than the default three episodes of each podcast on your PC and phone.

HOW LONG?
About 15 minutes – a little more if you're planning to make many adjustments.

HOW HARD?
You may need some assistance from your email provider, but using Zune is simple.

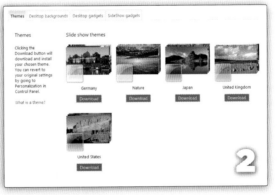

IN THIS CHAPTER

2

Installing Windows 7

INSTALLING WIN

Windows 7's install process is a huge improvement on previous efforts. The Windows XP installer was ugly and intimidating, and Vista kept asking questions all the way through the process. Windows 7 simply asks you what you want up front, then goes away and takes care of everything itself. In this chapter, we guide you through the different install options available: you can

ws

Windows®7

Install now

...w before installing Windows

...09 Microsoft Corporation. All rights reserved.

DOWS 7

upgrade directly from a previous version of Windows, or replace your existing system with a clean install of Windows 7 – while keeping all your old data and documents. We'll show you how to create a dual-boot setup, so you can keep access to your old OS, and how to install Windows 7 Service Pack 1, containing all the latest updates to the operating system.

HOW LONG?
Anything from half-an-hour to several hours, depending on the amount of data.

HOW HARD?
Quite straightforward, but you'll meet a few obstacles on the way.

HOW TO...
MOVE FROM WINDOWS XP

If you're moving from XP to Windows 7, here's how to make sure your files are safely backed up before the move, and transferred to the new system afterwards.

It isn't possible to perform a direct "in-place" upgrade from Windows XP to Windows 7, but that doesn't mean you shouldn't upgrade. You simply need to back up your personal files and folders before performing a clean installation of Windows 7, and restore them into the new operating system when you're done. That's easy to do, and these simple steps will show you how.

① START EASY TRANSFER Windows 7 comes with a tool called the Easy Transfer Wizard which makes it a breeze to back up your files in your old operating system, and to transfer them across to Windows 7. To access it, boot up your PC into Windows XP as usual, then insert your Windows 7 disc in the drive. Close the installation window if it opens automatically, and instead open Windows Explorer. Browse into the Windows 7 DVD, go into the folder named Support, then open the folder called Migwiz. In this folder you'll find a file called either MIGSETUP or MIGSETUP.EXE: double-click it to launch the Windows 7 Easy Transfer Wizard. The Welcome screen explains all the merits of Windows Easy Transfer; feel free to read it, then click Next to get started.

② CHOOSE YOUR STORAGE LOCATION If you only have a small quantity of data, it may fit onto a CD, a DVD or a USB flash drive, but if you've built up a large library of files the best option is a second hard disk – either inside your PC or externally connected via USB. If your PC is on a network, you can alternatively use another computer or a network attached storage (NAS) device. Choose the appropriate method from the choices given. On the next screen, confirm that this is your old computer.

③ CHOOSE FILES OR SETTINGS The wizard scans your system to see what files and settings can be transferred, and shows the results in a ticklist. It divides the files into those kept by the main user ("asus" in our example) and Shared items. If you want to see more details, click Customize to bring up a list of all the types of files due to be backed up, including Desktop items, Favorites and Program settings. If you don't want something to be moved to your new system, just deselect it. For finer control, clicking the Advanced button at the bottom will take you to a full file tree, so you can specify files and folders to keep.

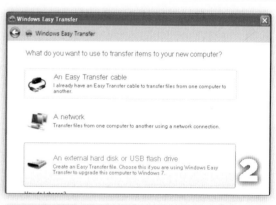

SAVE YOUR VITAL DATA Having chosen the files to keep, click through and you'll be asked if you want to protect your backup with a password. Unless you're dealing with sensitive files, you can skip on to the next step. You'll then be asked to name your set of files; choose something you'll recognise easily later, such as "Windows XP transfer files" and browse to where you'll save your data, as discussed in step 2. In our case, it's a USB stick.

FINISH WITH XP Once you've named the file and chosen the location, you can start the transfer. A window shows a progress indicator for each element. If you have a lot of data, now's the time to make a cup of tea. When the process is complete, you'll be told if any files didn't back up properly; if you need them, copy them manually onto a USB drive or other storage device so that you can transfer them yourself.

You've now completed the steps to get your data from your old PC to your shiny new Windows 7 system. If you're upgrading the same machine, or haven't already installed Windows 7 on your new PC, follow the steps on p24, then return to step 6 when you're ready to restore your saved files to your new system.

CONTINUE IN WINDOWS 7 In Windows 7, click the Start orb and go to All Programs | Accessories | System Tools. Click on Windows Easy Transfer to begin the second stage. Click through the Welcome window

and you'll be asked what method you'll be using. Select the storage you used earlier, and when asked whether this is your new or old PC click New to tell the wizard you already have your files backed up.

SELECT YOUR FILES When asked if your files have been saved to an external drive, connect or insert the drive or device containing your backup and click Yes. (If you chose another method, such as transferring over a network, make the appropriate choice.) Select the relevant storage type and you'll be asked where your files are. Locate your storage device and navigate to the folder you selected earlier. You should see the file you named in step 4 ("Windows XP transfer files" in our case) with the label "Easy Transfer File". Select this: if you entered a password in step 4, you'll be asked to provide it now.

RESTORE YOUR DATA Windows 7 scans your backup and shows a window as in step 3. Choose what to restore, or leave everything selected. If necessary, click Advanced to select all sorts of fancy tasks, such as transferring a whole user account from the old system or mapping an entire drive from XP. Click the Transfer button to begin the final stage. At the end, you'll see exactly what was transferred; the wizard will also present a list of the software it detected on your old system, with links to product websites and information on Windows 7 compatibility, so you can start reinstalling.

Tip

If you don't have a lot of files to transfer, and you don't need to transfer anything as complex as application settings or user accounts to your new PC, it can be just as simple to plug in a flash memory drive and manually copy across the files you need. You run the risk of missing files if your data is poorly organised, but being selective about what you keep is a great way of making a fresh start on your pristine new computer.

HOW LONG?
Half-an-hour to an hour.

HOW HARD?
Very easy: the Upgrade wizard takes you through the whole process.

HOW TO...
MOVE FROM WINDOWS VISTA

If you're currently running Vista, it's incredibly simple to upgrade your PC to Windows 7 – in fact, your files and settings won't even be touched in the process.

The best way to move to Windows 7 is always a clean install (see p24), as it ensures everything is precisely how Microsoft designed it to be from the start. If you want to take that route, simply follow the directions for moving from Windows XP on p20 – they'll work equally well in Vista.

But if you already have a Vista PC set up to your liking, it's very easy to upgrade directly to Windows 7, keeping all your programs and files in the same place – so long as you match the version of Windows 7 to your installed version of Vista. For example, if you're running Vista Home Premium, you'll need to upgrade to Windows 7 Home Premium. Vista Business becomes Windows 7 Professional, and so forth. Note that you'll need to install 32-bit (as opposed to 64-bit) Windows 7 over 32-bit Vista. If you want to check for certain which version is right, use Microsoft's Upgrade Advisor tool (see p10), which scans your current PC and gives you the upgrade information you'll need.

The upgrade process should leave your existing programs and data as they are, but if there are any files you absolutely can't afford to lose, it's a good idea to copy them onto an external hard disk or USB stick – or run Windows Backup – before you begin the upgrade process.

① START THE UPGRADE When you insert the Windows 7 disc, the upgrade process is similar to a full install. You can run a compatibility check online, which gives you a report similar to the Upgrade Advisor, but if you've reached this stage your PC should be ready for Windows 7.

② GET THE LATEST INSTALL FILES Click "Install now". You'll be asked if you want to go online to check for updates; if you have an internet connection it's a good idea to do so – there may well be updates for your hardware, as well as system enhancements released after the launch of Windows 7. After reading Microsoft's terms and conditions, tick the box to agree and then click Next.

③ CHOOSE THE UPGRADE OPTION Depending on your Windows 7 version, you may be offered the choice of a Custom (full) install or an upgrade. The process for a full installation is described on on p24, but if you want to move up to Windows 7 the easy way, click the Upgrade option to ensure Windows keeps all the important files from your Vista system in place.

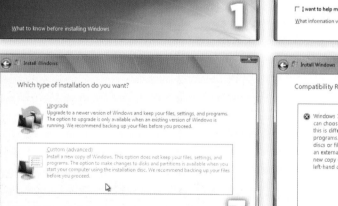

CHECK COMPATIBILITY The wizard will then check the compatibility of your system. Provided you've followed the instructions and bought the correct version of Windows 7 to upgrade to, all you should see here is a warning if any of your installed programs might have problems running properly in Windows 7. These issues can often be worked around later using Windows 7's Compatibility Mode, so don't worry too much about these warnings. If there are any critical issues – such as an incompatible version of Windows 7 itself – the installer will inform you and the process will be terminated before you can go too far and mess up your system.

BEGIN THE UPGRADE As long as no major compatibility issues have been found, you're now ready to begin the upgrade. Once it starts, it will proceed in a very similar fashion to a normal installation: you'll be given full details of what it's doing at all stages, and the system will restart several times. When it does, don't panic, just leave it to continue transferring its files until it asks you explicitly for some input. At that point, you're just a few steps from the Windows 7 desktop.

ENTER YOUR PRODUCT KEY You don't have to enter your Microsoft product key during the setup process – you have up to 30 days from installation to do so before you're locked out of your PC. But if you have it to hand, it makes sense to get this bit out of the way now. You'll find the 25-character code somewhere on the packaging of your Windows 7 DVD: simply type it out, exactly as it appears on the packaging, into the dialog box. Provided you're made no mistakes, the wizard will check it for a few moments and confirm that your copy of Windows has been activated successfully. Make sure you keep the code somewhere safe, in case you decide to use it to move your Windows 7 licence to a new PC in the future.

FINALISE YOUR SETTINGS You're almost there. Just choose your Automatic Update preferences: it's best to let Windows download and install its important updates automatically to keep your system secure and up to date. Then set the correct time and location, and you're done. The system may restart once more, and – a mere coffee break after you began – you'll see the new Windows logo, your desktop will appear, and you're up and running in Windows 7.

CHECK YOUR FILES If all has gone to plan, all of your files should be right where you left them, and all your applications should still be available. In the very rare instance that something's missing, get out the disk onto which you backed up your files earlier and simply copy them back. Alternatively, if you ran Windows Backup, you should be able to run a restore to bring them back. Then you're free to explore your shiny new Windows 7 environment. At which point, we suggest you head straight to chapter 3.

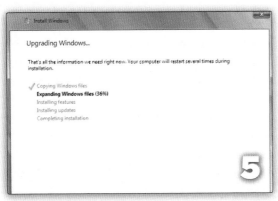

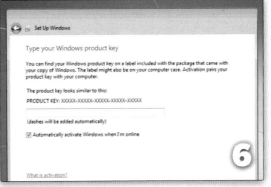

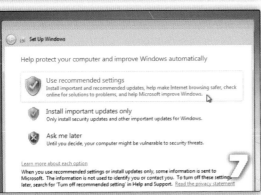

Tip

The Easy Transfer Wizard can move files from either Windows XP or Vista to Windows 7 (see p20) – and it can also be used to migrate between editions of Windows. For example, it can transfer your files from Vista Business to a new Windows 7 Home Premium installation. And if you happened to install the early Windows 7 beta version that Microsoft released for testing purposes, you can use the Easy Transfer Wizard to migrate to the full version of Windows 7.

2

Installing Windows 7

HOW LONG?
Should take less than an hour, and you can leave it alone to complete after the first few minutes.

HOW HARD?
The majority of the process is automatic, but read this guide first.

HOW TO...
CLEAN-INSTALL WINDOWS 7

A clean installation of Windows 7 is the best way to give your PC a totally fresh start – and you can do it without losing all your files and settings.

Windows 7 is the easiest version of Windows yet to install. The installer will guide you through just a few decisions at the start of the process, and will then go away and set up your new operating system without any need for your further involvement.

 CHECK YOUR VERSION Before you start to install Windows 7, you need to be certain you've made the right choice when it comes to the version. We cover this in detail in chapter 1, and our four-page guide starting on p12 should help you decide whether Home Premium, Professional or Ultimate are right for you.

If you do subsequently decide you've installed the wrong version, it's not the end of the world. As we discuss in chapter 1, you can always make use of the Anytime Upgrade scheme to gain access to extra features. This isn't the most cost effective approach, though. And you can't use Anytime Upgrade to move from a 32-bit version of Windows to 64-bit. If you choose a 32-bit installation now, then later on want to move to 64-bit – perhaps when you decide 4GB of memory is no longer enough – you'll have to perform a full reinstall. See p13 if you're in doubt.

 BACK UP YOUR STUFF If losing all your old files and settings is a bit too 'clean' for your liking, you can back them up using Windows 7's Easy Transfer wizard, then restore them to your new system after installation. You can do this following the process we describe on p20. Note, however, that while your personal files will be safe, you'll need to reinstall your applications once the new operating system is in place. If you're currently using Windows Vista you can avoid that by performing an upgrade instead of a clean installation: see p22 for how to do that. If you're running Windows XP, that option isn't available – the two systems are just too different – so you'll have to proceed with a clean installation.

 BEGIN INSTALLATION The Windows 7 installer can be launched from inside your old operating system, or you can boot your PC directly from the Windows 7 DVD. If convenient, it's a good idea to launch the installer within Windows, as this will allow the installer to download the latest updates, giving a better chance that all your hardware devices will be working the very first time you boot up Windows 7. If that's not practical, though,

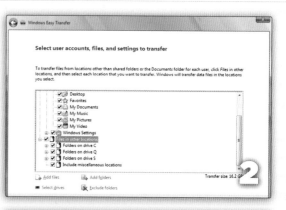

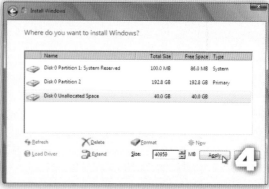

there's no harm in installing direct from the disc. To do this, simply insert it into your drive and restart the PC. If you get a message saying "Press any key to boot from CD or DVD", do so. If you don't see this and the installer doesn't appear, you'll need to access your BIOS and ensure it's set to boot from the DVD. Check your PC's manual if you're not sure how to do this. Whichever installation method you choose, simply follow the prompts until you see the initial Windows 7 setup screen, where you can alter the regional settings to the UK.

④ CHOOSE YOUR DESTINATION You'll be asked to choose between an Upgrade or Custom installation. We want the latter. Now choose where to install Windows 7: you'll see a display of all your local hard disks and partitions. This may vary according to how many drives are in your PC and how they're set up, but for most Windows machines it will be more or less the same. Unless you want a dual-boot (see p26) or virtualised (see p64) system, pick the main partition containing your existing Windows system. You'll need at least 16GB free, although we'd recommend at least double that. Be sure you've backed up your data (using Easy Transfer or manually), then select the appropriate partition and click Next.

⑤ WAIT... The install process is quite quick, so you can be using Windows 7 in as little as half an hour. Don't be alarmed if your system restarts several times during the process – that's normal..

⑥ ENTER YOUR DETAILS When Windows 7 starts for the first time, you'll be asked to enter your details, beginning with a name for your PC (so you can recognise it on a network). You can set a password for your user account: this is a good idea on a shared PC, and it's required to make full use of some online services (such as Windows Live Mesh – see p80). You'll also be asked to enter your 25-character product key, which can be found on or in your Windows 7 packaging. As long as the "Automatically activate Windows when I'm online" box is ticked, Windows 7 will authenticate itself automatically.

⑦ THE FINAL SETTINGS Next you'll be asked to choose Windows Update settings. For the sake of simplicity and security we suggest you let Windows install updates automatically. Then choose your location: this determines your default security settings (see chapter 8). If you choose "Home" you'll also be given the chance to create or join a Homegroup, which makes it easy to connect with other PCs on your network (see p98).

⑧ ENJOY And you're done. If you backed up your data, now's the time to restore it, and to install any applications you'll want to use in your new operating system. You can also start personalising Windows 7 according to your tastes – see chapter 3 – and set up your antivirus software. See p130 to learn more about why this is so important, and what your options are.

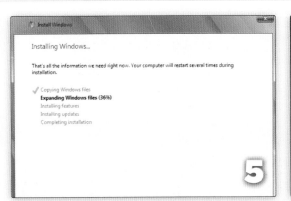

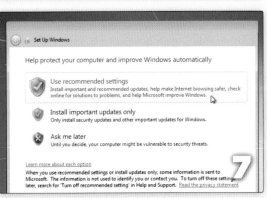

Tip

Windows Easy Transfer does exactly what it says on the tin, and works both when replacing an existing Windows installation on the same PC and when moving to a new Windows 7 PC. However, note that it only works when moving up from Vista, not from Windows XP. If you want to preserve files and settings from an XP system, follow our guide on p20.

HOW TO...
CREATE A DUAL-BOOT SYSTEM

*If you want to keep using older programs, a dual-boot system – retaining your
previous version of Windows – might be the best option. Here's how to set it up.*

HOW LONG?
An hour or so; longer, if
you take our advice and
back up your data first.

HOW HARD?
Be sure you understand
hard disk partitioning
before you try this.

Windows 7 is a big improvement over previous versions
of Windows, and we'd recommend that anyone who isn't
already using it should upgrade. However, in a few cases you
might need to retain access to an older version of Windows
alongside the current version. Perhaps you have some
unusual applications that only Windows XP or Vista will run
(although these should be few, as we explain on p56), or
perhaps you're reliant on older hardware devices that aren't
supported by Windows 7.

Fortunately, it's possible to get the best of both
worlds by keeping your existing operating system and also
installing Windows 7 on the same computer. You can then
choose which to run each time you start up.

It's called a dual-boot system, and to set it up
you'll need to make some fundamental changes to your hard
disk. The process isn't complicated, but it does carry a real
risk of losing all the data that's currently on your hard disk if
you make a mistake – so you'll need to understand what's
happening and prepare for it.

The procedure involves splitting your system hard
disk into two partitions: one that still contains your existing
Windows system, and a new blank partition, onto which we

can install Windows 7. To achieve this, you'll have to shrink
down your current system partition to leave a gap that's big
enough for the new Windows 7 partition.

Before starting this, you really do need to back up
everything. Altering partitions in itself won't erase your data,
but it can't be undone or reversed, and if, for instance, there's
a power failure at a critical moment, all your files will be gone.
Use your usual backup process in your existing operating
system to make sure everything is safely stored elsewhere.

You may also need to delete some files to
create space for the new partition. To see how much free
space is on your system disk, go to Start | My Computer,
right-click on your C drive and select Properties. Microsoft
recommends at least 16GB for a Windows 7 installation, but
we'd recommend aiming for at least 30GB of free space as
modern applications can eat up gigabytes of disk space.

Assuming you have enough free space to go
ahead, you'll need software that can resize the existing
system partition and create a new one. Vista has a suitable
utility built in, as we'll see below, but XP users will need third-
party software such as Easeus Partition Master, which you
can download for free from www.partition-tool.com

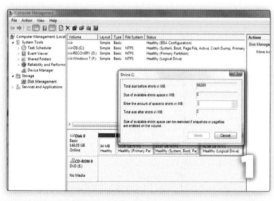

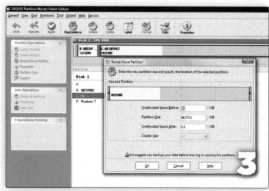

1 **PARTITIONING IN VISTA** If you're using XP, go to step 3. In Vista, use the built-in partition tool. Right-click Computer, choose Manage and then Disk Management. Right-click on your main disk (Disk0) and opt to Shrink Volume. This reduces the space used by the current partition, creating room for your new partition.

2 **SHRINK TO FIT** Windows 7 needs at least 16GB, so make sure you shrink your main partition by at least this amount, bearing in mind you'll probably need lots more space than this for new applications and files. A new volume will appear. Right-click this and choose New Simple Volume, then follow the default choices, naming your volume something obvious, such as "Windows 7" Unless you get an error message, head to step 4.

3 **PARTITIONING IN XP** If you're using XP, or you get an error in step 2, download a third-party partitioning tool such as Partition Master (www.partition-tool.com). Follow its instructions to complete a similar process to steps 2 and 3. If your PC already has the maximum of four active partitions (some Dell PCs do, for example), you'll first have to delete one you don't need.

4 **START THE WINDOWS 7 INSTALL** That's the hard part over with. Now you can simply insert your Windows 7 disc and proceed with installation in the same way as for a clean install (see p24). Insert the disc, reboot the PC and hit a key to boot into the installer. Follow the clean install (Custom) steps until you get to the "Where do you want to install Windows?" screen. Click Drive options (Advanced) at the bottom right.

5 **SELECT A PARTITION** Clicking this produces new buttons at the foot of the screen allowing you to delete selected partitions, format a partition or create one. You want to create a new one, so make sure you click on the newly unallocated space and then click New.

6 **PICK A SIZE** Choose a size for the new partition in the text area that appears. By default, the value is the whole of the available free space on the disk, which is what you're likely to want. If not, you can reduce it. The size is shown in megabytes, not gigabytes; 1,024MB is equal to 1GB. Remember, the recommended minimum free space for a Windows 7 installation is 16GB (16,384MB), but it's more practical to aim for 30GB or more.

7 **INSTALL AS NORMAL** The installation should now proceed in the same way as a clean install of Windows 7 (see p22), with a few reboots.

8 **CHOOSE ON STARTUP** Now, whenever you reboot your PC you'll see a Boot Manager screen that enables you to select either your old Windows XP or Vista installation, or the new Windows 7 system.

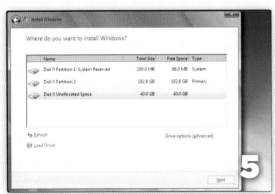

FAQ

Q: How much free hard disk space do I really need for Windows 7?

A: Microsoft officially recommends at least 16GB free hard disk space for installation. You may find your actual installation doesn't take up this much space, but remember this is just for Windows 7 itself – it doesn't take into account the space you'll need for applications, documents, files, photos, videos, games and anything else. We'd consider 30GB the bare minimum in reality.

WINDOWS 7 SERVICE PACK 1 INCLUDES ALL THE LATEST FIXES AND UPDATES
TO THE SYSTEM: INSTALL IT AND YOU CAN BE SURE YOUR PC IS UP TO DATE.

What's new in Service Pack 1

Right out of the box, Windows 7 is a very stable operating system. It makes the old jokes about Windows constantly crashing look ridiculous.

But in a system as complex as Windows 7, there will inevitably be some minor errors that crop up in unusual circumstances. What's more, hackers are always looking for new ways to break into PCs, so a system that was considered perfectly secure when it was originally set up might become susceptible to a freshly discovered vulnerability.

For those reasons, Microsoft is constantly releasing little fixes and improvements through the Windows Update service (see p136). These are normally installed on your PC one by one as they become available; but in February 2011 Microsoft released a huge bundle of updates called Windows 7 Service Pack 1, or SP1 for short.

PACK UP YOUR TROUBLES If SP1 didn't come preinstalled on your PC, you should install it right away (see p30). This won't make a visible change to the way Windows works. SP1 contains only "under the bonnet" improvements, designed to make your computer more stable and secure without interfering with the familiar Windows 7 experience.

Even if SP1 wasn't preinstalled on your PC, some of the included updates may already be installed on your system: SP1 brings together a total of 977 fixes and security updates that have previously been made available through Windows Update. The idea is simply to ensure that any gaps that may remain in your system are plugged.

NEW FEATURES Service Pack 1 also brings a few new updates to Windows 7 which haven't previously been available. The most exciting of these is support for Advanced Vector Extensions (AVX) – a series of programming "shortcuts" that can make some software run much faster. To take advantage, though, your computer needs to be equipped with an AVX-compatible processor. This essentially means you'll need a chip from Intel's new Core i3, i5 or i7 range (codenamed "Sandy Bridge") or one of AMD's forthcoming "Bulldozer" processors.

The other exclusive updates in SP1 are more pedestrian. There's a fix for a problem that can cause problems with sound over HDMI, and improvements to the process for saving documents in XPS format. Such updates are nice to have, but they're not exactly earth-shattering.

The real attraction of installing Service Pack 1 is peace of mind. Once it's installed, you can be confident that your already-stable operating system is completely up to date with nearly a thousand post-installation upgrades.

Tip

We've found Service Pack 1 to be rock solid, but if (for example) you're troubleshooting a problem with your PC, it's conceivable that you might want to temporarily remove it. You can do this by opening the Control Panel and selecting "Uninstall a program". Select "Service Pack for Microsoft Windows (KB 976932)" and click Uninstall to start the removal process. This option may not be available if SP1 came preinstalled on your PC.

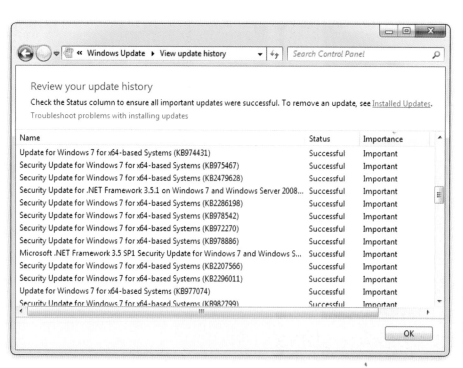

Windows 7 is constantly being updated, and many of the upgrades in Service Pack 1 may already have reached you through Windows Update – but you should still install the whole Service Pack, to be certain you're fully up to date.

Get your website online in minutes
and make @ name for yourself!

We offer a range of solutions that suit all needs, from **personalised email** with spam and virus protection to **business web hosting** including **FREE .uk domain** and **eshop facility**.

With over 10 years' experience we're the web host you can trust. With **free setup** and **24/7 phone** and **online support** we're here whenever you need us, day or night.

HALF PRICE ON SELECTED PACKAGES*

HOSTING NOW UP TO 50% FOR OFF 3 MONTHS*

Email hosting you@yourname.com

It's easy to create a personalised email address using your own domain. Plus get 50% off for 3 months with our exchange packages.

MAIL PLUS
£14.99pa (£17.99 inc VAT)
Annual payment applies

Professional email using your own domain
- ✔ 5 flexible mailboxes (50MB each)
- ✔ 2 Virus & spam protected mailboxes
- ✔ Fasthosts Webmail
- ✔ POP3 & IMAP access

EXCHANGE – HALF PRICE
£4.99pm (£5.99 inc VAT)
Normal price £11.99 inc VAT

Email hosting designed for any business
- ✔ 5 flexible mailboxes (50MB each)
- ✔ 1 Exchange mailbox (2GB each)
- ✔ Fasthosts Webmail
- ✔ Individual mailbox control panel
- ✔ Mobile access for real-time updates

ALL PACKAGES INCLUDE:
- ✔ Autoresponders
- ✔ Individual mailbox control panels
- ✔ Secure UK data centre
- ✔ Catch-all email

Check online for details on easy mobile access

Web hosting

Create a professional looking website quickly and easily with our free and simple to use website builder. Plus get up to 50% off for 3 months.

PERSONAL STANDARD – 10% OFF
£4.49pm (£5.39 inc VAT)
Normal price £5.99 inc VAT

- ✔ **5GB** web space
- ✔ Unlimited bandwidth†
- ✔ Choice of Windows or Linux (no extra cost)
- ✔ Virus & spam protected email
- ✔ **FREE** website builder
- ✔ **FREE** instant setup

BUSINESS STANDARD – 30% OFF
£6.29pm (£7.55 inc VAT)
Normal price £10.79 inc VAT

- ✔ **25GB** web space
- ✔ Unlimited bandwidth†
- ✔ Choice of Windows or Linux (no extra cost)
- ✔ **FREE** website builder
- ✔ **FREE** instant setup
- ✔ **FREE** .uk domain (worth £5.90)
- ✔ **FREE £105** advertising vouchers
- ✔ **5** MySQL databases
- ✔ ASP.NET 3.5 with AJAX extensions
- ✔ OneClick Installer (Linux only)

goMobi now available *our **new** mobile website builder***

We have a wide range of domains available **from £2.95pa. Secure yours today!**

Buy now at
fasthosts.co.uk/hosting
0844 583 0760

World Class Web Hosting

HOW TO...
INSTALL SERVICE PACK 1

Windows 7 Service Pack 1 is very easy to install, but the process involves a few steps. We walk you through downloading and deploying the update.

HOW LONG?
The update takes a while to download, and installing isn't exactly nippy either.

HOW HARD?
Mostly a simple case of clicking a few buttons in a right order.

Microsoft offers Windows 7 Service Pack 1 through the Windows Update service, so if you're patient you may find it comes to you automatically. Computers are also starting to be sold with Windows 7 SP1 pre-installed. It's quite possible, therefore, that you might already have the update without having had to lift a finger. If you don't have it, though – or you're not sure – here's what to do.

 CHECK IF YOU ALREADY HAVE IT If your computer already has Service Pack 1 installed, this will be noted in the System information window, accessible from the Control Panel; click on "System and Security" then System. If you're not certain that it's already installed, look here: if you have SP1, the words "Service Pack 1" will appear below the copyright information at the top of the window. Our example PC in the picture below hasn't had the update applied, which means we'd better install it ourselves.

LAUNCH WINDOWS UPDATE The easiest way to get SP1 is via Windows Update – a very useful service which we describe in more detail on p136. You can also download the installer from Microsoft's website,

but doing it through Windows Update is much simpler, as the mechanism is already built right into Windows.

To start, simply launch Windows Update from your Start menu: if you see a button labelled "Check for updates", click it. You may be presented with a selection of updates that don't include Service Pack 1: you should allow Windows Update to install these, and to reboot afterwards if it wants to. Service Pack 1 won't appear on your list until you've installed some necessary prerequisite updates, so keep trying – it should appear eventually.

TIME TO INSTALL Sooner or later, Windows Update should give you the option to install Windows 7 Service Pack 1. As you'll see, the size of this update can vary considerably, from a quite reasonable 44MB right up to a huge 533MB. That's because a large proportion of the fixes and upgrades included in SP1 have previously been available through Windows Update, and if you already have them installed on your PC there's no need to download and install them again. The actual amount of data that you need to download will be determined once you start the update.

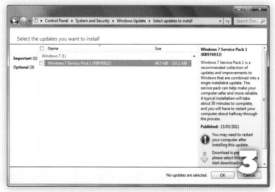

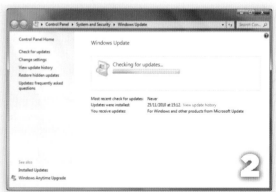

INSTALLING MANUALLY If you've tried running Windows Update over and over again, and it simply won't give you the Service Pack, you can download the installer from Microsoft's website (www.microsoft.com/downloads) and run it yourself. Be warned though that if you decide to take this route, you'll have to download an enormous installer. At nearly 2,000MB in size, it's many times larger than the download you'll receive via Windows Update. That's partly because it contains every single Windows 7 update that's been previously released – regardless of what's already on your system. The installer also includes a whole load of updates for Windows Server 2008 R2, which is an entirely different operating system. From Microsoft's point of view it makes sense to bundle everything into a single download that can be used to update both operating systems. From your point of view, though, it's a big waste of time. Depending on the speed of your internet connection, you can expect to spend an hour or more waiting for all these redundant updates to download.

 CREATING A RESTORE POINT Installing Service Pack 1 is a major change to your system, so Windows creates a restore point before continuing. We haven't heard of Service Pack 1 causing any problems after installation, but if you do run into difficulties you can simply use Windows 7's System Restore tool to roll your system back to this restore point and carry on as before. For more information about System Restore, see p167. It's also possible to uninstall Service Pack 1 from the Programs and Features window in the Control Panel: as we note on p28, you need to look under "S" for Service Pack.

 INSTALLING THE UPDATE There's very little for you to do now: the rest of the procedure ticks along fairly automatically. It can take five or ten minutes for Windows to download and install the update, so this would be a good time to go and make yourself a cup of coffee. You can also continue to use your computer during this time, although its performance might be bogged down a little by the installation process.

RESTARTING YOUR PC Once Windows Update has finished installing SP1, it will prompt you to restart your PC. You might think this is the end of the process, but there's more churning to go, as Windows completes all the SP1 updates that couldn't be applied while the system was in use. You'll typically have to wait several minutes for the computer to shut down, and another few minutes for it to start up again.

CHECK IT'S WORKED Windows 7 with Service Pack 1 looks outwardly identical to the original, unpatched version; but if you go back to the System window you'll see the words "Service Pack 1" have appeared, confirming that you're now fully updated.

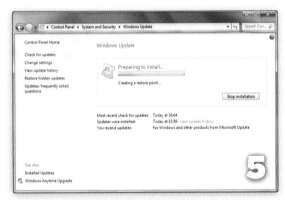

Tip

Technology never stands still. Service Pack 1 brings you up to date as far as February 2011, but each month there will doubtless be more new updates to install – so it's important to keep checking Windows Update for the latest enhancements. There may even be new service packs in the future: Windows Vista has received two service packs so far, while XP is on its third, and the old Windows 2000 system went up to SP4.

IN THIS CHAPTER

3

Windows 7 The basics

WINDOWS 7: THE

Past versions of Windows could be fairly accused of making the basics more complicated than necessary. Windows 7 sweeps away much of the confusion and clutter and delivers a clean, fast and attractive operating system. The most visible improvements have taken place on the desktop, the screen that you see when you first start your PC. From the revamped

BASICS

Taskbar to the Jump Lists that sprout from your favourite applications, Windows 7 delivers both speed and sophistication. In this chapter, we'll explain what Windows 7's unique features do and how to get the best out of them. We'll also take a look at the powerful Libraries feature and explain how to keep your family safe with user accounts.

3

Windows 7
The basics

The only default icon on the desktop is the **Recycle Bin**. You can add shortcuts to files and programs as in previous versions (see p36), although the new Taskbar and Libraries make it less likely you'll want to.

Gadgets – small applications such as clocks, calendars and mini-photo galleries – can be placed anywhere on the Windows 7 desktop. Click and hold on your desired gadget and drag it to wherever you want it. Find out more about Gadgets on p40.

Recycle Bin

Control Panel ▸ All Control Pan

Go online to

• Discover new feature
• Find out everything y

Go online to find out what's new in Windows 7

Choose when to be notified about changes to your computer

Change the size of the text on your screen

The **Start menu** gives a list of your most commonly used applications. It can be opened by clicking on the Start Orb or by pressing the Windows button on your keyboard. If you want to make an application a permanent fixture on your Start menu, right-click on the program's name and select Pin to Start menu. Alternatively, select the Remove From This List option if you don't want the software to show here. The little arrows next to the programs' names activate the Jump Lists (see p38).

The right-hand side of the Start menu provides one-click access to **common locations** such as your Documents, Pictures and Music folders. The **Control Panel** hosts a bunch of useful tools – such as the option to uninstall unwanted software – while Devices and Printers controls anything attached to your PC.

Paint

Getting Started

Calculator

Windows Media Center

Sticky Notes

Snipping Tool

Remote Desktop Connection

Magnifier

Solitaire

WordPad

▶ All Programs

Search programs and files 🔍

PC Pro

Documents

Pictures

Music

Games

Computer

Control Panel

Devices and Printers

Default Programs

Help and Support

Shut down ▸

Click **All Programs** to see a list of every piece of software installed on your PC. Windows 7 has several applications pre-loaded to get you started.

The enhanced **Instant Search** is a fast way to find programs or files on your PC. Start typing and results for matching programs, documents, photos or other files will instantly appear.

Like in Vista, the **Start Orb** is the equivalent of Windows XP's Start button. Click this to pop open the Start menu or, ironically, when you want to shut the PC down.

The Windows 7 **Taskbar** has been completely revamped compared to earlier editions. Running programs are now represented by chunky square icons, and your favourite programs can be 'pinned' to the Taskbar, so you don't have to go hunting around the Start menu to find them. You can also change the order of icons on the Taskbar by dragging and dropping to your desired positions.

Windows 7's **Getting Started** screen can help you with most of the basic tasks you need to undertake after installing a new operating system, including customising settings and adding new user accounts. If the Getting Started screen doesn't appear on startup, find it by typing 'getting started' into the Start menu's Search box.

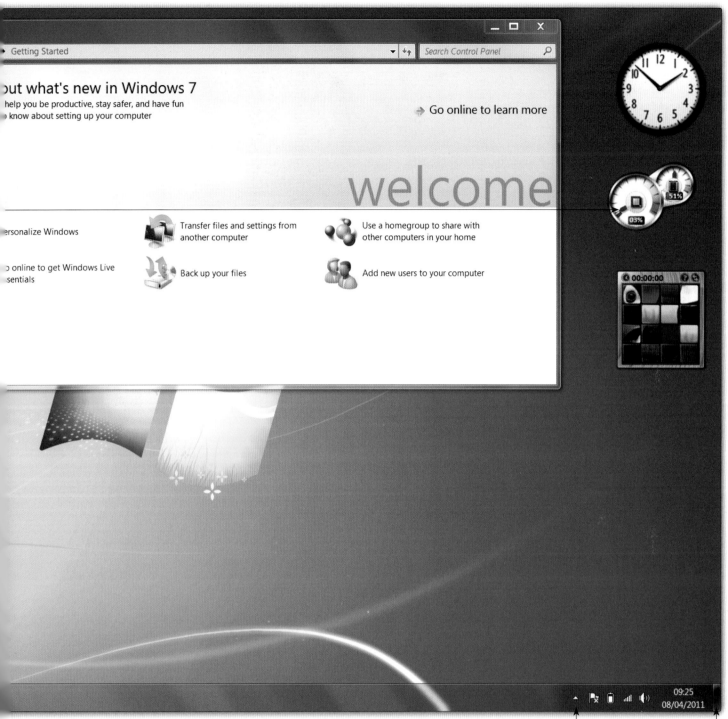

Getting Started

▼ ↵⁺ *Search Control Panel* 🔍

out what's new in Windows 7

help you be productive, stay safer, and have fun
know about setting up your computer

➜ Go online to learn more

welcome

ersonalize Windows

Transfer files and settings from
another computer

Use a homegroup to share with
other computers in your home

online to get Windows Live
sentials

Back up your files

Add new users to your computer

09:25
08/04/2011

The Windows 7 desktop

The desktop includes a number of new or redesigned features from
previous versions of Windows. If you're running Windows 7 on a netbook
or low-powered PC, don't be alarmed if you can't see the translucent
window effects we show here – Windows turns them off automatically if
your PC doesn't have the graphical grunt to cope.

The **notification area**, or
System Tray, shows programs
that are running in the
background, plus details of
your network connection,
volume level and other useful
info. Click the up arrow to
access hidden notifications
and to customise notifications.

Hover over the handy new
Show Desktop button and any
open programs will temporarily
disappear to reveal your
desktop and Gadgets.

3

Windows 7
The basics

Personalise the desktop

Most people like to stamp their personality on their PC by adjusting the appearance of the desktop. Windows 7 makes it easy to add a splash of character.

Many of its customisation features can be found by right-clicking on the desktop and selecting Personalize. You can also access these settings via the Control Panel, which is available from the Start menu. The simplest way to start tinkering is to use Windows 7's themes, as we explain on the opposite page. But there are a few basics you need to know first about controlling the appearance of the desktop.

THE TASKBAR The bar at the bottom of the screen has been completely revamped from older versions of Windows. The text descriptions of programs that are currently open have been replaced by chunky icons. Most people quickly get used to this, but if you want to go back to the old way, you can: right-click on the Taskbar, click Properties, and select "Never combine" from the Taskbar buttons dropdown menu.

The best thing about the Taskbar is that even programs that aren't currently in use can be shown here, giving you one-click access to your favourite software. To add a program to the Taskbar, open the program, then right-click on its icon and choose "Pin this program to Taskbar".

Unlike in previous versions of Windows, you can also shuffle the icons on the Taskbar into your preferred order. Left-click and hold on a Taskbar icon and drag into your desired position. It will stay there for good.

You don't have to keep your Taskbar at the bottom of the screen. Shift it the top or either side by right-clicking on the Taskbar, choosing Properties and taking your pick from the Taskbar location dropdown menu.

DESKTOP ICONS The first time you open Windows 7, you'll find only the Recycle Bin on the desktop, and perhaps a few other software icons installed by your PC manufacturer. If you want to add shortcuts to your favourite software here, find a program on the Start menu, right-click its name, select Send To and choose "Desktop (create shortcut)". You can do the same with your favourite files or folders.

DISPLAY RESOLUTION Windows 7 should select the correct resolution for your screen. If it looks fuzzy or you want to experiment, right-click an empty space on the desktop and select Screen Resolution. Adjust the sliding scale. If you pick an unusable option, don't worry: Windows gives you 15 seconds to revert back to your previous display setting.

Tip

Today's widescreen monitors offer very high resolutions, which can make on-screen text so fine as to be almost unreadable. There's no need to artificially bump down the resolution – a new feature in Windows 7 allows you to simply make the text bigger.

1. Right-click on the desktop, choose Screen Resolution and then click on the link that says "Make text and other items larger or smaller".

2. Choose from the options to make the text and other items either 125% or 150% of their current size. You will need to restart your PC for the changes to take effect.

3. Now Windows text and desktop icons look bigger, without any loss of clarity or sharpness.

HOW TO...
CHOOSE OR CREATE A THEME

1 **CHOOSE A THEME** Windows 7 comes with a series of default themes – ready-made packages of complementary desktop backgrounds, sounds and screensavers. These include an excellent UK pack with stunning photography of beauty spots including Stonehenge and the White Cliffs of Dover. Take your pick by right-clicking on the desktop, choosing Personalize and selecting one of the Aero Themes. Each theme contains a selection of photos, and your background will change periodically as it cycles through them. To move on to the next photo, right-click on the desktop and choose "Next desktop background".

2 **DOWNLOAD NEW THEMES** Microsoft is making a series of alternative themes available for download. In the Personalize menu, click "Get more themes online" at the far right. Early examples include a serene Isle of Lewis pack. Click on themes to download them to your computer. Once downloaded, they'll be available from the My Themes section.

3 **BUILD YOUR OWN THEME** Beautiful as Microsoft's Windows 7 themes are, the best way to stamp your personality on your PC is by creating your own. First, a little preparation: save all the photos you want in your new theme into a single Pictures folder. Now open that folder, right-click on one of those photos and choose "Set as desktop background". Close the folder, right-click on the desktop and choose Personalize, and you should see your photo appears as an unsaved theme.

To add more photos to the theme, click the Desktop Background link at the foot of the screen and browse to the folder containing your pictures. Select the pictures you want to add, holding down the Control button as you click them. Tweak the timing settings if you like, then click Save Changes (this can take a while to process). If you wish, you can also change the colour of the transparent "glass" on the desktop windows to match your photos, as well as the Windows sounds and the screensaver, using the options provided. When you've finished tweaking, click Save Theme and give it a name.

4 **SHARE YOUR CREATIONS** You can share your saved theme with friends and family, or upload it to a website for others to download (make sure you own the copyright to the photos before doing so). In the Themes menu, right-click your chosen theme and select "Save theme for sharing". Give it a name and save it. You can now email the file to other users or make it available for download. Beware: if you've used a lot of high-resolution photos, the file may be too large for some people to receive in their mailboxes.

HOW LONG?
About 15 minutes – a little more if you're planning to create your own theme.

HOW HARD?
It's blissfully simple to tweak the appearance of your PC and even share the results with others.

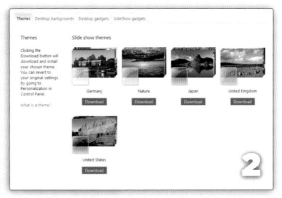

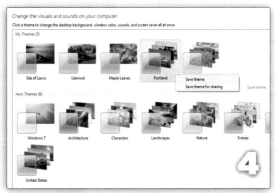

Introducing Jump Lists

One of the greatest strengths of Windows 7 is it makes it easier to find what you want on your computer – and one of the ways it does this is with Jump Lists. It's a feature that's new to Windows 7, and it works with the new Taskbar. Right-click on a program's icon in the Taskbar at the foot of the screen, and you'll see a list sprout upwards – hence the name Jump List. Alternatively, hold down the left mouse button on a program's icon and drag the mouse upwards. If you're using a touchscreen, hold your finger on the program's icon and swipe upwards to activate the Jump List.

Jump Lists aren't only accessible from the Taskbar. Click on the Start orb and hover over a program's name, and you'll see Jump Lists emerge from this menu too. In the vast majority of cases, the Jump List will feature items that you've recently opened using that particular program. So, for example, in Microsoft Word it's a quick way of opening a document you were working on yesterday: hover over the document's title and left-click to open, instead of having to plough through your folders.

With applications such as Windows Media Player, Jump Lists can also be used to access basic controls, such as "Resume previous list" to continue playing your music from where you last left off. Alternatively, right-click on the Internet Explorer logo and its Jump List gives you the option to start surfing in InPrivate mode, which won't leave any trace of your web session lingering on your PC. There are plenty more applications that make use of Jump Lists – just try right-clicking and see what you can find!

You also have some control over what appears in the Jump Lists. If you have a file or document that you open regularly – say, an expenses form or a welcome letter that you send out to new members of your club – you can "pin" it to the Jump List so that it's always ready.

There are two ways of doing this. If the document you want to keep is already in the application's Jump List, click the little pin icon next to its name. If it isn't, open the folder containing the relevant document and drag it down onto a blank space on the Taskbar.

It isn't only files and documents that can be pinned to Jump Lists. If there's a folder you want quick access to, you don't have to create a shortcut on your desktop: just drag its icon down into the Taskbar and onto the Windows Explorer icon (the yellow one that looks like a bunch of folders). You'll be offered the option to pin the folder there.

If you decide you don't want an item pinned to a Jump List any more, it's easy to remove: just hover over its name and click the little pin icon.

Tip

You can also use Jump Lists to quickly take you to commonly used folders. Right-click on the Windows Explorer icon (by default, this is found to the right of Internet Explorer's icon in the Taskbar) and you'll see your ten most frequently opened folders listed.

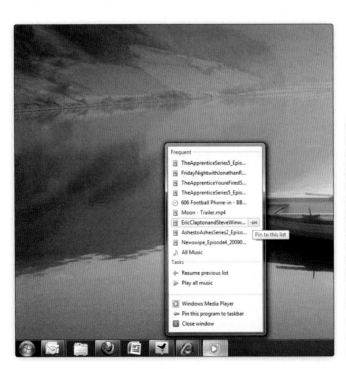

Jump Lists offer quick access to documents and tasks related to a particular program, such as playlists and playback controls in Windows Media Player.

Internet Explorer's new private browsing mode can be accessed this way, and programs from other makers should soon start to offer Jump Lists.

3

Windows 7
The basics

FILL YOUR DESKTOP WITH LOTS OF HANDY LITTLE APPLICATIONS – FOLLOW OUR GUIDE TO FINDING AND INSTALLING THE BEST WINDOWS 7 GADGETS.

Introducing Gadgets

First seen in Vista, Gadgets have become a key feature of the desktop. These tiny utility applications cover everything from the ridiculously trivial (virtual fortune cookie?) to the genuinely indispensible (see our top picks, below).

Windows 7 gives you free rein to place your Gadgets wherever you like on the screen. Along with all the other new features in Windows 7, such as the revamped Taskbar and Jump Lists (see p38), there's less need than ever to clutter your desktop with shortcut icons – so you should have plenty of space to play with.

KEEPING TRACK OF YOUR GADGETS Microsoft has made it easier than ever to keep an eye on your Gadgets, allowing you to quickly check the latest news headlines, for example. In Windows Vista, Gadgets were forever hidden away underneath all your other windows, so in order to see them you had to minimise whatever you were working on. Windows 7 introduces a new Show Desktop button at the bottom right of the screen. Hover the cursor over this and all your windows fade away, allowing you to take a glance at

your Gadgets. Move away, and you're swiftly back to where you left off. The Gadgets menu is also easier to find than it was in Vista: right-click on a blank spot on the desktop and you'll see Gadgets listed among the options.

WHERE DO GADGETS COME FROM? Microsoft provides a dozen Gadgets to get you started in Windows 7, including a very handy headline reader and a picture slideshow that elegantly scrolls through the snaps in your Pictures folder. But the majority of Gadgets are supplied by third-party developers that have created hundreds of tiny tools to choose from. You can access this bountiful supply via Microsoft's website: see opposite for instructions. You may see some older Gadgets that were created for Vista, but they should work in Windows 7 as well.

A word of warning: third-party Gadgets should be treated with caution, because, as with any software, there's a small chance they could pose a security threat. Make sure you have security set up (see chapter 8) before downloading more, and be wary of entering login details into Gadgets.

Tip

Microsoft's Gadgets aren't the only type of desktop applet. Google offers a vast range with its Google Desktop service, which is free to download from http://desktop.google.com. Yahoo's similar Widgets are available free at http://widgets.yahoo.com. There's nothing to stop you running Google or Yahoo's applets alongside Microsoft's Gadgets, but it might impact the performance of low-powered computers such as netbooks.

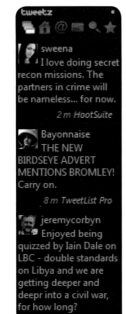

The **Tweetz** gadget streams the latest Twitter updates, so you can keep up to date with important news – and less serious matters.

With the **My eBay Toolbar** gadget you can keep an eye on auctions and ensure you're not outbid – without being glued to your browser.

The **Google** Gadget does just what you'd expect. Simply type in your search terms directly from the desktop – there's no need to fire up your web browser first.

The **Currency Converter** is great for anyone who handles foreign currency at work. It's handy for holiday money too.

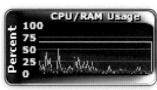

Techie types can keep an eye on their computer resources with this compact **Speed Test** gadget.

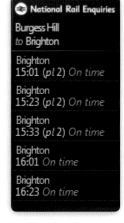

Live Departure Boards is a convenient way to keep an eye on your train times.

Listen while you work with the official **BBC Radio** Gadget, which lets you tune in to a range of BBC radio stations via the internet.

HOW TO...
DOWNLOAD MORE GADGETS

① **VISIT THE ONLINE GADGET GALLERY** The easiest way of getting to Microsoft's Gadget website is to click on the link from Windows 7's Gadgets menu. Right-click any blank space on the desktop, select Gadgets, then click on "Get more Gadgets online" at the bottom of the window. This will take you to the Desktop and SideShow Gadgets library. SideShow gadgets are designed to be viewed on secondary displays – we needn't worry about those for now. There's plenty to choose from in the main Desktop Gadgets category.

② **TAKE YOUR PICK** In your browser you'll now see a selection of popular gadgets, which you can click to download immediately if you so wish. You'll also see a link labelled "Get more desktop gadgets"; click on this and you'll be presented with the full range of Gadgets, divided into themes such as "Fun and games" and "Search tools". To help sort the wheat from the chaff, find the category you're interested in and click "Sort by rating" at the top of the list, to bring the most popular Gadgets to the top of the pile. If you want to find one of the Gadgets we've recommended opposite, pop its name into the search box at the top and click the green Gallery button. You might have to scroll through a couple of pages to get the precise Gadget you were looking for. Although most Gadgets are free, some do cost money.

③ **DOWNLOAD MORE GADGETS** Once you've found a Gadget you like the look of, click the Download button. At this point you'll be presented with a warning message advising you to download Gadgets only from developers you trust. This is Microsoft's way of covering its back when pointing you to Gadgets developed by other companies. Check your security software is running, and click Install. You'll now see another pop-up asking whether you want to Open or Save the file; click Open, and in the next box click Install. The Gadget should now appear on your desktop.

④ **CUSTOMISE YOUR GADGETS** Once a Gadget is installed, you can move it to wherever you like on your desktop by clicking on the little grid of dots that appears when you hover over it and dragging it into place. If, when you hover over the Gadget, you see a little icon with an arrow pointing to the top-right corner, clicking this will show a larger version of the Gadget. You'll also notice a little spanner icon, which gives access to the settings for that particular Gadget. This is where, for example, you can set the radio station you want to listen to in the BBC Radio Gadget. If you don't want a Gadget on your desktop any more, click the "x" icon. It will still be available from the Gadgets menu, unless you choose to completely uninstall the item.

HOW LONG?
You can spend ages browsing the list of Gadgets, but each only takes seconds to install.

HOW HARD?
The process couldn't be much simpler: the only problem is you're spoilt for choice.

3

Windows 7
The basics

 MOST OF US NOW HAVE FILES, PHOTOS AND MUSIC ON A SECOND PC OR AN EXTERNAL HARD DISK. THAT'S WHERE WINDOWS 7'S LIBRARIES COME IN...

Introducing Libraries

Libraries are quite simply one of the best things about Windows 7. They may seem a little counter-intuitive at first, but within a week or two you'll wonder how you ever put up with the old, fiddly way of working.

When you install Windows 7 four Libraries are set up for you: Documents, Music, Pictures and Video. Each contains all the folders and files you'd previously have kept in My Documents (in Windows XP) or Documents (in Vista). What's different is that a Library isn't tied to what's contained on your PC's main hard disk. As you'll see later, it can also include files from anywhere else – perhaps from an external hard disk, or another computer on your network.

To use the Library metaphor, not only can you instantly grab any book from your own bookcase, you can also grab more from your local library. This means you don't need to duplicate files from other computers and drives; you can access them just as if they were sitting on your hard disk (so long as your computer is linked to that external device).

To see this in action, find your list of Libraries in the left-hand pane of Windows Explorer, and click on the blue triangle beside Documents. You'll see two entries appear beneath it: My Documents and Public Documents. These are the actual hard disk folders; right-click on My Documents and select Properties and you'll see it lives in C:\Users\Name, where Name is your Windows username. If you left-click a folder on, say, your desktop and drag it into the Documents Library, the folder itself will be moved to the default save location. You'll get a tooltip-style message to let you know about this.

CUSTOMISING LIBRARIES As they stand, Libraries aren't terribly useful – you need to tailor them to your system. First, you can add folder locations to a Library. This is really the point of Libraries: to organise documents and files that may be on different physical media into one handy view.

Each Library view has an "Includes" label at the top right. By default, each Library location includes two folders: My Documents and Public Documents, My Video and Public Video, and so on. But click the "Library locations" link and you can add a folder to bring its contents into the Library view from anywhere. Remember, this isn't copying or moving folders, just allowing you to view them within a single window. Yet you can interact with them as normal here. Deleting or manipulating a file within a Library view affects the underlying physical file, wherever it may be.

The power of Libraries is that you can add folders from almost anywhere: different partitions, external hard disks, even network locations. The only limitation is that you can't add folders on "devices with removable storage", such as a USB flash drive or a DVD-R in your optical drive.

Tip

We can't emphasise this enough: hard disks fail. And with them go photos, music, crucial documents and video. Can you really afford to live without them? Use Libraries to set up a simple backup regime, even if it's just copying your whole photo library to an external hard disk every week.

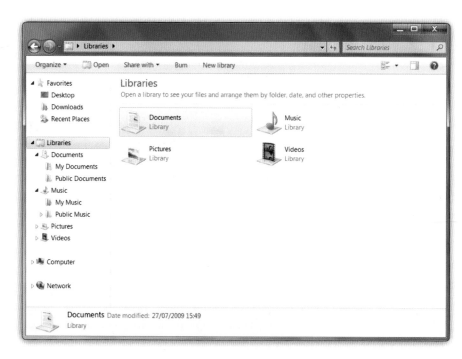

This is how your four Libraries will look by default, but there's an immense amount of opportunity to shape them to your needs.

HOW TO...
TWEAK AND SET UP LIBRARIES

Here's how to set up your own Libraries. Why bother? Well, the benefit of adding an external hard disk to a Library will be obvious to anyone who has a large media collection and has ever tried to upgrade their PC. With your media files on an external device, you can just attach your drive to the new machine, add the location to the Library – and immediately find all your files exactly where you'd expect them to be.

It also means that as your data inevitably grows and fills up your drives, you can just plug in a new drive and add that to the Library. And by setting the default save location to the new disk, you have a super-easy way to get unlimited storage without having to copy files around or mess about with expanding partitions and suchlike. Bliss.

Just remember that the more disks you have, the more chance there is of one of them suffering a failure, so always back up your vital files.

 ADD FOLDERS By default, the only folders in each library are the standard Documents locations under C:\Users\. The power of Libraries lies in the ability to add folders. To do that, click the "Includes 2 locations" link at the top of any library view.

BEYOND YOUR PC Click Add to start expanding the scope of the Library. You can add folders from almost any location, including network folders.

Here we've browsed on the network to find a folder. The only things you can't add are removable storage: flash memory drives and optical drives (CDs and DVDs).

 WHAT SAVES WHERE? An initial difficulty with Libraries is what happens when you actually want to move or save a file into the Library, as Libraries represent the contents several folders at once. So where do your files go? The answer is simple: into the default save location. In the Documents Library Locations dialog, one of the folders will be marked as the default save location. That's the actual folder on your system that any files dragged into the library will be saved to. To change the default save location, all you need to do is right-click on a library folder and select "Set as default save location".

CUSTOM LIBRARIES You're not limited to the default Documents, Video, Music and Pictures libraries. You can easily create your own. To create a custom library, click on the top-level Libraries icon, right-click and select New | Library. Enter a name and you're away. New libraries don't include any folders when they're first created, so you'll need to add them as in step 2. Bear in mind that if you right-click on an already created Library and select New Folder, that's what you get – a new folder in the default save location.

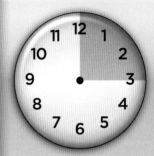

HOW LONG?
15 minutes is a safe bet. You may want to set aside more time to get to grips wih custom Libraries.

HOW HARD?
It's a bit of a mind-bender at first, but once you understand how Libraries work you'll quickly get to grips with using them.

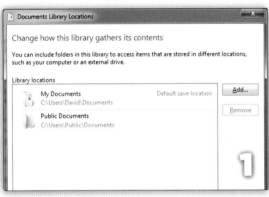

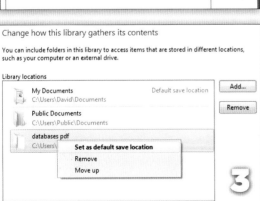

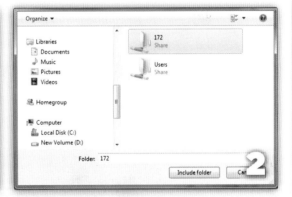

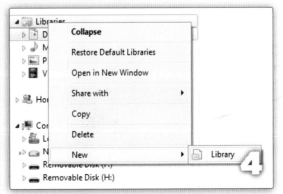

Introducing user accounts

One of the most common security blunders people make with family PCs is to let everyone log in to an Administrator account, giving children the power to delete vital Windows files that could prevent the computer from working, and allowing them to rifle through your private documents.

Even worse, it grants children permission to install their own software. This leaves your PC wide open to attack when they decide to load that tempting free game they found online, which turns out to be a scam that steals your bank account details.

To help prevent younger (or even older) users running wild, Microsoft offers several security measures, one of which is individual user accounts. Each person can have their own account and password on the PC, which they enter when they sit down to use it, giving them access to all the files and documents they need, while limiting their access to features that could compromise security.

The other advantage of giving children their own accounts is that you can apply separate parental controls for each child, preventing them from using the computer late at night, for example. See p122 for more on setting up Windows 7's Parental Controls.

TYPES OF ACCOUNT There are three types of account in Windows 7. Administrator is the default that's set up for the first person on the PC. Administrator accounts have full control over the computer, with the ability to add new software and hardware, make changes to key Windows settings, and set up and delete accounts for other users.

On a family PC, it's sensible to have only one Administrator and everyone else on Standard user accounts. (As the administrator, you might even decide to set up your own Standard user account, as we discuss on the opposite page.) Standard users can make use of any of the software already on the PC, create and delete their own files, and personalise the desktop with their own themes, only displayed when they log in. They also have their own web browser bookmarks and toolbars, so Dad's setup isn't overrun with links to gaming and social networking sites.

Standard user accounts are banned from installing their own software, however. If a Standard user attempts to install a piece of software, they'll be prompted for the Administrator's password before being allowed to proceed.

GUEST ACCOUNTS Finally, there's the Guest account, which is designed to be used by visitors to the house who need access to a computer. They too are barred from installing software and making any changes to key files and settings. You can switch on the Guest account by going to Start | Control Panel | User Accounts and Family Safety | User Accounts. Then choose "Manage another account" and click on the Guest account icon.

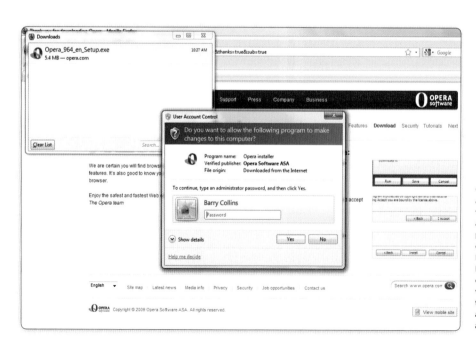

Only Administrator accounts are allowed to install software and make other potentially significant changes to the PC. Ensuring other users log in with Standard or Guest accounts will go a long way towards preventing accidental damage and security breaches.

HOW TO...
SET UP A STANDARD ACCOUNT

CREATE A NEW ACCOUNT Type "user accounts" into the Start menu and click User Accounts. Now click "Manage another account" and "Create a new account". Type the name of the person whose account this will be into the Account name box, and make sure Standard user is selected. Then click Create Account.

PASSWORD-PROTECT THE ACCOUNT Ideally, all the user accounts on your computer should be protected by a password, so people can't log in as each other. If younger users forget theirs, the Administrator can reset it. To set a password on the account you've just created, return to "Manage another account", click the name of your new user and choose "Create a password". You'll be asked to type the password twice, plus a hint (such as "favourite footballer"), which will be shown on the login screen should the person forget their password. You can also change the user's picture and set Parental Controls (see p122) from this menu.

CHANGE ACCOUNT TYPES For the ultimate in security, even the Administrator should do their day-to-day computing using a Standard account. That makes it harder for you to make mistakes, and can limit the risk of malware installing itself on your PC – though be warned that there are plenty of threats that can get

you even when you're using a Standard account – see our discussion of online security on p130.

If you've already spent time tailoring your Administrator account to your needs, you don't need to start from scratch. Simply create a new Administrator account with a strong password, which you can use when you need to make sweeping changes to your system. Now go back to the User Account menu for your own account and select "Change the account type". Choose Standard user, and all your settings and documents will remain in place under the new, safer Standard account.

It's worth noting that Windows 7's User Account Controls also provide a certain degree of protection (see p128 for more on this) in Windows 7, so advanced users may now regard using a Standard account as overkill.

DELETING ACCOUNTS Administrators have the power to delete user accounts when necessary. To do this, go to the User Accounts menu, select "Manage another account", click on the account you wish to erase and select "Delete the account". Be warned: deleting someone's account will delete their documents, music, photos and other files – unless you select the Keep Files option which isn't the default choice. Make sure you select this, or double-check there's nothing worth keeping in this user account before opting to Delete Files.

HOW LONG?
It takes only a few minutes to set up Standard user accounts for all the family.

HOW HARD?
It's simple to add this vital layer of protection – just beware of data loss when deleting accounts.

3
Windows 7 The basics

 WITH WINDOWS 7'S ENHANCED SEARCH TOOLS, YOU CAN JUMP STRAIGHT TO WHAT YOU NEED – WHETHER IT'S ON YOUR PC OR EVEN ON THE INTERNET.

Introducing Windows Search

We've seen how Windows 7's Libraries conveniently bring all your personal data together in a few virtual locations (see p42). But if you use your PC regularly, you'll quickly build up a large collection of data, and it can still be a pain to find the file you're looking for. Windows 7's Search can scan all your files in a flash and show only the ones you want.

FINDING A SPECIFIC FILE Running a simple search in Windows 7 is easy. Imagine you're looking for a file called *Robyn's Plans for April.doc*, and you know it's somewhere in your Libraries. Start by going to Windows Explorer and clicking on Libraries in the left pane to see your Libraries. Look to the top-right of your Explorer window and you'll see a field labelled Search, like in a web browser. Type "Robyn's Plans for April" into this (you don't need to press Return). A dropdown menu will appear as you type, giving you some extra options, which we'll discuss – but ignore that for now. You should see a list of related files appear in the main view, and if you use Outlook or Windows Mail you'll also see any relevant messages and contacts found in your email archive.

What if the file you wanted isn't there? Perhaps you didn't save the file into a Library after all. If you didn't, Windows won't find it, as by default it only searches within your selected folder. In the main Explorer pane you'll see options to broaden the search to your whole PC, specify other locations to search, or even search the internet.

Searching your whole computer can take a long time. Windows keeps an index of your personal folders, so it can locate their contents in moments; but when you start searching other folders, Windows has to inspect each file. You can choose which folders are indexed by opening the Control Panel and clicking "Change how Windows searches".

FINDING MANY FILES If you still can't find your file, perhaps you accidentally saved it under a different name. If you enter just the word "plans" into the Search field, Windows will show you all files within the current folder that include that word. Hopefully, this list will include the file you're looking for: if so, you can double-click to open it right away, or right-click it and select "Open file location" to view its folder.

If you'd find it useful to have all your plans at your fingertips, click the "Save search" button above the main display. Provide a name for this search when it asks, and you'll see that name appear under Favorites in the navigation pane of your Explorer window. In future, you can click this link and Windows will immediately re-run the search, showing all files with "plans" in their names – even new ones – in the folder you originally searched.

see p42

Tip

You can also use the Windows Start menu to search. Click the Start orb to open this and you'll see a text-entry box labelled "Search programs and files". Type your keywords in here and Windows will show you all the programs and personal files it can find with matching names or descriptions. It's a simpler way of running a search, and can be a time-saver as you don't need to take your hands off the keyboard.

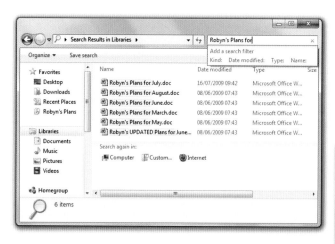

Windows Search makes it easy to find files, especially if you keep them in Libraries. Notice that it will find all files whose names contain the specified words; to match only the whole phrase, enter it within quote marks, such as "Robyn's Plans for".

As well as searching for files by their names, you can even find phrases within files such as Word documents to track down the content you're looking for.

HOW TO...
CUSTOMISE YOUR SEARCHES

① CUSTOMISE THE VIEW You can view your search results in several ways. Click the "Change view" button towards the top-right of the Explorer window to cycle between various views. You can also click on the dropdown arrow next to the "Change view" button to choose your own display format. The Extra Large Icons view is handy if you're searching for pictures, since it shows thumbnails of all the images found without you needing to open them. The Content view shows excerpts from the text found inside each file, so it can be useful for identifying word processing files or pages you've saved from the web.

② FILTER YOUR SEARCHES As you type your terms into the Search box, you'll see a dropdown menu appear offering filters to narrow down your results. These filters change intelligently depending on the active folder: if you're in the Documents library, for example, you'll see an option to search by Author; move to the Music library and the filters include Artist name and Length. Click on a filter to see the options you can apply: Authors, for example, will let you pick authors from a list, while Length options range from "Very short (under 1 min)" to "Very long (over 60 mins)". You can apply as many filters as you like, enabling you to home in on the file you need even if you don't know its name.

③ ADVANCED FILTERS Once you get adept at using filters, you can control them manually. For example, type "author:Robyn" as a search term and the results will be narrowed down to documents created by Robyn, even if that filter isn't normally offered for that folder. All the filters in Windows 7 can be used in this way, and you needn't worry if you don't know how to use each one: once you type the colon, Windows will pop up a list of options that you can choose from using the mouse. There's a huge range of filters available, and you can visit www.pcpro.co.uk/links/win7filter for a list.

④ FEDERATED SEARCH Windows 7 also features a new Microsoft technology called Federated Search. Besides searching your own files, you can also use the Windows interface to search websites. To take advantage, you'll need to download a tiny piece of code called a Federated Search Connector for each site you want to search. These are available for sites including YouTube, Flickr, Amazon and Microsoft Bing. Advanced users can even create their own connectors, as we explain on p54. Once you've installed a Federated Search Connector, it will appear like a saved search in your Favorites. Click it and you can search websites and other online resources as easily as rummaging through your own computer.

HOW LONG?
It generally takes just a second or two to find files, but you might need ten minutes to get the hang of the features.

HOW HARD?
You could spend hours learning the filters and creating Connectors, but simple searches are easy.

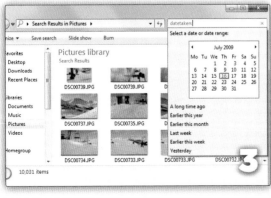

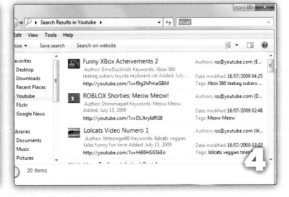

WINDOWS 7 INCLUDES UPDATED PAINT, WORDPAD AND CALCULATOR TOOLS, EACH WITH A SNAZZY INTERFACE AND PLENTY OF GREAT FEATURES.

Windows 7's bundled applications

They might never match the power of full-blown third-party software, but the applications that come with Windows 7 do an admirable job for basic tasks – and they're free.

For basic document editing there's WordPad, while Paint handles simple image editing. Both now have the easy-to-use Ribbon interface, as found in Microsoft Office. Plus there's the Calculator, with a range of advanced operation modes. You'll find them all in the Start menu, under All Programs | Accessories, along with the other free utilities Microsoft provides as part of Windows 7.

WORDPAD Windows' top text-editing app has had a redesign, and the toolbar now looks like a professional word processor. It's divided into two main subsets, Home and View, so you can make adjustments without having to dive into dropdown menus. As in Microsoft Office, the Font and Paragraph tools take centre stage, along with Insert and Edit options. Click the View tab to adjust the zoom and turn word wrap on or off.

There's also a Quick Access bar in the top-left corner, which can be customised to hold the options you regularly use. WordPad can save documents in the XML-based format used by Microsoft Word 2007 and 2010, or in Text and Rich Text formats that any editor can open.

PAINT Windows Paint may lack the features of a proper photo-editing package such as Adobe Photoshop Elements, but for basic picture creation and manipulation it's a fun tool. (It's also handy for pasting screen captures made with the PrintScreen key.) Everything you need now sits in the accessible Ribbon, with rotating, cropping and resizing options beside Tools, Shapes and Colours.

There's a useful colour editor, and the main menu provides shortcuts to send the current picture in an email or set it as your desktop background. As in WordPad, a customisable Quick Access bar at the top-left carries your favourite tools. Images can be saved in all the most commonly used formats, including JPEG, PNG and TIF.

CALCULATOR You might not think a humble Calculator could have any exciting secrets, but it's worth a closer look. If you open the View menu you'll find a Scientific modes, plus – new in Windows 7 – Programmer and Statistics options, which change the button panel to reflect appropriate functions.

And the Calculator isn't limited to simple sums; it can perform unit conversions and work out date differences, and even comes with quick tools for mortgage calculations, vehicle leasing and fuel economy.

Tip

You may soon find you outgrow the bundled apps that Microsoft provides, but that doesn't mean you have to spend lots of money. See chapter 5 for our guide to the top programs you can download to enhance Windows for free.

From the Calculator's **View menu** you can choose a button layout, select Worksheets and see your calculation history.

You can **copy and paste** numbers straight into the Calculator from other programs, and do the same back out when you have the result.

As well as the Scientific view seen here, there are now separate **Programmer and Statistics views**, each replacing the buttons with functions relevant to those tasks. The usual number pad is always present, and if you don't want advanced functions you can switch to Basic view to hide them.

You won't see this by default, but go into the View menu (see left) and select a **Worksheet** and you'll be greeted with a selection of useful quick calculation tools like this mortgage calculator. Other options include a unit converter and a fuel economy calculator.

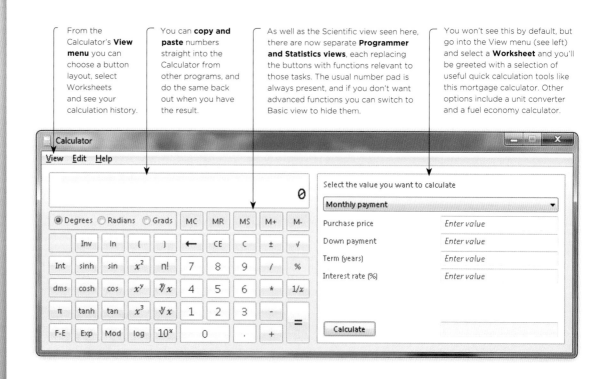

WHAT'S NEW IN...
WORDPAD

The **Quick Access** bar holds the Undo and Redo buttons by default, but you can customise it to hold any of your favourite options.

You can **find and replace** words to save time in long documents. The only key tool that WordPad still sorely lacks is a word count.

The **File menu** lets you quickly attach a document to an email or open recently edited documents.

The new **Ribbon** interface divides the main tools into tabs instead of dropdown menus, so the tool you need is only ever one click away.

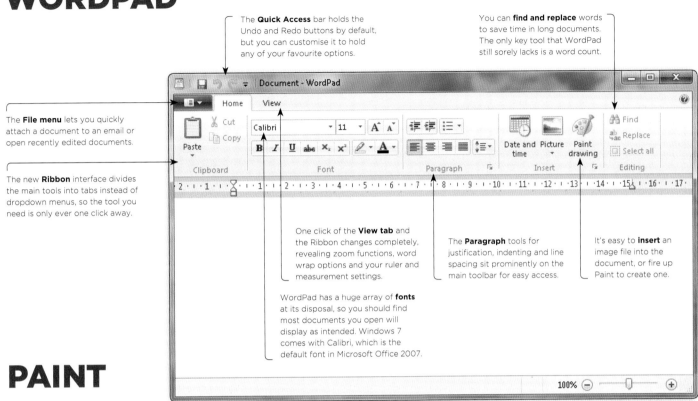

One click of the **View tab** and the Ribbon changes completely, revealing zoom functions, word wrap options and your ruler and measurement settings.

The **Paragraph** tools for justification, indenting and line spacing sit prominently on the main toolbar for easy access.

It's easy to **insert** an image file into the document, or fire up Paint to create one.

WordPad has a huge array of **fonts** at its disposal, so you should find most documents you open will display as intended. Windows 7 comes with Calibri, which is the default font in Microsoft Office 2007.

PAINT

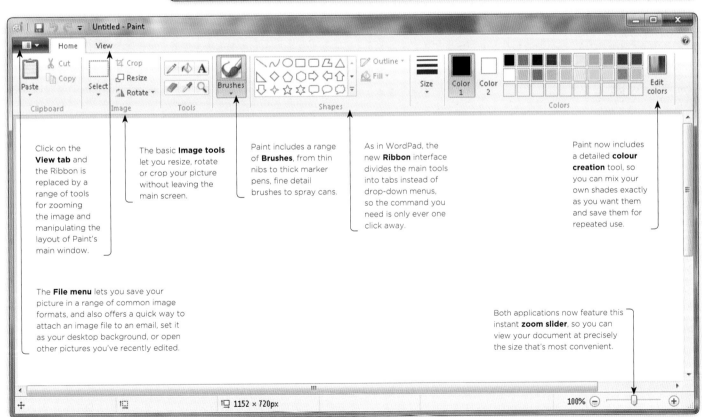

Click on the **View tab** and the Ribbon is replaced by a range of tools for zooming the image and manipulating the layout of Paint's main window.

The basic **Image tools** let you resize, rotate or crop your picture without leaving the main screen.

Paint includes a range of **Brushes**, from thin nibs to thick marker pens, fine detail brushes to spray cans.

As in WordPad, the new **Ribbon** interface divides the main tools into tabs instead of drop-down menus, so the command you need is only ever one click away.

Paint now includes a detailed **colour creation** tool, so you can mix your own shades exactly as you want them and save them for repeated use.

The **File menu** lets you save your picture in a range of common image formats, and also offers a quick way to attach an image file to an email, set it as your desktop background, or open other pictures you've recently edited.

Both applications now feature this instant **zoom slider**, so you can view your document at precisely the size that's most convenient.

IN THIS CHAPTER

4

Advanced features

ADVANCED FEAT

We've now covered the basics of Windows 7, but there's much more to it than a few tweaks. With just a little technical know-how you can speed up your day-to-day work with keyboard shortcuts; calibrate your monitor so that it displays colours more accurately; create virtual hard disks – and even install Windows 7 directly onto a virtual drive. In this chapter we'll show you how,

URES

and reveal what the enhanced Aero interface has to offer. It goes way beyond glossy effects – from shaking a window so that the others fall away, to instantly tiling windows and moving them between screens. And you'll discover why PC manufacturers and users alike are excited about the touchscreen technology built into Windows 7.

Unleashing Windows Aero

Windows 7's Aero Glass interface is certainly pretty, but don't be fooled into thinking it's purely cosmetic. It also provides a range of new features that make the operating system quicker and easier to use. Many of these aren't visible at first glance – they're hidden away, only becoming apparent when you drag windows in a certain direction or activate a keyboard shortcut. On these pages we'll show you eight secret Aero shortcuts you can use to get even more out of Windows 7.

1 **WINDOWS SHAKE** Often you can find yourself with a dozen application windows open. This makes moving between programs laborious, and can distract you from the document you're working on. In Windows 7 you can easily "shake away" the clutter, minimising all the open windows except the active one. To do this, click and hold any blank space in the bar at the top of the window you're working on; drag it down slightly if the window is full-screen. Then shake the mouse gently from left to right. You should see all the other windows disappear. Don't worry if you have unsaved work in any of those windows – they haven't been closed, just minimised to the Taskbar at the bottom of the screen. Click on the program's icon there to re-open the window.

2 **GO FULL-SCREEN** If you're working in a window and want to make it full-screen, there's no need to find and click the fiddly little box icon at the top right. Just drag the window's top bar to the very top of the screen; the window instantly fills the screen. To return it to its original size, drag it back down.

3 **SNAP TO THE EDGES** Sometimes you want to work in more than one window at once: for example, you might need to refer to a web page while writing a document. Windows 7 makes it easy to show two windows side by side. Click on the bar at the top of the first window you want and drag it to the far left of the screen; the window snaps into place, filling half the screen. Now do the same with the second window, but drag it to the right. The windows should be butted up. The only time this won't work is when you have more than one monitor on your PC. In this instance, use keyboard shortcuts instead: hold down the Windows key and press the left or right arrow key as appropriate.

4 **SHOW THE DESKTOP** Keeping an eye on the news headlines or your train times using a Gadget (see p40)? You don't have to minimise all your windows to take a peek at your desktop; just hover the mouse over the translucent vertical bar next to the clock in the bottom-right corner and all your open windows temporarily melt away, revealing your Windows desktop and all its Gadgets.

Aero isn't just a pretty face – it adds convenient features that you'll use every day once you get to know them. Among the new options in Windows 7 are Shake (1), which fades out other windows to let you focus on what you're doing; the ability to make a window full-screen (2) just by dragging it to the top; snapping windows to the left and right for an instant side-by-side setup (3); quickly showing the desktop (4); and switching through application windows using Windows Peek (5). If none of this floats your boat, you can switch off Aero (8) and pretend your PC is stuck in the 1990s.

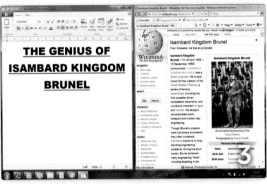

5 WINDOWS PEEK
By default, Windows 7 doesn't show names for the various icons in the Taskbar, so it can be tricky to find the window you're looking for. A new feature called Windows Peek can help. Hover over any icon in the Taskbar and up pops a miniature thumbnail image of that window. Move your mouse over this thumbnail and Windows shows you the position and contents of the window itself. This is handy when you have multiple web pages open in Internet Explorer: each tab gets its own thumbnail, so you can just click the one you want to open.

6 TASK SWITCHER
If you don't want to scroll through thumbnails with Peek, there's an easier way to flip through your open apps. Hold the Alt key and press Tab to invoke the Task Switcher. You'll now be presented with thumbnails of all your open windows slap-bang in the middle of the screen. With Alt still held down, keep pressing Tab to move to the window of your choice – or simply click on a thumbnail with the mouse to switch directly to it.

7 FLIP 3D
Task Switcher has a bigger, flashier brother called Flip 3D. Instead of seeing thumbnails of your open windows, you can flip through them in a full-screen three-dimensional carousel. Just hold down the Windows key and press Tab. Then keep on pressing Tab and watch the pseudo-3D windows you have open flit past you. It's the epitome of style over substance, and no more efficient than the Task Switcher, but we're all entitled to show off now and again, aren't we?

8 SWITCH AERO OFF
If you've had enough of translucent glass windows, preview thumbnails and whooshing graphics, it's easy to switch off the Windows Aero effects and adopt a simpler look. Right-click on the desktop, choose Personalize, and select either Windows 7 Basic or Windows Classic from the available themes. The Basic theme looks like the regular Windows 7 interface but without the graphical effects, while the Classic theme makes your desktop look like Windows XP – now that's retro, man.

Introducing Federated Search

Searching websites has been a staple of internet browsers for some time – we're all familiar with using search engines such as Google and Microsoft Bing. But, for the first time, Windows 7 makes it possible to search the web without using an internet browser at all. The term "Federated Search" may sound complicated, but it's easy to configure and use from an ordinary Windows Explorer window.

Why would you want to? Well, it's convenient not to have to open up a web browser. And Windows 7 searches internet sites in the same way as it searches your hard disk: by sending information as you type it. This means you don't even have to finish a word before results appear in your search window, so it's the fastest way to get results.

SETTING IT UP Windows 7 doesn't come with Federated Search set up by default, but it's well worth taking just a few minutes to get it working. Adding an internet search requires you to download a file called a search connector. Lots of these are already available; enter "windows 7 search connector" into your favourite search engine (via your web browser, for one last time) and you should find plenty. Connectors are freely available for practically all popular websites, including eBay, Google News, YouTube and Flickr. Search connectors are typically just a few kilobytes in size so they download almost instantly.

Once you've found a connector from a site you trust, double-click it and you'll be prompted to install it; just click Add and you're done. We take you through the process in more detail on the opposite page.

USING IT When you want to use your newly installed search connector for the first time, hold down the Windows key and press F for Find – or just type something into the Start menu and click the "See more results" link. You'll see a window appear with a navigation bar on the right, giving options for all the places you can search. Your search connector will be included in that list. Select it and you'll be prompted to begin typing a search term in the standard box.

You'll see results come back looking like a list of files; single-click on an item and a live preview of the web page will load in the right-hand pane. It makes finding the result you want quick and easy, because you don't need to open a web browser, or go back to your results every time you finish looking at a page.

Tip

If you want a search connector but can't find a suitable ready-made one online, you can make one yourself. It's relatively simple and takes only a few minutes for each website; instructions can be found at www.pcpro.co.uk/links/win7connector

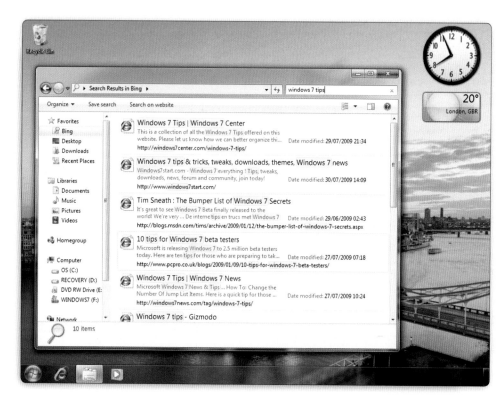

Once you add one or more connectors for your favourite online search engines, you can search the web from within Windows 7 just as easily as searching on your own hard disk.

HOW TO...
ADD A SEARCH PROVIDER

① **FIND A CONNECTOR** Finding a new search provider couldn't be easier, and the number available is growing all the time. Popular websites such as Flickr and YouTube already have search connectors. Enter "windows 7 search connector" and the name of a search provider into any search engine, via your web browser, and you'll get plenty of results. Connectors are available from a variety of sources, including expert users as well as internet companies, but be sure you trust the provider of any connector you download.

② **INSTALL YOUR CONNECTOR** We opted for a Flickr search connector from www.istartedsomething. com/flickrsearch, which not only provides a connector for the Flickr photo-sharing site, but also allows you to determine how that connector sorts your results: you can search by the date a picture was taken, or how interesting it's judged to be by Flickr's servers. Once you've downloaded it, just double-click on the resulting file and you'll be prompted to add it to Windows 7.

③ **SEARCH** This is where the fun starts. Hold down the Windows key on your PC's keyboard and press F. By default you'll be taken to a screen that wants to search your PC, but pay attention to the list of locations under the Favorites banner (which only appears

after you type something into the search box). This normally holds default locations such as your desktop and places you've added manually, but now you'll see a new icon called Flickr Search. In our case, we're feeling nostalgic for Cuba (where we spent a memorable holiday a few years ago), so we click the Flickr Search icon and type "cuba".

The results appear after just a few seconds, sorted by whatever criterion you selected when you downloaded the connector. If you click on any of the preview images, the far right-hand pane will show the Flickr page that hosts the image. It's a live preview, which means it appears on your PC as it is currently on Flickr's server. If you click any of the links, your default internet browser will launch and the page will be loaded in that.

④ **CUSTOMISE YOUR VIEW** The results page is very flexible. Not only can you grab the edge of any of the panes and drag it around to fit on the screen, but you can also view more or less about your results, either by clicking the thumbnail button near the top right or by holding down Ctrl and moving your mouse wheel (up to make the thumbnails bigger, down to make them smaller). The smaller they are, the more you can see on one page. At the smallest size you also get information about the page on which the item appears, plus a few of the tags applied to it and the name of the author.

HOW LONG?
A matter of moments to find and install the search connector of your choice.

HOW HARD?
Dead easy; just think twice before installing search connectors from unknown sources.

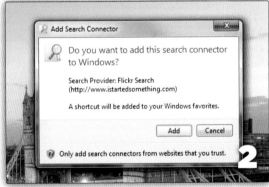

4

Advanced features

Introducing Windows XP Mode

Tip

You may not need Windows XP Mode to run older applications. If a program doesn't run straight away, try right-clicking on its icon and selecting "Troubleshoot compatibility". Windows 7 will guide you through a process of choosing compatibility settings that may well get your application working.

Tip

By default, Windows XP Mode runs at a reduced screen resolution in the relatively primitive 16-bit colour depth. This is unsuitable for photo-editing tasks and other graphical applications. You can fix it by going to Tools | Disable Integration Features, then changing the settings in the Desktop Properties of your XP desktop.

Almost all applications that were written for Windows XP should work perfectly on Windows 7. But there are some fundamental differences between the two systems, and there's no guarantee that a program written for one will run on the other.

That's a potential problem for businesses. Many companies rely on applications and services designed for Windows XP, and they can't afford to upgrade to Windows 7 if it means losing access to that software.

Wisely, Microsoft has taken steps to ensure that all software designed for Windows XP can still be used in Windows 7. The Professional, Enterprise and Ultimate editions of Windows 7 support a feature called XP Mode, which is based on Microsoft's Virtual PC 7 tool. When activated, it creates a full virtualised Windows XP system on your Windows 7 PC, within which you can install and run any programs that require the older OS. You can even access all your hard disks, optical drives and USB devices straight away from within your virtual XP system, without any of the additional configuration this would usually require.

Windows XP Mode isn't supplied with Windows 7 as standard, but it can be downloaded – along with the version of Virtual PC 7 it needs to run – from www.microsoft.com/windows/virtual-pc/default.aspx

THE BAD NEWS Not all Windows 7 systems can run XP Mode. To use it, your computer processor must support either Intel's VT technology or AMD-V. That should include all recent desktop processors, such as Intel's Core i3, i5 and i7 series, and AMD Athlon II and Phenom II chips. But if you have a lightweight laptop or an older system it's worth performing a web search to check your processor qualifies.

Virtualisation must also be enabled in the PC's BIOS. Check your manuals or the website above for details if you don't know how to do this.

Finally, as we've noted, XP Mode is only available in the business-orientated and Ultimate editions of Windows 7, so Home Premium users are out of luck.

RESURRECTING THE DEAD Once you have XP Mode up and running, you'll be faced with a window containing the old-fashioned XP desktop and not much else. If you want to maximise screen space, or hide Windows 7 from users, just select View Full Screen from the Action menu at the top.

Although your Windows XP system is a virtual machine, it's still able to connect to the internet, and it's still susceptible to virus infections and the like. Therefore, the very first thing you should do is install some sort of security software on your virtual XP machine. Depending

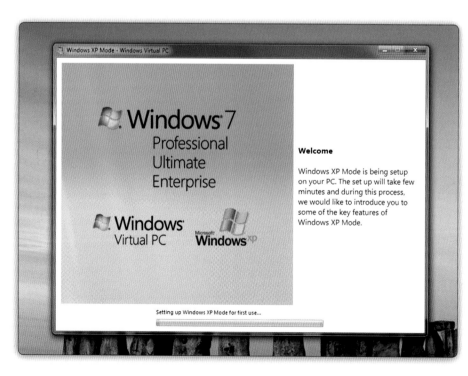

Installing Windows XP Mode gives you two PCs for the price of one – you can run even the oldest and fussiest XP programs within Windows 7 without them knowing they're not on an ordinary Windows XP system. Unfortunately, it's only available with the Professional, Enterprise and Ultimate editions of Windows 7, so Home Premium users will have to rely on Windows 7's inherent ability to run most XP (and Vista) software without any extra help.

on your licence, you may be able to install the same security suite you're using on your Windows 7 system. Alternatively, you can download and install a free antivirus tool such as Microsoft's free Security Essentials tool – see p130 for our guide to this handy enhancement.

Once that's done, it's time to set up your XP-loving, Windows 7-hating applications. You do this in exactly the same way as you would on a standard Windows XP machine. Go to My Computer within XP and look under <Your PC> to access your "real" PC's hard disks and optical drives: from here you can install whatever applications you like, then use them just like you could in the good old days.

Here's where XP Mode gets clever. Once an application has been installed to your XP Mode virtual desktop, you can launch it directly from your standard Windows 7 desktop. Go to Start | All Programs | Windows Virtual PC | Windows XP Mode Applications, and you'll find a list of any programs installed on your virtual XP machine. Select one, and it will load straight onto your desktop, just as if it were running directly under Windows 7. In fact, the only way you'll even know your applications are running in the XP Mode virtual machine is that they'll appear with a classic Windows XP-style frame, rather than a Windows 7 Aero window. It's impressively seamless.

XP Mode gives you two ways of running applications: from inside a virtual XP desktop (top right), which you can either run in a window or full screen, or virtualised within the Windows 7 desktop (below right). Here, the application window can be used just like any Windows 7 program, without explicitly treating it as a virtualised XP application.

Running virtualisation software such as Virtual PC 7, on which Windows XP Mode is based, often means some fiddling around to get your peripherals and storage working from the virtual operating system as well as your main one. Fortunately, XP Mode simplifies this.

Only half a gigabyte of RAM is allocated to Windows XP Mode by default – after all, 512MB was a lot of memory in those days. If you need more, and there's plenty available in your PC (bearing in mind you also have Windows 7 running), you can adjust this.

USING EXTERNAL DEVICES Normally, getting a virtual system to interact with external hard disks, USB drives and other peripherals can be tricky, but the technology behind XP Mode does the work for you.

When you start the XP Mode desktop, you'll see a USB menu at the top. Click it to list any USB devices connected to your PC. Printers and scanners may first need to be "attached": this option forces XP Mode to install drivers for new hardware.

By default, USB storage devices, such as memory sticks and hard disks, are shared between your Windows 7 system and the Windows XP virtual system. You'll find them listed with your host system hard drives as <Drive X> on <Your PC>. Alternatively, you can attach them to the virtual PC only, making it simpler to access them from Windows XP.

A LITTLE MORE POWER XP Mode is brilliant at what it's designed for, but it isn't built for speed. Its graphics are powered by a generic graphics adapter simulator, rather than by the real drivers for your PC's specific display hardware, so you can forget about games, and graphics-intensive applications and effects may be slow.

Memory is also limited by default to 512MB. This should be enough for the kind of business applications XP Mode is designed to run, but you can allocate more. To do this, shut down the Virtual PC by selecting <Ctrl-Alt-Del> from the menu bar and choosing "Shut down". Now (in Windows 7) go to Start | All Programs | Windows Virtual PC | Windows Virtual PC. Right-click on Windows XP Mode and choose Settings. Click on Memory and allocate the desired amount in the Memory (RAM) box provided.

4
Advanced features

Introducing Device Stage

Windows 7 includes a new feature called Device Stage that makes it easier to use and manage the various devices you connect to your PC. When you plug in a supported media player, digital camera, mobile phone or printer, the Device Stage screen appears. (You can open it yourself by selecting View Devices and Printers from the Control Panel, then double-clicking on a device.) As in our example image below, you'll see a picture of your device alongside a range of tasks and options specifically tailored to that very model.

The precise options you see here are down to the hardware manufacturer. The obvious choice is to provide information and shortcuts to common tasks: our all-in-one printer shows us the printer status, the number of documents in the print queue and the sort of paper loaded, as well as providing direct links for changing settings and scanning documents.

Manufacturers might also choose to embed links to their online services, manuals and software: HP, for example, could have provided a direct link to buy new ink cartridges for this particular printer, or a link to the latest driver. Mobile phone manufacturers could include a facility with Device Stage to record your own ringtone, synchronise contacts, or perform specific tasks using your model's dedicated PC software.

MIXED BLESSING Device Stage is a perfect opportunity for manufacturers to make life easier by putting features and services in a consistent, accessible place. Unfortunately, manufacturers haven't taken full advantage of it – our HP Photosmart printer, for example, doesn't offer any online functions. We've also found many printers and storage devices just show up with a default set of actions, and generic icons – in our image below, the printer picture is attractive, but it doesn't resemble the real printer.

GETTING IT WORKING Device Stage works by downloading device information over the internet, using the Windows Update service. If you don't use the recommended settings for Windows Update, it may not appear for your devices.

When you open the Devices and Printers view, you may see a yellow bar along the top of the window, advising you that "Windows can display enhanced device icons and information from the internet." Click on this and you'll be given the option to enable Device Stage. If you still can't see the interface, open your Windows Update settings and ensure your PC is set to automatically download updates from the internet. The box labelled "Give me recommended updates the same way I receive important updates" should be ticked.

This is what Microsoft describes as a **photorealistic image** of your device – although HP's C4200 series printers don't actually look anything like this.

Customize your printer shows the kind of options you'd get by clicking Advanced in a Print dialog, such as ports and sharing.

If your device contains removable storage, such as the memory card readers in this printer, you can click **Browse files** to view the contents.

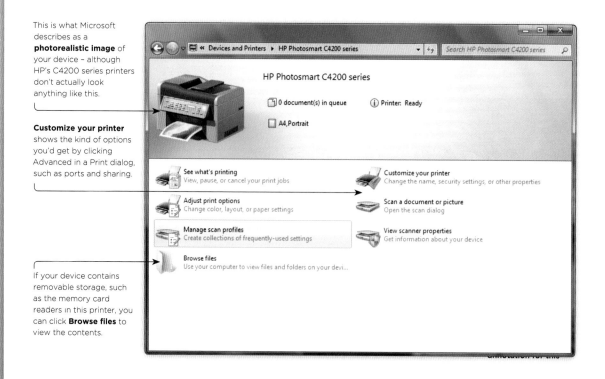

HOW TO...
CREATE A DESKTOP SLIDESHOW

Desktop slideshows let you select multiple wallpapers, so instead of looking at a static desktop background you can watch it change through the day.

① GET PERSONAL Desktop slideshows are supported in all editions of Windows 7 except Starter, and you can use any selection of images – in JPG, PNG, GIF or BMP formats – stored on your PC. To choose pictures, go to Control Panel | Appearance and Personalization | Personalization | Desktop Background. Or right-click on the desktop, select Personalize from the dropdown menu, then click the Desktop Background link at the bottom of the window.

② CHOOSE DEFAULT IMAGES There are several ways of choosing which images to include in your slideshow. By default, you choose from the Windows Desktop Backgrounds that Windows 7 installs on your hard disk. Clicking on the name of a theme or folder (for example, Landscapes) will select every background image included in each theme. You can also lasso a selection of images, or simply click on whichever images you like, one by one, while holding down the Ctrl key. Using the Select All and Clear All buttons, you can either pick all the images in the current Picture Location or remove them all from your selection.

③ CHOOSE YOUR OWN IMAGES Alternatively, use the Picture Location menu to select photos from your own Pictures Library or other Libraries and locations on your PC. Alternatively, use the Browse button and navigate to your favourite shots using the standard Windows Explorer file browser interface.

It's also possible to create a desktop slideshow from any group of images. Open a folder in Windows Explorer, click to select some photos, then right-click and choose "Set as desktop background" from the menu.

④ TWEAK YOUR SLIDESHOW SETTINGS Do you want your desktop background to change every minute, every hour, or just once a day? The dropdown menu below the label "Change picture every:" allows you to set how long each background image will stay on your desktop before neatly transitioning to the next. By default, the desktop background rolls on from one selected image to the next, from folder to folder or theme to theme, until it gets to the end and cycles back to the beginning, but check the Shuffle box if you'd rather see your pictures in random order.

HOW LONG?
Two minutes to pick new backgrounds, but you can easily waste a lot more time...

HOW HARD?
Very easy, and messing about won't do your PC or pictures any harm.

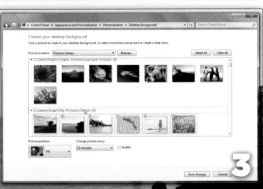

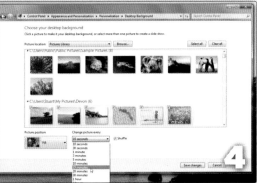

MICROSOFT HAS TRIED AND FAILED WITH TOUCHSCREEN INTERFACES BEFORE, BUT WINDOWS 7 FINALLY GETS IT RIGHT – IN SPECTACULAR FASHION.

Working with a touchscreen

Touchscreen PCs are growing in popularity. Many all-in-one "lifestyle" PCs now come with a touchscreen as standard, so you can play music and video without having to fiddle with the keyboard and mouse. There's also a growing market for standalone monitors with touchscreen capabilities, so even regular PCs can get in on the action. And then of course there are the ranks of laptops and Tablet PCs that use touch as their primary interface.

Windows 7 is the first version of Windows to come with full support for finger-based touch – in fact, it's the first mainstream desktop OS of any kind to offer that capability. Its predecessor Vista allowed Tablet PC users to make "flicks" with an electronic stylus, but that's a far cry from intuitively controlling your computer by simply swiping and pressing with a finger.

Windows 7 even supports multitouch, so it knows when you put more than one finger on the screen at a time and responds accordingly. If you have a touchscreen

PC, an instant way to test this is with Microsoft's supplied Paint program: load it up, drag four fingers across the page, and you'll see four lines of virtual ink trail behind. It's an experience as life-changing as the first time you moved a pointer with a mouse instead of the cursor keys.

MAKING GESTURES It's fun to draw with several fingers at once, but the real power of a multitouch system lies in gestures. Gesture controls are commonly associated with mobile devices such as the Apple iPhone and iPad, but they're every bit as useful in Windows. If you put two fingers on the screen while an image file is open and push them apart, you'll zoom in. Pinch your fingers together and the image becomes smaller. You can also rotate images by moving your fingers around your thumb.

This works both in Windows Explorer – you can also move windows around by pulling them about by their title bars – and in applications. Drag your finger up

Windows 7's **virtual keyboard** now responds to multitouch on compatible screens, so key combinations, such as holding Shift while pressing a letter key to get a capital, work just like on a physical keyboard.

While you type, Windows **predicts** words you might be aiming for, based on its own dictionary and also on what you've entered previously – so it won't keep offering words you never use.

a list of files, as if you were sliding a piece of paper away from you, and you'll scroll smoothly down the list. Within applications, you can scroll through documents by touching the screen. If you try to scroll beyond the end of a list of files or the end of a document, the window will give a little joggle to show that you can't go any further. Zooming works well in a web browser, and it's great in Windows Live Photo Gallery too (see p74). Placing a finger on the screen and tapping with another is equivalent to a right-click.

FLICKING OFF The "flick" concept, which seemed to have died out with the Tablet PC, is back in Windows 7, and here it makes a lot more sense. To flick, place a finger on the screen, then lift it off as you move it. Flicking right or left will skip to the next or previous image in a gallery. Place a finger on an application shortcut on the Taskbar and flick upwards, and the Jump List for that application will open (see p38). Flicks also work in most web browsers to take you forwards and backwards through your browsing history.

WRITTEN EXAMINATION One thing fingers aren't good for is writing, but there's now even better support for users who want to create and edit documents using a stylus. Windows' handwriting recognition has always been pretty good, and Windows 7 continues the tradition. When activated, the Tablet PC Input Panel peeks onto the screen from the left-hand side, and Microsoft claims its accuracy has improved since Vista. We're inclined to agree: despite our messy handwriting, Windows 7 did a good job of turning even joined-up script into correct editable text.

If it does make a mistake, it's easy to make corrections. If you need to break a word into two, for example, draw a vertical line where you want the break; to join up two words, draw a curved line beneath them. If you need to correct a word after Windows has misinterpreted it, you can simply tap it with the stylus, tap the incorrect letter, and write the correct one over the top of it.

KEY CONCEPTS If handwriting isn't your thing, the onscreen keyboard in Windows 7 is also incredibly capable. (Note that the keyboard within the Tablet PC Input Panel, which we're describing here, is subtly different from the onscreen keyboard; find both of these by typing their names into the Start menu's search box.) With a multitouch screen, you can hold down the onscreen Shift key to type capital letters, for example. It's possible to achieve great speeds, though the lack of tactile feedback means you may never quite manage to touch-type.

Windows also makes suggestions, so if you get part of the way through a word and pause, you'll be given a few likely ways to complete it along the top of the keyboard. These are drawn from a comprehensive dictionary, and Windows will also modify its suggestions as you use the touchscreen features, either by writing with a stylus or tapping at the onscreen keyboard. Eventually Windows will suggest words that aren't merely a fit with the letters you've just entered, but are also likely guesses based on what you've typed in the past.

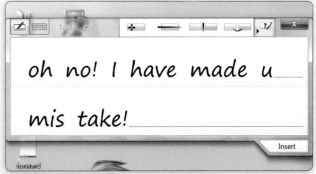

Windows 7's handwriting recognition can convert scruffy scribbles into accurate text. It can be used anywhere you'd normally type.

Any mistakes in the resulting text – whether your fault or Windows' – can easily be corrected. Instead of appearing in separate boxes, the letters instantly replace your writing. To change any word, just tap it, tap the incorrect letter within it, then write over the top.

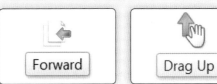

Further gestures split or combine words. Here we're drawing a curved line to join two word fragments together. Similarly, drawing a vertical line through a word splits it at that point. A horizontal line through a word deletes it. Animated examples show you how.

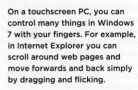

On a touchscreen PC, you can control many things in Windows 7 with your fingers. For example, in Internet Explorer you can scroll around web pages and move forwards and back simply by dragging and flicking.

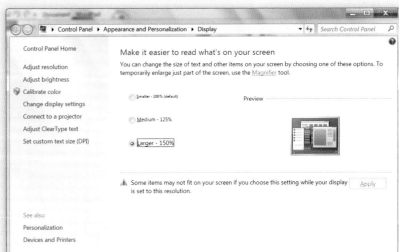

If your text and icons are too small to interact with easily, use the options in Appearance and Personalization to make them bigger onscreen while leaving the overall display resolution unchanged.

4

Advanced features

HOW LONG?
Basic calibration is a brief process, though you could get carried away and spend hours tinkering with settings.

HOW HARD?
You don't need any specialist knowledge, but finding the perfect colour balance and contrast can be fiddly.

HOW TO...
FINE-TUNE YOUR DISPLAY

If your monitor's left at its default settings, you may not be able to enjoy the full effect of Windows 7's graphical interface. Here's how to take control and get bright colours and sharp text using the Display Color Calibration tool.

Some displays look perfect out of the box – but most don't. Whether you're using a huge 27in LCD display or a diminutive laptop panel, it's likely that you can improve the quality of your display with a few simple adjustments .

There are several reasons to do this. First, it can help make text appear as sharp as possible – nobody likes squinting at fuzzy words. Second, it can add vibrancy and warmth to your desktop, and to the graphics in general. That may sound trivial, but it can have a big effect on the experience of using your computer, making everything you do more engaging and enjoyable.

Lastly, if you ever edit digital photographs on your PC, you'll want to make sure your monitor displays them accurately. If your screen makes them appear too dark or too light, or gives them a colour cast, what you see on your PC will be different to what everyone else sees when they look at them – and it'll be different to what you see if you have them printed.

Windows 7 contains a monitor calibration tool that can help you set up your display perfectly, and on these pages we'll show you how to use it.

① LAUNCH THE CALIBRATOR The Display Color Calibration tool is a new feature in Windows 7, but Microsoft has kept oddly quiet about it (perhaps wanting to foster the idea that Windows works perfectly out of the box). It's even hard to find in the Control Panel unless you know where to look – it's hidden in the left-hand pane in the Display settings. The easiest way to find it is to open the Start menu and type "calibrate". Once you've launched the program, you'll be asked you to drag it onto the monitor you want to calibrate. This only applies if you have more than one monitor connected to your PC: if you're using a single monitor or a laptop screen, hit Next to continue.

② ADJUST THE GAMMA The first task in the Display Color Calibration tool is to adjust your gamma. In simple terms, gamma is a setting that governs how light Windows makes your light colours, and how dark it makes your dark colours. Different monitors reproduce shades of grey in different ways, so in order to display smooth gradients from white to black, Windows needs to know what gamma setting is right for your monitor.

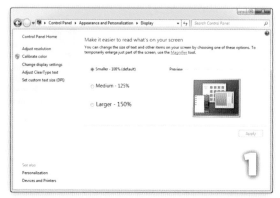

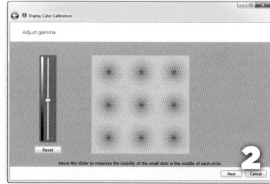

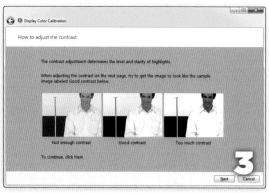

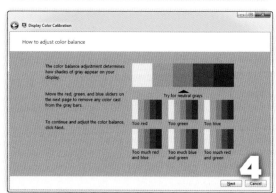

This is worked out in a clever way, using a pattern of circles. The areas on the outside of the circles are a neutral grey, while the centres of the circles are made up of alternating light and dark lines. If the centres look lighter than the neutral grey then your gamma is too high; if they look darker then it's too low. All you have to do is adjust the slider until the black and white lines look similar in intensity to the grey. When they do, you've found the correct gamma setting for your monitor.

On some displays you may find that deliberately setting your gamma below the correct point makes your desktop appear richer and more solid. There's nothing wrong with this – but remember that, if you want to edit photographs or videos, what you see on your screen is darker than it will appear to other people.

③ SET BRIGHTNESS AND CONTRAST Now that Windows is using the correct gamma settings, it's time to turn your attention to the monitor. The next two calibration tasks will show you two images containing extremes of dark and light, and you'll be invited to adjust the settings on your monitor to make them appear correct. If you don't want to do this, or if you're using a laptop that doesn't have the option to adjust these settings, use the option to skip this part.

Unlike the gamma calibration, there isn't exactly a "correct" setting here. If you make the display too dark you may find that details in games and images are lost in the murk – and if you make it too bright they may get "burnt out." You probably won't be able to find settings that make all the detail in the sample pictures perfectly visible. That's OK – just pick the best compromise you can.

④ COLOUR BALANCE Very few monitors produce perfectly neutral tones: it's quite common to see a slight blue or purple cast. Windows can adjust its colour output to compensate for this, so you get cleaner whites and greys. This is achieved in the last step of the Display Color Calibration process.

Adjusting the colour is very simple: at the bottom of the window you'll see three sliders, one for red, one for green and one for blue. At the start, the sliders will all be set over to the far right, indicating that each colour is contributing to the display at its full intensity.

Grab a slider and drag it to the left and the intensity of that colour in your display will be reduced. Don't go mad: you'll find that reducing any of these colours by too much will have a rather drastic and unwanted effect. The trick is to nudge the colours down by just enough to neutralise a colour tint, without overdoing it and creating the opposite problem. If you experiment with the sliders for too long, your eyes may well get confused as to what's really neutral: it's worth stepping away from your computer for a few minutes, then coming back fresh to check that your whites and greys really are white and grey.

Once you're happy, click Next to accept your new colour settings. If you want to, you can go straight on from here to tune your ClearType text settings – see box, right.

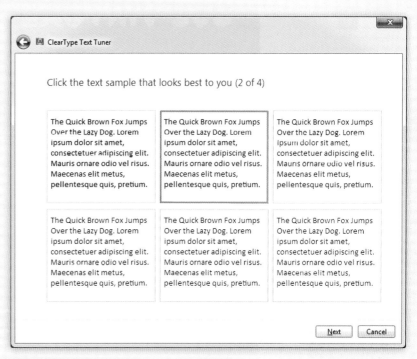

The ClearType Text Tuner launches after you've calibrated your colours, or you can run it at any time from the Control Panel. You'll see a few samples of text and will be asked to choose which looks best. This helps Windows make text look as sharp as possible on your particular monitor. The Tuner also ensures that your monitor is running at its native resolution, so graphics as well as text look their best.

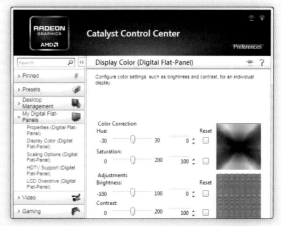

Depending on the graphics hardware inside your PC, you may find you have additional options for adjusting colour, gamma and other settings within the manufacturer's software. In this example, an AMD Radeon graphics card gives us a different way of adjusting the colour and brightness of our display. You may also be able to save settings for future use, so you could have different settings depending on where you use your laptop. Normally these settings will override any adjustments you make in the Display Color Calibration tool.

If you're serious about getting the most accurate colour from your PC, you can invest in a colour calibrator. These devices attach to your monitor and "watch" the colours it produces, with far greater accuracy than the human eye is capable of. They can then automatically adjust your computer's colour settings to be as near to perfection as possible. This is great for design professionals and artists, but expect to pay £60 for basic devices such as the Datacolor Spyder3Express (pictured) and £300 for fully featured units.

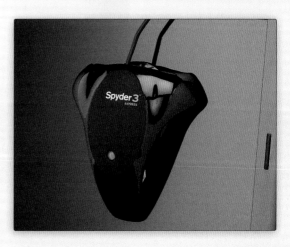

4

Advanced features

HOW LONG?

Allow at least an hour to complete the setup.

HOW HARD?

If you don't consider yourself an advanced Windows user, don't mess with this feature.

HOW TO...
USE VIRTUAL HARD DISKS

You can install Windows 7 independently of your existing system by using one of its best new features: virtual hard disks. They have lots of other uses, too.

Windows 7 is the first operating system that really lets personal users exploit virtualisation: the idea of separating the system you're using from the underlying resources. One example is Windows XP Mode (see p56), which runs older programs in a virtual XP environment. Another is the ability to create virtual hard disk images that behave like physical disks, even though they're really just files on an existing hard disk. All versions of Windows 7 allow you to create virtual hard disks, but only Ultimate allows you to boot from them.

We've looked at achieving something similar with a dual-boot system (see p26), but creating a virtual disk is much quicker than the lengthy process of resizing and moving disk partitions. And if you decide you don't want the new partition, you can just unmount the disk with a quick command and delete its associated virtual disk file. Finally, backing up the contents of your "disk" is as simple as copying a single file – which is essentially what it is.

DISKPART The key to creating virtual disks is a command-line tool called DiskPart. It's included with Windows 7, and you can start it by entering **diskpart** at the command prompt. We'd stress that this is

a very powerful tool that, if used carelessly, can completely wipe all the information on your hard disk. If you're not confident opening and using the command prompt in Windows, you shouldn't be playing around with DiskPart.

A new command line window will open (after you've clicked Yes at the UAC alert), with the usual C:\> command prompt replaced by DISKPART >.

LIST DISKS You can now start issuing commands. To start with, type **list disk**. When you hit Return, you'll see a list of disks on your system, along with their status, size and free space.

CREATE THE IMAGE The first step in creating a virtual disk is issuing a "create" command, with a few parameters to set the size and the type of disk. The command goes like this: **create vdisk file=filename maximum=xxx type=[fixed/expandable]** Filename specifies a name and path for your new virtual disk, such as C:\DATAVDISK.VHD. Maximum is the size of the disk in KB. If you select type=fixed, a virtual disk file is immediately created that fills the entire maximum size and

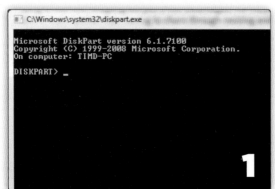

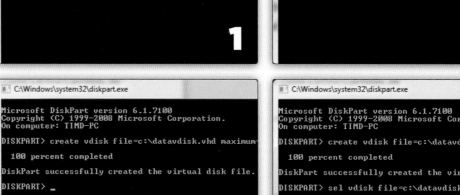

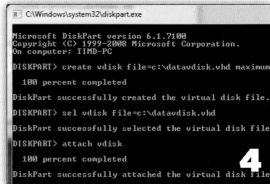

won't change. With type=expandable, the file starts at just a few KB and grows as required up to the maximum. Note that its size is always reported to the OS as the maximum, for instance when you right-click on the disk and choose Properties to see the free-space pie chart.

So to create a disk that starts tiny but could go up to 30GB, you'd enter **create vdisk file=c:\datavdisk.vhd maximum=30000 type=expandable**. When you do this for the first time, Windows 7 will automatically install a driver called Microsoft VHD HBA. Look in the location you've set for the disk (in our example, the root of C) and you'll find a virtual disk file with the name you specified.

 SELECT THE DISK The disk won't pop up in Windows Explorer just yet – there are still a few more steps to complete. You first need to select that disk so it has focus in DiskPart, and to do this you use the "sel" tool: **sel vdisk file=c:\datavdisk.vhd**. Now attach the disk file to the system by typing **attach vdisk**.

 CREATE A PARTITION So far, the virtual disk is like a blank, unpartitioned and unformatted drive. We need to create a primary partition, select it, make it active and format it using the following commands:

create part primary
sel part 1
active
format fs=ntfs quick

 ASSIGN THE DISK Now a single magic word will make the disk visible to Windows: **assign**. A new disk immediately pops up in Windows Explorer and you can use it just like any other drive.

 CLEVER INSTALLATION At this point, Ultimate owners might wish to perform a clean install of Windows 7 (see p24). Alternatively, use DiskPart with your existing Windows installation. To start installation, put the Windows 7 DVD in the drive, reboot, and hit a key to run Setup when you're prompted. Once you get to the welcome screen, the clever part begins. Your virtual disk needs creating, so hit <Shift+F10> to pop up a command prompt. Type **diskpart** to start the DiskPart tool.

 INSTALL WINDOWS 7 Now to create your virtual disk. Type **create vdisk file=c:\win7disk.vhd type=fixed maximum=30000**. Give the disk the focus by typing **sel vdisk file=c:\win7disk.vhd**. Now attach it to the system with **attach vdisk**. Enter **exit** twice to exit both DiskPart and the command prompt.

Proceed with the installation as normal, opting for Clean install and selecting the virtual hard disk as the installation drive. As far as the system is concerned, the virtual drive acts as a fixed disk. After installation, you effectively have a dual-boot system, but if you select Windows 7 as the OS it boots from the virtual disk image. To back up the whole system any time, just copy the file!

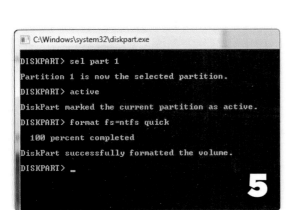

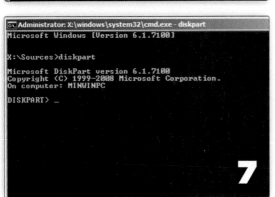

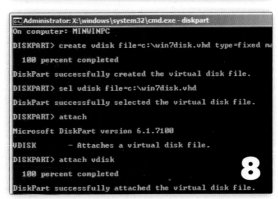

Tip

As you might expect, you can't delete a virtual hard disk file while it's mounted in Windows. That's just as well, since it prevents nasty accidents. To remove a virtual disk, fire up DiskPart and make sure you have the correct disk selected. Use the **list disk** command to check: the currently selected disk is marked with an asterisk. Then enter the **remove** command by itself. The disk will disappear from the Computer view and you'll then be able to delete or move the file.

Advanced features

 YOU CAN COMPLETE TASKS MORE QUICKLY IF YOU AVOID USING THE MOUSE. HERE ARE THE HANDIEST KEY SHORTCUTS TO BE FOUND IN WINDOWS 7.

Windows 7 keyboard shortcuts

Press the Windows key to open the Start menu. Begin typing when you let go, and Windows will search for whatever you enter. Try the first few letters of the name of a program, for example. Once the correct item appears, press Return.

To jump to an advanced search, including any search connectors you've installed (see p54), hold down the Windows key while pressing F.

To minimise all the currently open windows, giving a clear view of the desktop and your Gadgets, press <Windows+D>. Hit it again and your windows will reappear as before.

Press <Windows+E> and Windows Explorer shows your Computer window.

Pressing <Windows+L> locks your PC – ideal if you're going out and don't want others to access it. You can also switch users.

A favourite of Windows pros, <Windows+R> brings up the Run dialog box. Enter an application name or folder to open it.

Holding down the Windows key, keep pressing T and Windows will cycle through all the programs sitting in your Taskbar.

If you know you want to launch, say, the third program in the Taskbar, press that number with the Windows key and it will instantly activate.

If you want to start a new instance of a program – say, you already have Internet Explorer open, but you want to open a separate browser window – press Shift and the number of the program in the Taskbar to launch it afresh.

Similarly, press Alt with a number and the Windows key to open the Jump List for that program. Could be handy.

Windows' Aero Flip 3D effect always looks great in computer showrooms. Impress your friends by activating it using the <Windows+Tab> keyboard shortcut.

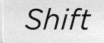

This one requires nimble fingers, but if you have a huge desktop spanned across multiple monitors it's a godsend: use this triple combination to move a selected window from one screen to another in an instant.

The Windows key plus the up arrow maximises the window you're working on. And yes, the down arrow minimises it.

Even better, the Windows key plus the left cursor arrow will move a program to the left of the screen; the right arrow moves it to the right.

Tip

You can carry on adding your own keyboard shortcuts until you run out of keys, and you're not limited to assigning them to applications – you can also launch specific files or folders by creating shortcuts to them and assigning key combinations to the shortcuts, as explained on the opposite page.

HOW TO...
CREATE YOUR OWN SHORTCUTS

If you're not satisfied with the ability to pin a program to the Taskbar or find it with a quick search, use this method to assign a keyboard shortcut to it.

Probably the shortcut we use most, this quickly selects which monitor is active. You can duplicate your display, extend it, or switch to an external monitor or projector alone. Great when setting up a PC for a presentation.

Opens the Ease of Access Center, ready for you to start up tools such as the Narrator, Magnifier and On-Screen Keyboard.

One for laptop users only: <Windows+X> launches Windows Mobility Center.

And finally, here's another way to minimise all your windows at once. Unlike with <Windows+D>, you can't repeat it to restore them; instead, use the same combination with the addition of the Shift key.

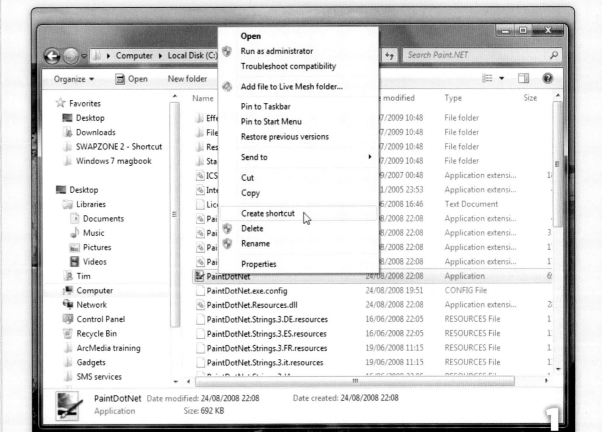

1

2

① **FIND YOUR APPLICATION** First, navigate your way to your chosen program. You'll probably find it hiding away in C:\Program Files. Our example is the excellent free utility Paint.NET, which is installed by default to C:\Program Files\Paint.NET. Having found the application file, right-click it and select Create Shortcut.

② **ADD A KEY COMBINATION** You may be prompted to save the shortcut to the desktop; click Yes. Right-click on the newly created shortcut icon and select Properties. You should see this dialog (left), which controls everything from the compatibility level of the file – for example, telling Windows 7 that this program must be run in Windows XP compatibility mode – to its displayed name. Here, click on the Shortcut tab. We're interested in the "Shortcut key" box, so click on this. Whichever key you next hit will be the nominated shortcut key to work in combination with Ctrl and Alt.

Click OK. You may be prompted to enter the Administrator password before your shortcut takes effect. This done, you can press <Ctrl+Alt+1> (or whichever key you chose) and your program will instantly launch. Note that certain keys aren't valid – Esc, Enter and the spacebar – and that if the program already has a shortcut associated with it, your new key combo may not work.

TRY 3 ISSUES

PC Pro's team of expert journalists deliver more pages of news, reviews and advice than any other PC magazine – every month.

We'll keep you up-to-date with the latest industry news, whilst our reviews will help you to avoid costly purchasing mistakes.

OF **PC PRO** FOR £1

Stay ahead of the latest IT developments with 3 issues for just £1

If you enjoy reading *PC Pro*, your subscription will automatically continue at just £24.99 every 6 issues by Direct Debit – **a saving of 17%** on the shop price.

Save 17%

ABOUT PC PRO

➜ Essential Reviews

PC Pro leads the way for exclusive reviews, ensuring that you are continually up-to-date with the latest products and technology trends. We review more hardware and software than any other PC monthly and represent the first stop for any serious technology vendor looking for a definitive and independent analysis.

➜ Keep up with the latest technology

If there's a technology you need to know about, *PC Pro* will have it covered. From the latest processors to trends in business, from in-depth software guides to provocative features, our team of experts provides insight and analysis based on decades of experience.

Every edition of *PC Pro* comes with a **BONUS DVD** containing software, applications, games and utilities

IN THIS CHAPTER

5

Enhance Windows 7

ENHANCE WINDO

Windows 7 is a streamlined operating system. By that we mean it's efficient, but also stripped-down: when you install it, there's no email client like Outlook Express, no photo manager and no MSN Messenger. You can download the latest versions of these applications (and more) as part of the free Windows Live Essentials pack. These useful tools integrate tightly

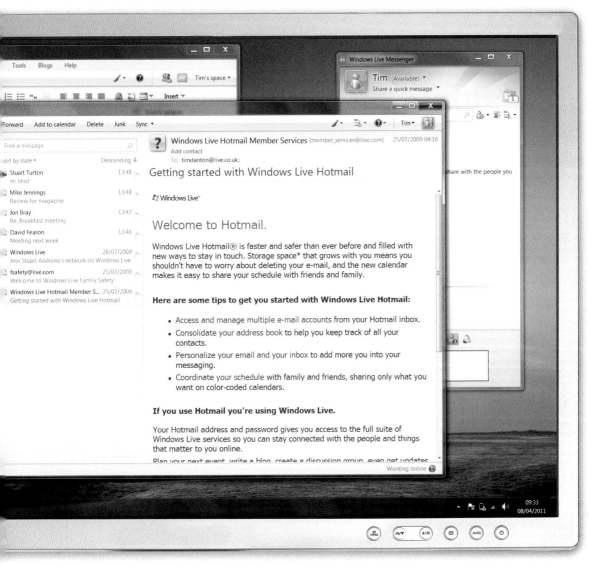

WS 7 FOR FREE

with Microsoft's online Live service, so albums created in Photo Gallery can be dropped into emails or posted on your Windows Live Spaces blog. In this chapter we examine what each Live Essentials application offers, and round things off with our pick of the excellent non-Microsoft additions to Windows 7 that you can also download for free.

WINDOWS LIVE MAIL IS A SURPRISINGLY POWERFUL OFFLINE MAIL APPLICATION, WITH BUILT-IN ANTI-PHISHING AND A HANDY CALENDAR TOO.

Introducing Windows Live Mail

If you currently use a webmail service such as Microsoft's Hotmail or Yahoo! Mail, then Windows Live Mail (not to be confused with the Windows Live Mail webmail service) is your ticket to freedom. Instead of relying on a constant internet connection, Windows Live Mail downloads email to your hard disk, so you can refer to it whenever you want, and indexes it, making it easy to find messages. Alternatively, if you prefer to use the email supplied by your internet service provider (such as BT or TalkTalk), you can receive and reply to email in Windows Live Mail rather than using a web browser. It's much easier and more integrated.

PHISHING TRIP There are numerous websites out there that are designed to look like a trusted site – such as an online bank – and encourage you to enter your details, which they record and then use to hijack your account. To hook you, they send emails purporting to be from, say, Barclays, telling you to check your balance or update your information.

This is "phishing", and Windows Live Mail has extra features to beat it. Messages from suspicious sources are partially blocked, allowing you to see plain text but not links or images. This helps to protect you from objectionable content, as well as reducing the chances of you clicking on a fraudulent link without thinking. Viewing an image could confirm back to the scammers that your email address is working, encouraging them to target you again.

ADDING PICTURES If you email a lot of pictures, you'll also appreciate Live Mail's close ties to Windows Live. When you add pictures to a message, they aren't simply attached, as in Outlook, but are sent to a Microsoft Live server, while the body of your message and the image thumbnails go to the email recipient. The resulting email is smaller and faster for the recipient to download. To see your full set of pictures, they simply click on one of the image thumbnails and are taken to an online slideshow.

DATING GAME There's no longer a separate calendar application supplied with Windows 7 or the Windows Live suite. Instead, Live Mail now includes a full-blown calendar. You can invite people to events on your calendar via email. If you want other people to be able to see your appointments, you can set up an online calendar at http://calendar.live.com and then edit it with the Windows Live Mail application.

Tip

Live Mail has a surprising number of features for a free application. For instance, you can click "Add to calendar" to copy the contents of an email into a new calendar entry, avoiding the need to flick between the Calendar and Mail sections of the applications. To set up a service that sends upcoming calendar appointments to your mobile phone as text messages, click on the Menu button, then on Deliver my reminders.

This is the main Windows Live Mail interface. If you look down at the bottom of the left-hand navigation bar, you'll see extra options for features such as the Calendar, Contacts, RSS feeds (from news sites and blogs) and – a relic of the 1990s, surely – internet newsgroups.

Introducing Windows Live Writer

If you've ever wanted to share your thoughts, photogaphs and videos with the world, Windows Live Writer makes it easy to create your own online blog, from setting it up to posting text, photos, video clips and more.

Blogging is about far more than just text, which is why Windows Live Writer – despite its name – offers numerous ways to add pictures, video and other extra titbits to your posts. It's easy to create a blog, or you can work with a blogging service you already use.

Keeping a blog is almost obligatory these days, but it can be hard work. Signing up, managing the design and keeping it updated all takes time. Windows Live Writer ties in closely with Windows Live Spaces and, with minimum fuss, allows you to edit a blog from a user-friendly text editor. If you've used WordPad or Microsoft Word, it will feel familiar.

MAKE A DEBUT When you first start Live Writer, you'll be asked which blogging service you currently use. If you're already signed up to WordPress, for instance, this is the place to give Writer your details. Alternatively, if you click the option labelled "I don't have a blog; create one on Windows Live for me", you'll be prompted to enter your Windows Live details. Once that's done, you'll be greeted by a standard-looking text editor. Tap in a few lines, hit the Publish button at the top left and your first post will appear.

MAKE IT SHINE Blogging isn't just about words. The right-hand toolbar has a number of options to spice up your new blog. This starts with Pictures, which embeds single images and can produce spectacular results. Hit Photo Album, for instance, and a selection of your images will be transformed

into a single image, with a link that takes your readers to your Live photo albums. Alternatively, clicking Video lets you select a video from YouTube to embed in your post. Writer is also smart enough to look at any videos you've created using Windows Movie Maker.

Finally, clicking Maps brings up Microsoft Virtual Earth. Drag the map around until it looks how you want – centre it on the location you're blogging about, for example – then click Insert and the map will appear. The only limitation is that your readers can't drag the map around within your page; instead, clicking it will take them to Virtual Earth.

MAKE IT COMPLICATED Writer also conceals some surprisingly complex and powerful tools. Click "Add a plug-in", on the Insert menu, and you're taken to a website where you can get free add-ons for services such as Flickr, or a tool that lets you add files for your readers to download.

Finally, take note of the three tabs at the bottom of the screen. Clicking on Preview will allow you to see what your post will look like in a web browser, while Source, for the more ambitious blogger, lets you edit the source code of your post to get it looking exactly the way you want.

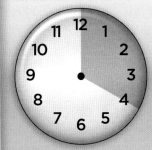

HOW LONG?
Setting up your site and organising your content can take a while, but it's rewarding to share the fruits of your labour.

HOW HARD?
Starting and updating your blog is simplicity itself, but to get the best from Writer's advanced features it helps if you're familiar with the basics of HTML – the language in which web pages are created.

THE WINDOWS LIVE PHOTO GALLERY CAN KEEP YOUR PHOTO COLLECTION ORGANISED – AND IT CAN EVEN DIGITALLY TOUCH UP YOUR PICTURES.

Introducing Photo Gallery

With the advanced handling of image thumbnails within Windows 7, you might wonder whether you need a standalone photo gallery application at all. But over time we all end up with more and more digital images, and in need of a tool like Windows Live Photo Gallery. It can help you organise your pictures, so you can find the ones you want effortlessly, by date, by tags or by who's in them. It can also help you correct some common problems, and join together two or more photographs to make a perfect composite or a broad panorama. It's not the only application of its type: one popular alternative is Google's terrific Picasa (see p82), but Photo Gallery is well worth a try.

GET IT SORTED When you first launch Photo Gallery it will scan all the pictures it can find on your hard disk and display them in a simple thumbnail view, sorted by date (as pictured below). This is a convenient way to start organising your library, but it's not terrifically versatile – for example, if you take several photos of the same subject on different dates, you'll have to scroll around to find them all.

Photo Gallery makes it easier to find the picture you're looking for by letting you attach tags to each image. A tag is a short description that describes something about a picture, and each image can have as many tags as you like.

So, for example, you might tag a seaside photograph with "beach", "Torquay" and "holiday". In future, you could simply search for all photographs tagged "beach" and have them all at your fingertips, regardless of when they were taken.

If your images are divided up into folders, Photo Gallery will automatically tag them with these folder names as it imports them. To add custom tags to an image, click on the "Descriptive tag" icon in the Ribbon along the top of the window. The tags bar should appear at the right. Select one or more photos with the mouse – you can hold down the Shift key while clicking to select a whole range of images. Then click on "Add descriptive tags" at the right, type in some text for your tag and press Return. If you want to add more tags, click on "Add descriptive tags" again and repeat the process. In this same pane you can also add captions to your photgraphs, geotags specifying where they were taken and people tags saying who's in them.

Once you've done this, you can now search by tags, as well as by date: click on the Find tab at the top of the window and you'll see a Tags dropdown, from which you can choose to view only pictures bearing a particular tag. You can also sort by people, if your photos have this information attached. Click on the View tab and you can see your whole library sorted by tag, or by person.

Tip

Photo Gallery supports plug-ins, so it's possible for Microsoft and others to add extra features in the future. You can check for new plug-ins by going to the Create tab, clicking on the "More tools" dropdown and selecting "Download more photo tools". At the time of writing there are three plug-ins available: a collage generator, a tool for turning your photos into a 3D map and an advanced panorama generator, offering more features and control than the standard tool built into Photo Gallery.

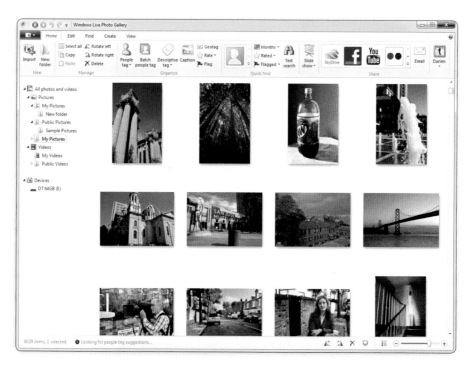

What makes Live Photo Gallery such a clever tool is that it's easy to use – anyone can quickly understand the way it organises your photographs. And it has a number of extra tools if you want to tap into its power.

DON'T I KNOW YOU? Tagging all the people in your photo collection can be a slow business, but Photo Gallery can help you out. In the Home tab, click on "Batch people tag" and Photo Gallery will group together all the pictures it thinks are of the same person, making it easy to select them all and tag their every appearance in one go. The groups it comes up with appear in a row along the top of the window: click a group, tag it, then click Close when you're done.

SHARE YOUR SHOTS When it's time to show off your work, you can easily turn a selection of images into a slideshow. If you just want to watch this on your own screen, select the pictures you want to include, then click the little projector screen icon at the bottom of the window. You can also export a slideshow as a video: go to the Create tab and click on Movie to transfer your images to Windows Live Movie Maker (see p76) to add music, apply effects and transitions and preview your video before you hit "Save movie".

If you want to share your pictures online, you can do this too: select the images you want to upload and hit one of the big "Publish" icons – by default you'll see options for SkyDrive (see p78), Facebook, YouTube, Flickr and MSN. Click the dropdown and you can download support for more services, such as SmugMug and TwitPic.

There are several other ways to distribute your images: you can email pictures or upload them to a blog from directly within the program. You can also send them directly to a professional photo printing company, and have glossy prints delivered to your door a day or two later – for a fee, of course.

TOUCHING UP Photo Gallery isn't designed for serious photo editing, but it contains some great touch-up tools. Click on the Edit tab to access them. The Auto adjust button will try to correct several common errors in one go, and it's always worth trying – if you don't like the effect you can always hit Revert and use the tools manually.

One tool worth special mention is the Retouch tool. If there's a spot on your picture, or an unwanted intrusion such as a bird flying past, click on the Retouch tool and drag a box around the offending area. Photo Gallery will do its best to remove the obstruction.

If you can't get your picture to look right, try the Photo Fuse feature, which combines the best elements from multiple snaps – great for family portraits where people keep looking in different directions. You'll find this under the Create tab, along with a Panorama feature that can stitch together multiple images to create very high or wide pictures. These tools work best with source pictures taken from the same angle, with the same lighting conditions.

TRY IT AND SEE Photo Gallery is an unassuming application with an emphasis on fun – but with its powerful organisation features and touch-up tools, it may well be the only photo management application you need. On these pages we've given a brief overview of what it can do, but the best way to appreciate its power is to try it yourself.

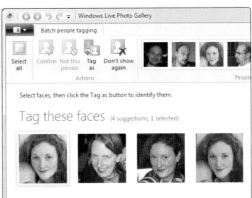

Photo Gallery can automatically fix common photographic problems such as red-eye, colour casts or overexposure.

The Batch face tagging tool tries to automatically identify when the same person appears in multiple photographs, though its hit rate isn't quite perfect.

The Photo Fuse tool combines two or more images into one photograph containing the best bits of both. The result should look better than any of photos you really took. (We won't tell if you don't.)

5

Enhance Windows 7

MICROSOFT'S FREE VIDEO-EDITING TOOL PROVIDES EVERYTHING YOU NEED TO TURN YOUR DIGITAL FOOTAGE INTO A COMPLETE CINEMATIC EXPERIENCE.

Introducing Movie Maker

Many mobile phones these days come with built-in video cameras, and handheld camcorders are becoming cheap and commonplace. It's easy and fun to capture memorable moments from your life and share them, whether that's through a web service such as YouTube, by creating your own DVD or simply by sharing a video file with your friends.

Windows Live Movie Maker is the perfect tool for tidying up your footage, adding a soundtrack and captions and publishing the result via whatever medium you prefer. It can accommodate more ambitious video projects too: you can splice together as many different clips as you like, with sophisticated transitions, to build up a proper cinematic narrative.

GETTING AROUND Windows Live Movie Maker uses a simple layout that's similar to what professional video-editing packages use. At the right of the window you'll see a preview of your movie: most of the time this will be paused while you're editing, but when you want to make a change you can immediately preview it here.

At the left-hand side of the window you'll see all

the video clips (or still photographs) that you've imported, arranged from left to right, top to bottom. This shows the order in which they'll be played. If you want to rearrange them, simply drag them around. The thick vertical black line shows the "now" time – think of this as where your movie is paused, and where any edits you specify will be applied. You can move it by clicking anywhere on the timeline. By default it moves in large jumps of several seconds: if you want to position it more precisely, put it near to the point you desire, then use the left and right advance buttons beneath the preview window to fine-tune its location.

WHO'S GOT THE BUTTON? Along the top of the window you'll see all of Movie Maker's editing tools, presented in a clean Ribbon interface. It's from here that you'll import videos, photos and music, apply transitions and visual effects, add captions and finally publish your movie. The Video, Music and Text Tools groups (as seen below) will only appear once you place clips, audio files and captions into your project. You'll find the all-important Open and Save commands under the blue tab at the far left of the window.

Tip

Movie Maker offers an AutoMovie feature that will automatically apply transitions, titles and visual effects to your movie. These are a good way to quickly preview different types of effect when you're just starting out – but we don't recommend you use this feature for your own movies. Such templates quickly grow familiar and dull, and they're no substitute for your own creativity.

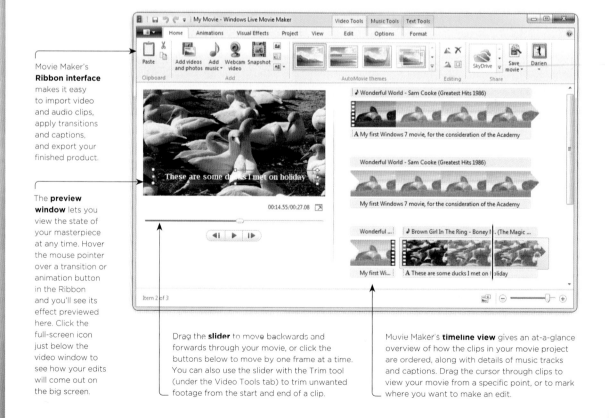

Movie Maker's **Ribbon interface** makes it easy to import video and audio clips, apply transitions and captions, and export your finished product.

The **preview window** lets you view the state of your masterpiece at any time. Hover the mouse pointer over a transition or animation button in the Ribbon and you'll see its effect previewed here. Click the full-screen icon just below the video window to see how your edits will come out on the big screen.

Drag the **slider** to move backwards and forwards through your movie, or click the buttons below to move by one frame at a time. You can also use the slider with the Trim tool (under the Video Tools tab) to trim unwanted footage from the start and end of a clip.

Movie Maker's **timeline view** gives an at-a-glance overview of how the clips in your movie project are ordered, along with details of music tracks and captions. Drag the cursor through clips to view your movie from a specific point, or to mark where you want to make an edit.

HOW TO...
MAKE YOUR FIRST MOVIE

① IMPORT AND ARRANGE CLIPS If your video clips are on your hard disk, you can import them by clicking "Add videos and photos" under the Home tab. If they're still on your camera or phone, you can click on the blue tab at the far left and select "Import from device". Your images and movies will be imported into Windows Live Photo Gallery (see p74), from which you can bring them into Movie Maker. Once you've imported the clips for your movie, drag them into the desired order in the timeline view. If you need to crop off extraneous footage from the start or end of a clip, use the Trim tool under the Video Tools tab. You can also use the Split tool to break one clip into smaller chunks, which you can then reorder as you wish.

② ADD SOUNDS AND TRANSITIONS Click Add music under the Home tab to overlay audio files over your clips – you can specify how each one starts and ends from the Options tab that appears under Music Tools. (Remember that if you use copyrighted music, you can't legally distribute your video to others.)

Next, it's time to apply smooth transitions between clips. This is done from the Animations tab: click on the clip you want to transition to, then hover over any of the transition options to preview the effect. When you find one you like, click to apply it. You can specify how quickly the transition takes place by changing the Duration setting.

③ EFFECTS AND CAPTIONS The Visual Effects tab lets you apply effects such as adjusting the colours or warping the image. Many of these effects aren't very practical, but there are 26 to play with, so it's worth having a browse to see if any of them can enhance your scenes – simply hover the mouse over one to see its effect. The Brightness adjustment at the right of the Ribbon can help you compensate if a clip has poor light balance.

This is also a good time to add titles and captions to your movie, if you want them. To do this, go back to the Home tab and click on Title, Caption or Credits to add whichever elements you desire. The Format tab will now appear under Text Tools. Click on any text element (on the timeline below the video clips) and you can edit its appearance, as well as applying optional animations and specifying how long captions should remain on screen for.

④ PUBLISH AND BE DAMNED When your movie is ready for public consumption, you can send it directly to YouTube (or a different online service) by clicking the icon in the Home tab. Movie Maker will automatically convert your movie to an appropriate format and upload it. For more options, click the Save Movie dropdown just to the right: you can save your movie as a standalone file, email it to a friend or export it to Windows DVD Maker, ready to be burnt to a disc.

HOW LONG?
Assembling your first project and learning the ropes will take a while. But once you get more familiar with the software, you'll be knocking out blockbusters in five minutes flat.

HOW HARD?
Though Movie Maker keeps things simple and intuitive, there's still a learning curve.

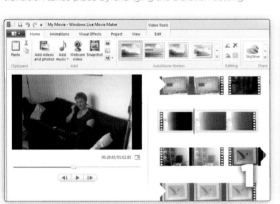

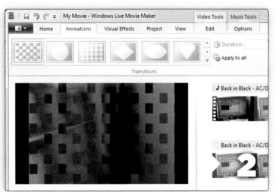

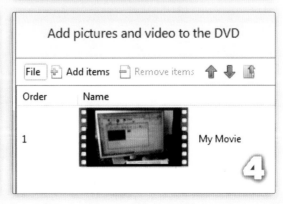

MICROSOFT'S ONLINE STORAGE SERVICE OFFERS AS MUCH SPACE AS YOU'RE LIKELY TO NEED – FOR FREE. AT HEART, IT'S ALL ABOUT SHARING.

Introducing SkyDrive

SkyDrive from Microsoft gives you an enormous 25GB of online space, dwarfing the 1 or 2GB you get free with rival services such as Dropbox (www.getdropbox.com). All you need is a browser and a Windows Live ID, and you can access your space from any PC with an internet connection.

Uploading files is easy. Sign into Windows Live using your Windows Live ID (you already have one if you use Hotmail, for example), click the More link at the top of the homepage, then select SkyDrive from the menu. There are four folders – Documents, Favorites, Shared Favorites and Public – and you can add your own via the Create Folder link. Choose a folder, then click "Add files". You can upload five at a time by clicking Browse and navigating to your file(s). To download files, sign in, access your SkyDrive, find the relevant folder, click on a file, then click Download.

It's possible to use SkyDrive as a safe online store for vital files and documents, or as a space to transfer files between PCs. However, since SkyDrive can't actively schedule backups or synchronise updated files, a service such as Live Mesh or Mozy (www.mozy.co.uk) might be a better option. SkyDrive scores highly on two other counts, though. First, that 25GB capacity makes it better suited to today's large media files than more restrictive services. Second, SkyDrive is more than just a dumb online space: it's designed to let you share files, photos and documents.

GROUP THERAPY SkyDrive integrates with the sharing and collaboration features of Windows Live, so you can make files available to the world at large or to your contacts. These can be divided into categories, so family members don't get confidential business reports and colleagues don't get baby photos, and members are alerted when you add or change files. SkyDrive is especially well suited to photo sharing. You can upload individual images, or even create galleries and upload them to your online space. Share your holiday snaps with friends or contacts in your network and they'll get a message announcing your new uploads. They can view your images singly or in a slideshow, and add comments to tell you exactly how silly you look in your favourite beach shirt.

If you want informal comments on a speech, sales pitch, letter or report, this is a quick-and-dirty way of getting a document out there and feedback back in. Why not use the Description field to give your contacts an idea of what you're doing and what you're expecting from them?

Tip

When you first create a new folder in your SkyDrive, you can only share it with the Public, your Network or yourself. Once it's there, however, click on the link next to "Shared with:" and then click Edit Permissions. This will allow you to restrict access to a particular category of contacts (for example, family or co-workers) or even to specific individuals.

With its more-than-generous 25GB of free storage space, SkyDrive lends itself well to photo sharing; but there's no reason why you can't use it for more businesslike purposes, such as sharing notes on a big project between a number of colleagues.

Introducing
Windows Live Messenger

Formerly known as MSN Messenger, what started off as a simple instant messaging application is now a great all-round communication tool.

When it launched ten years ago, MSN Messenger was a simple program for sending short messages to friends. Since then, it's grown to become a real-time communications client that's just as much at home with voice and video calls as text-based chat.

Messenger matches all the major features of third-party conferencing tools, such as Skype and Google Video Chat. It works with your existing Windows Live identity, and can share contacts with Windows Live Mail and SkyDrive. The main window makes it easy to set your current status (Available, Busy, Away, or the sneaky Appear Offline) and check the status of your contacts. To start a conversation, just double-click on a name; to initiate a PC-to-PC voice or video call, click the Show menu button to the right of the Search bar, then Actions | Call A Contact's Computer Or Video | Start A Video Call.

Even text chat is as rich as it gets. Static emoticons are supported by animated "winks". During chat, you can switch to video or voice, and even play a selection of simple games with your contact. You can send files to other users during a conversation, or publish them to your SkyDrive from within Messenger.

Over the past few years, Microsoft has tried to make Messenger a sort of hub for your social networking, both in Windows Live and outside. As well as a Search bar and links to MSN services, you'll find What's New updates on changes within your Windows Live networks, plus a Facebook button that lets you make and check updates to the social networking service without leaving Messenger.

TEAM EFFORT The program's real sharing power lies in its group features. You can create groups with the same ease as adding contacts: click the button next to the Search bar, then select Create a Group and follow the simple instructions. Once you have a group, you can invite contacts to join it, then use the group as a place to have online and offline discussions and share photos and files.

It's easy to set up text chats with multiple users: each group gets a Windows Live web page and a shared calendar. It's a great way to share interests or keep in touch with family or friends – or it can turn Messenger into a business tool for simple collaborative projects or maintaining communications between colleagues.

Finally, don't forget Live Messenger isn't tied in to desktop Windows. The browser-based client works on most mobile phones, and you can download dedicated clients for the iPhone and iPad, Android phones and Tablets and – soon, we're promised – Windows Phone 7 devices.

It's easy to set up chats between **multiple users** for a family confab or virtual meeting.

Extras like **animated smileys** make chat more fun – though you're not forced to use them, of course.

You can send messages to friends even when they're **offline**.

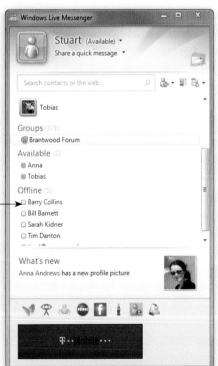

5

Introducing Windows Live Mesh

Microsoft's SkyDrive service provides 25GB of free online storage (see p78), so offering a second service for sharing files between your PCs might seem a redundant move. Live Mesh, however, is a different sort of service to SkyDrive – potentially a more useful one.

At its simplest level, Live Mesh is a means of ensuring that every Windows PC, laptop and netbook that you use (as well as every Apple Mac system) can access the data you need to do your work and live your life.

On another level, it's a system for sharing and collaborating. Sure, you can share photos or documents with SkyDrive or a third party service such as Dropbox (www.dropbox.com), but Live Mesh goes further.

And as the icing on the cake, it also features a fantastically easy-to-use remote access service, enabling you to use your own PC from another via the internet with almost no configuration required.

All this might sound complicated, but Live Mesh is easy to understand. Imagine you have the service installed on two PCs, and each PC has a folder called "Project Files". Using Live Mesh you can synchronise these folders, so that whenever you update a file within the folder on one computer, the copy on the other PC is automatically updated too. For anybody who uses more than one PC in their day to day life, the benefit is obvious: you always have

immediate access to your most up-to-date files, regardless of which computer you're using. And Live Mesh isn't limited to two PCs: you can create a whole network of connected computers – a "Mesh", as Microsoft would have it.

SIGN ON Considering how powerful Live Mesh is, setting it up is surprisingly easy. First you simply download and install the service as part of Windows Live Essentials. You'll then be prompted to enter your Windows Live ID and password: this protects your files, so make sure your password isn't easily guessable. Finally, select "sync a folder" and choose a folder to share with your other computers. If you want to share multiple folders, you can repeat the process as many times as you like.

Once that's done, you can set up synchronisation to many other PCs by simply installing Live Mesh and going through the same process. You can also install it on a Mac to share files across platforms – the Mac installer is a free download from the Microsoft website.

The Live Mesh interface also includes an option to sync your Internet Explorer favourites between PCs, which could be handy if that's your browser of choice (see chapter 6). If you're running a recent version of Microsoft Office, Live Mesh will optionally sync your styles and templates too. A small touch, but a nice one.

Live Mesh keeps your documents and media synchronised between all your PCs. Even if you work across multiple computers, you can be sure you're always working with the latest versions of your files and can get access to them from wherever you may be.

LIVE DEVICES That covers *your* systems, but what happens if you need to access a file from somewhere else? Well, when you set up a folder to sync in Live Mesh, by default it will sync not only to your other PCs, but also to your SkyDrive account (up to a maximum of 5GB). You can access this from anywhere by going to the Windows Live Devices website (http://devices.live.com) and signing in. Click on "SkyDrive synced storage" from the Live Devices web page and you can browse and download whatever files you need.

You'll see that the Live Devices site also lets you access your Live Mesh computers, so you can connect to them remotely – which brings us on to the last great feature of Windows Live Mesh.

GRAB THE REMOTE Provided you allow it, Live Mesh can act as a powerful remote access tool, enabling you to take full control of any Windows PC running Live Mesh. Hook up your work system and your PC at home, for example, and you can find and open documents, send and receive emails and run most applications on your home machine from the comfort of your office desk – or vice versa, if you don't have a particularly security-conscious IT department.

Setting this up is very simple, but there are a few things you need to check. First, the computer you want to connect to must be running Live Mesh – that goes without saying. It must also be fully powered on: Live Mesh is clever, but it can't wake up a computer that's asleep or switched off.

The computer you want to connect to must also have a Windows password set. That's for your own security – Microsoft wouldn't want just anyone to be able to take control of your PC.

Finally, you need to enable Remote Access within Live Mesh, which is switched off by default (again, for your security). To do this, open up the Live Mesh interface from the Start Menu – you'll find it under All Programs | Windows Live. Click on the big word "Remote" at the top of the window, then click the link labelled "Allow remote connections to this computer". The service takes a few seconds to start up, and then you're done.

As you'll see if you have other computers running Live Mesh, this is another way to start a remote session, rather than going through the Live Devices website. If a computer's available, you'll see a link underneath its name which you can click on to connect.

The Live Mesh remote access service is very similar to the standard Windows one (see p168): while you're using the remote PC, no-one else can use it, nor can they see what you're doing – anyone standing over the machine will just see a login screen.

Remote access is terrifically convenient if you ever need to run a work application that isn't installed on your home PC – or vice versa. But be realistic about which applications you can use. The connection between your home PC and your away system won't be fast enough to keep up with rapidly moving graphics, so if you're hoping to use it to watch BBC iPlayer or play 3D games, you're likely to be disappointed.

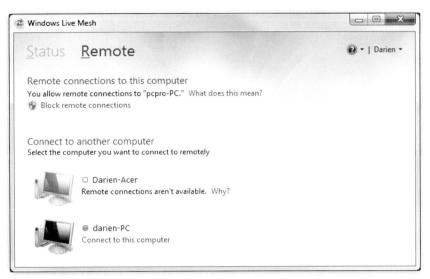

Live Mesh's remote access interface is extraordinarily easy to use – you just have to remember to enable remote connections to your computers ahead of time, so they're available when you need them.

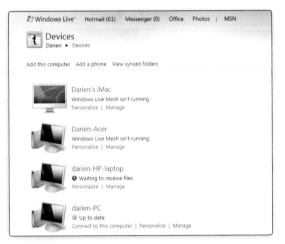

You can also access your Live Mesh computers in a browser, via the Windows Live Devices website. Even systems that aren't switched on, which don't have Remote Access enabled, can be administered from here.

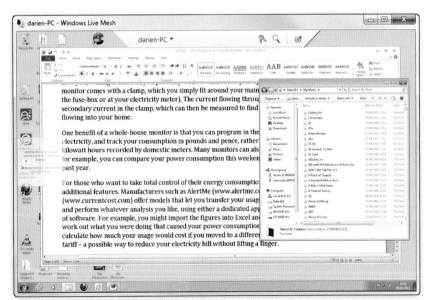

Once you're connected via remote access, you'll enjoy the novel sight of your PC desktop appearing in a window, which you can drag around and resize just as if it were a regular application.

5

Enhance Windows 7

GET MORE OUT OF YOUR WINDOWS 7 PC WITHOUT SPENDING A PENNY: HERE'S OUR GUIDE TO SOME OF THE BEST FREE DOWNLOADS ON THE WEB.

The best free apps for Windows 7

Windows 7 includes a great range of software to work, play and communicate, but adding some third-party applications can really broaden your PC's horizons. On these pages you'll find a smörgåsbord of superb free software to download.

Tip

▲ Besides the software we list on these pages, there are some other downloads that are so fundamental they're effectively part of the operating system. Your web browser is one: see chapter 6 for a guide to choosing and installing your browser. Many people install Apple's iTunes music and video manager too – we discuss that on p106. Lastly, it's vital to install some kind of virus protection, and this too can be had for free. See pp130-132 for our guide to Microsoft's free security suite, and some of the third-party alternatives.

▲ Google Picasa

Windows Live Photo Gallery (see p74) can organise your photos, but Picasa does a more comprehensive job scouring your hard disks for images and filing them in order. You can then organise them into albums, with handy searchable descriptions. Its built-in editing tools provide a range of corrections and adjustments to your images, and even add special effects. You can also create slideshows and screensavers, order prints from UK services, and upload pictures to web albums. **http://picasa.google.com**

Pidgin

Windows Live Messenger is great for communicating via Windows Live or Yahoo, but what if you have friends on AIM, Google Talk, ICQ or Apple iChat? Pity the fool who has to monitor half a dozen different chat applications. Pidgin is a free alternative chat client that can connect to all of these services at once. You can even hold several conversations on different services at the same time, all from one simple interface. Just enter your details for each of the various chat services and Pidgin presents you with a single unified "buddy list".

For those who want a little bit more from their chat client, there's a whole range of optional plug-ins too, which can further extend Pidgin's capabilities. You can add extra notifications, customise the appearance of the interface, tweak your security settings and even integrate your Pidgin conversations with other services such as Facebook and OKCupid. You'll love it when a plan comes together. **www.pidgin.im**

◀ Paint.NET

Windows 7 comes with the basic Paint program, but Paint.NET is a much more advanced tool, with more than enough features to keep amateur photographers happy. It's also blessed with a user-friendly interface, and will run on any modern PC. Noteworthy features include adjustment and retouch tools that rival commercial image-editing packages, plus the ability to build up and manipulate parts of an image in Photoshop-style layers. There's a range of special effects too, and a strong community of users is constantly adding extra features in the form of free plug-ins. **http://paint.net**

7-Zip

If you regularly download files from the internet, you'll know that a lot of things come in compressed formats such as Zip or RAR. This means there's less data to transfer, so the load on the network is less and you get your files more quickly. Compression is also handy if you need to keep a lot of files together without filling up a DVD or USB flash drive. Windows 7 has built-in options for creating compressed folders, but 7-Zip is easier to use: once it's installed, you can simply right-click on any regular file or folder and you'll see options for creating a compressed archive. Right-click on a compressed file and you can extract it there and then. 7-Zip works with many different types of compressed file, including ISO disc images, so it's a great enhancement for Windows. **www.7-zip.org**

▼ OpenOffice.org

If you're using your PC for business purposes, you've probably already invested in Microsoft Office. For everyday use, though, that's an avoidable expense. OpenOffice.org is a completely free alternative office suite that will suit many individuals and small firms just fine.

OpenOffice.org includes all the tools you need to do business: a word processor, a spreadsheet, a presentation designer, a database and even a structured drawing tool. These applications work in similar ways to their Microsoft Office counterparts, so it's easy to get started. And they're largely compatible with the files created by Microsoft applications, so you can happily use OpenOffice.org to exchange documents with people using Word, Excel, PowerPoint and so forth.

OpenOffice.org doesn't match every single feature in Microsoft Office, and its interface is comparatively basic next to the Ribbon used in Office 2007 and 2010. But OpenOffice.org's suite of applications are still highly capable, and strong online documentation along with an enthusiastic user base provide the reassurance of comprehensive support should you get stuck. **www.openoffice.org**

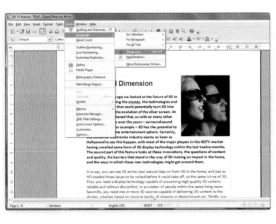

▲ Google Earth

A stunning technical and educational resource, Google Earth brings the entire world to your desktop. If you've ever wanted to explore downtown Buenos Aires, or watch the sunset over the Gateway to India, Google Earth can take you there. It features a complete map of the world, with satellite images, 3D models of many landmarks and a wealth of fascinating and practical information, from geographical facts to driving directions. Look upwards and you can explore the moon and the surface of Mars, or enjoy a guide to the night sky, complete with live telescope views and expert commentary. The historically minded can also survey archive images of major cities and compare them to the present day reality – fancy taking a stroll through Ancient Rome? Google Earth is an incredible resource for anyone interested in our amazing planet. **http://earth.google.co.uk**

CCleaner

The more you use your computer, the more unwanted files accumulate. These include temporary files saved by your web browser, deleted files lingering in the Recycle Bin, diagnostic files created by Windows... the list goes on and on. This eats up hard disk space, and it can slow down your PC, as your

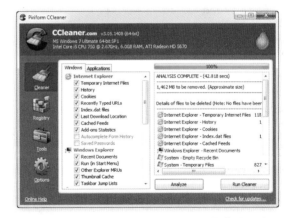

programs trawl through redundant files to find their data. CCleaner automatically finds and removes these unwanted files, helping to restore your PC to tip-top condition.

It doesn't stop at deleting files, either. CCleaner can also scan your system Registry (the database of settings used by Windows and applications) and fix or remove any invalid settings that have been left behind by old programs. This too can help speed up your PC.

Lastly, CCleaner keeps an eye on which programs are running when you start up Windows, and provides an easy interface to disabling them, or uninstalling them altogether. It all adds up to a great housekeeping tool – the only question is why all CCleaner's features aren't built in to Windows. **www.piriform.com/ccleaner**

WinDirStat ▶

The name's short for Windows Directory Statistics, and that's what this free disk-analysis tool gives you – a clear, comprehensive breakdown of all the directories in your system. It's ideal for anyone wondering where all their hard disk space has gone. You get a list of all the folders on your PC, to browse, as well as an easy-to-understand block diagram, colour-coded to show different file types, exposing the relative sizes of your folders and directories. It's a great way to track down those pesky files and folders that keep filling up your hard disk. **http://windirstat.info**

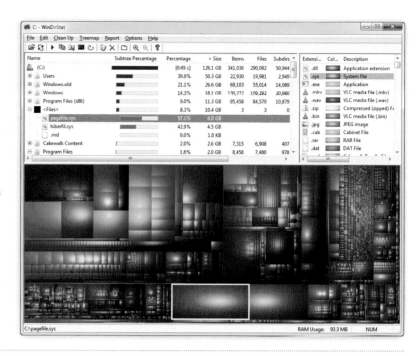

Tip

▲ If you want to find more free software online, there are plenty of places to look. Start with reputable libraries of freeware, shareware and demo programs such as www.tucows.com, and open-source software repositories such as www.sourceforge.net. Even advanced tasks can be catered for without shelling out: for example, Google's SketchUp (http://sketchup.google.com) is a comprehensive 3D drawing system, while Audacity (http://audacity.sourceforge.net) offers excellent sound-recording and editing tools. But double-check the source before downloading any software, or there's a risk you could end up exposed to malware – see chapter 8.

▼ FileZilla

FTP is a system for transferring files directly between computers. If you just use your PC for everyday web surfing, you may never need to use it, and if you only have to download the odd file once in a while you can do this from your web browser.

For those who need to make more regular file transfers, though, FileZilla is a great tool. It lets you store the details of sites you frequently connect to in the Site Manager, so you can reconnect to them with a single click; or you can just enter your connection details into the Quickconnect bar at the top. After that, it's a simple question of selecting a folder on your computer on the left, navigating through the FTP site on the right, then dragging the files you want from one to the other. A tabbed interface even lets you connect to multiple servers at once. If you have lots of files to transfer, FileZilla can save you a huge amount of time and bother. **http://filezilla-project.org**

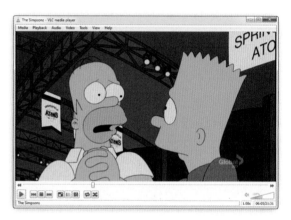

▲ VLC Media Player

VLC plays music and video files, as well as DVD media. To that extent, it's a direct replacement for Windows Media Player. But VLC offers many advantages over Windows' own player. For a start, it supports an enormous range of video formats – if you're having trouble playing a file, just throw it at VLC and the odds are it'll work like a charm.

VLC also supports advanced playback features, such as bookmarks and subtitles. If your disc or video file has multiple audio tracks – perhaps an audio commentary, or a dubbed dialogue track in a different language – VLC lets you choose between them.

The software can even apply a variety of post-processing filters to make your movies look the best, and if you're having trouble with audio that's out of sync with the picture, VLC can fix that too. Useful video effects, such as cropping and zooming, rub shoulders with more frivolous adjustments, such as colour inversion. VLC does it all: if you've the slightest interest in watching video on your PC it's well worth a download. **www.videolan.org**

◀ Songbird

On a basic level, Songbird is a free library manager for your collection of music, video files and photos. Just like Windows Media Player or iTunes, you can use it to organise your downloaded tracks, convert CDs into audio files, create custom playlists and synchronise them with a portable media player. What makes Songbird special is that it's based on the Firefox web browser (see p90) – and just like Firefox, it can accommodate any number of add-ons to gain new capabilities. For example, when you install Songbird, you'll be given the option of downloading the 7digital Music add-on, which recommends new music based on the songs you've been playing. With the Last.fm Radio add-on, Songburd can stream recommended music directly into your player.

Add-ons can offer "real-world" services, too. The Concerts add-on will keep track of the artists in your music library, and let you know when they're playing near you, while the New Releases add-on keeps you up to date with forthcoming albums. The possibilities are limitless, making Songbird far more than a simple Media Player replacement. **www.getsongbird.com**

HandBrake

With built-in support for the widely used H.264, XviD and DivX codecs, Windows 7 is the Microsoft's most video-friendly operating system yet. But there are still some formats it doesn't support; and even if your file will play in Windows, that doesn't mean you'll be able to transfer it to a portable player, tablet or phone – such devices are notoriously finicky about which video file formats they'll accept. HandBrake can help, by converting video files into a wide range of formats compatible

with PCs, iPods, handheld games consoles and so forth – it comes with presets for Apple devices, which can be easily adjusted to work with other media players. Handbrake can't convert encrypted files, or data copied from commercial DVDs – that's illegal. But for getting the odd file to work with your player, it's a great tool. **http://handbrake.fr**

▼ Recuva

If you've ever accidentally deleted a file you meant to keep, you'll appreciate the value of a tool like Recuva. By carefully scanning the data that's left behind on your hard disk, it can recover deleted files – even after you've emptied the Recycle Bin. In certain scenarios that could be a life-saver – not bad for a free tool!

Recovering files in this way is most likely to work if the disk hasn't been written to since the file was deleted – otherwise there's a chance your precious data will already have been overwritten. So don't put off installing Recuva until you need it, as the very process of installing it could cause you to lose your data for good. We suggest you download Recuva sooner rather than later, for the sake of your own peace of mind . **www.piriform.com/recuva**

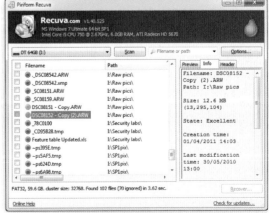

▲ SiSoftware Sandra Lite

Unless you're the kind of person who builds their own computers, you may not know exactly which components are in your PC. Even if you know what's supposed to be there, it's hard to be certain that everything is set up correctly, and performing the way it should be. This free edition of Sandra – the "System Analyser, Diagnostic and Reporting Assistant" – provides a thorough breakdown of every last component in your PC, with lots of technical detail, without you having to go near a screwdriver. This can be highly valuable when you're planning an upgrade, if you need to check if a program is compatible with your system or if you need to contact technical support. Sandra also includes numerous benchmarking tools, so you can check exactly what each component in your system is doing for you and compare its performance to that of different types of hardware. **www.sisoftware.co.uk**

IN THIS CHAPTER

6
Internet & networking

INTERNET AND

Windows 7 is designed for a networked world, and in this chapter we'll show you how to get up and running online – both on the internet and on your home network. However you use Windows, you're certain to want a web browser, so we start with an overview of the major options: there are more choices than many people realise, each with its own strengths

NETWORKING

and weaknesses. We'll also explain how to set up a wireless network and connect your Windows 7 PC to it with maximum speed and security. Finally, we'll explain how Windows 7's HomeGroup feature makes it a breeze to share files and even printers between multiple PCs, and walk through the steps involved if you need the flexibility to share individual items.

Introducing Internet Explorer 9

Windows 7 comes with Internet Explorer 8, a fully-featured web browser for visiting your favourite sites. But there's now a newer version offering improved performance and a cleaner look – and there are plenty of alternative browsers as well, as we'll discuss on the following pages. First, we'll tell you how to install and get the best from Internet Explorer 9, or IE9 as it's known for short.

BROWSER BALLOT When you start up Windows for the first time, you may see a requester inviting you to choose your web browser. This is called the "browser ballot", and it makes it easy to to configure Internet Explorer as your default browser, or to install a different option. As we'll see, though, there are good reasons to stick with Microsoft's own browser. At the time of writing, it's still the older Internet Explorer 8 that's offered, but we expect Microsoft will soon update this to the latest version 9.

For now, therefore, if you want to install IE9, you have to download the installer yourself. That's easy to do: simply visit www.beautyoftheweb.co.uk, click the orange Download Now button and follow the on-screen prompts. That slightly unusual address is indeed the official Microsoft site: the company simply wants to draw attention to the graphical powers of IE9.

SURF'S UP IE9 works much like previous versions and other browsers, but it's designed to be as minimal as possible, so as not to distract from your favourite sites. Along the top you'll see an address bar, where you can type or paste web addresses. If you type in something that isn't an address, IE9 will carry out a web search instead – so, for example, if you don't know the address of a taxi firm in North London, you can just type "north london taxi" and find one. As you type, IE9 will also display a dropdown containing the titles of any pages you've previously visited that contain your phrase: just click on a title to jump back to that page.

TABBED BROWSING To the right of the address bar you'll see one or more tabs. Tabs let you keep multiple pages open within one browser window. Press <Ctrl+T> to open a new tab, without losing your original webpage. You can also open a tab by clicking the mini-tab to the right of the tab titles.

You can open any link in a new tab by holding down Ctrl while you click it, or by clicking the wheel of your mouse. Internet Explorer colour-codes your tabs, so you can see at a glance which tabs are part of the same session.

These are IE9's basic features, but there's plenty more to discover. We look at some of the more advanced additions on the opposite page.

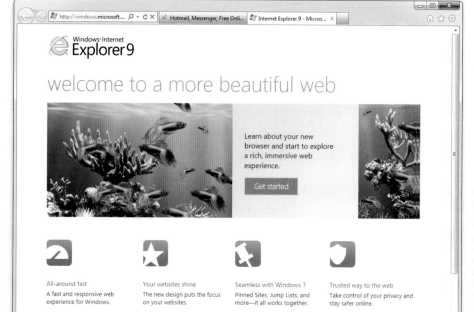

Microsoft's Internet Explorer 9 is the most minimal version yet. With almost no buttons or menus, the website itself is the star of the show. But behind that simple front-end, IE9 still has some powerful features hidden away.

HOW TO...
USE IE9'S ADVANCED FEATURES

(1) MOST POPULAR SITES Internet Explorer 9 keeps track of the sites you visit – not in a sinister way, but just so that next time you start the program or open a new tab, you can get back to your favourite pages right away. Your most popular sites are automatically updated as you browse, with an activity monitor below each entry showing how frequently the page is updated – to give you an idea whether it's worth checking back. If there's a site you don't want to appear here, simply click the little close icon at the top right of its pane, and it'll be gone for good. At the bottom you'll see a few more options, including "Reopen last session", which restores all the tabs you had open last time you were using IE9 – helpful if you were interrupted.

(2) INPRIVATE BROWSING Another option you'll see beneath the list of popular sites is InPrivate browsing. InPrivate mode is indicated by a blue button in the address bar. When you browse in InPrivate mode, nothing you do is recorded – a useful option if you have an online banking account, for example, and want to be sure your details won't be left behind on your PC. It's also useful if, for any reason, you don't want other people to be able to see which sites you've been visiting. Remember, however, that this includes you – if you visit a page in an InPrivate window and later want to find the information in your browser history, it won't be there.

(3) DOWNLOAD MANAGER The Download Manager is a new feature in IE9 that's enormously helpful if you regularly download files from the web. It gives an at-a-glance view of all the files you've recently downloaded, as well as any that are still in progress. You can also open or launch downloaded files and programs with a single click, and search for a particular download by typing into the search box at the top right of the window. Click on Options and you can select the default location where downloaded files will be saved. You can open the Download Manager at any time by pressing <Ctrl+J>.

(4) PINNED SITES Most of us have a few websites that we use all the time – common examples might be webmail, social networking sites or online business applications. Internet Explorer 9 lets you give these sites their own taskbar icons, so you can access them directly, in just the same way that you'd launch a regular program. To "pin" a site to the Taskbar, simply open it in IE9, then drag its tab down to the bottom of the screen. An icon will be automatically created, using the site's own logo where possible. Click on it to open the web page, or right-click to have the option to visit it in InPrivate mode. When you launch IE9 in this way the browser will also attempt to match its window colours to those of the site – not a particularly useful feature, but cute all the same.

HOW LONG?
IE9 is quick to install (though you may need to restart your PC), and then you can simply click on its icon and go.

HOW HARD?
The basics are very intuitive, but if you want to make the most of IE9 there are a few controls and shortcuts to master.

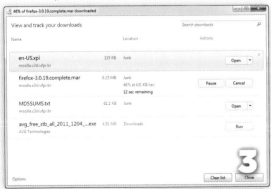

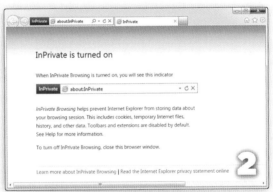

IF INTERNET EXPLORER IS NOT FOR YOU, TRY THE FREE, OPEN SOURCE
MOZILLA FIREFOX – THE WEB'S SECOND MOST POPULAR BROWSER.

Introducing Firefox 4

Firefox 4 is the latest edition of the free web browser published by the Mozilla Foundation. It's a powerful and fully featured alternative to Internet Explorer. You can choose it from the Windows 7 "browser ballot" (see p88), or you can download the installer from www.getfirefox.com.

Firefox isn't the only non-Microsoft browser: we'll look at some other options on the following pages. It is the most popular one, though, thanks to a long-held reputation for being faster and more secure than Internet Explorer.

In truth, that's no longer the case. Internet Explorer 9 has much better security than its predecessors, and it's slightly faster than Firefox. That's proved by the free SunSpider benchmark, which measures how quickly a browser can execute the sort of code that drives rich, interactive websites. On our test PC, Firefox 4 completed the tests in 327ms, while IE9 shaved that down to 303ms. It's not a big gap, though: either browser will be perfect for sites such as Google's Gmail or Google Docs. Which one you choose will be a matter of personal preference.

FIREFOX FEATURES Firefox looks similar to Internet Explorer, but it does a few things differently. Next to the address bar, you'll see a separate search box, which makes it easy to search Google, Bing or other resources such as the

Chambers Dictionary, eBay or Wikipedia (although you can search directly from the address bar if you prefer). Go online and you can install extra search engines, and you can also choose from hundreds of downloadable graphical themes, known as "Personas", to give your browser a distinctive look.

Those who use several different computers will appreciate Firefox 4's sync capabilities, which can automatically share your browsing history, passwords, bookmarks and even open tabs between different PCs.

Firefox also pioneered some of IE9's more advanced features. For example, Firefox has for many years had a Private Browsing mode, equivalent to IE9's InPrivate browsing, that lets you surf without your steps being recorded in your computer. The Download Manager was also originally a Firefox innovation.

WELCOME ADDITIONS The jewel in Firefox's crown is its huge library of add-ons, which can provide almost any feature, from simple things such as multi-language spellchecking to radical enhancements such as changing the way websites display. Those that add major new features are known as "extensions": on the opposite page you'll see some of our favourites, but there are thousands more to choose from: visit http://addons.mozilla.org to see them all.

Tip

As you use Firefox, it will learn the sites you frequently visit. By default you'll see a "Most Visited" button to the left of the Bookmarks Toolbar: click it and you can instantly hop to any of your regular sites, or open them all at the same time, each in its own tab.

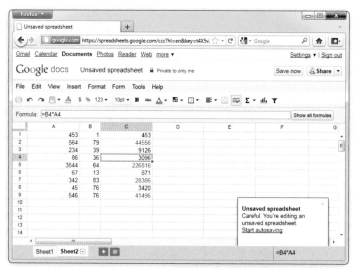

The most popular rival to Microsoft's Internet Explorer, Firefox is a free application that's faster and – in many ways – better, with a neat layout that makes it easy to work with modern online services such as Google Docs.

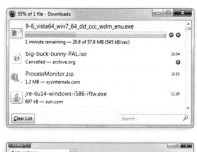

Firefox's Downloads pane (above right) helps keep track of files retrieved from the internet, while add-ons (above), developed by numerous third parties, provide even more features.

HOW TO...
USE FIREFOX EXTENSIONS

There's an extension for everything: some are frivolous or highly specialised, while others can benefit almost everybody. Here's a selection of our favourites.

 FLASHBLOCK You've seen web pages that present graphics and sound using Adobe's Flash plugin. It's become an integral part of the web. But there's no denying that some sites get carried away, obscuring the content you want to read. Flashblock puts you back in control: with this extension installed, Flash animations load up "frozen", and won't display until you click the Play button. It's a simple but excellent tweak.

FIREGESTURES The standard browser controls are easy to master, but once you start using multiple tabs, and paging back and forth in your browsing history, things can get fiddly. FireGestures lets you ignore Firefox's buttons and menus, and navigate with mouse gestures. For example, to go back to the previous page you hold down the right mouse button and drag to the left, no matter where on the screen your pointer happens to be. You can switch between tabs by dragging up and to the side, or using a rocker motion on the mouse buttons. The controls can be customised, and you can download scripts for more actions. Before long you'll wonder how you ever got by without mouse gestures.

 FOXLINGO One of the great things about the web is that it's truly global, and since you're lucky enough to understand English you can access a huge proportion of international information. All the same, there's a lot more out there in foreign languages – and FoxLingo's translation toolbar can help you read it. The extension uses free online resources to translate selected text or an entire web page between 53 languages, and also offers quick links to many other language resources, including dictionaries, text-to-speech translators and proofreading services. You can even enter search terms in English and find pages in other languages.

GREASEMONKEY Greasemonkey is an amazing extension that can dramatically improve the way websites look and function. It works by downloading a page from the web, then adding in its own custom scripts to provide new features. Anyone can write a script (although it takes a little programming expertise), and there are already hundreds available for free. The features they add are as diverse as showing larger pictures in Facebook; adding features to Twitter; finding song lyrics on YouTube; and changing Google from white to black. Greasemonkey can even save you money, as there are numerous scripts designed to alert you automatically when better deals are available online.

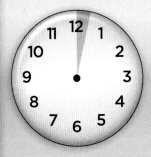

HOW LONG?
Adding a Firefox extension is a two-minute job, although you can happily spend hours downloading scripts and configuring gestures.

HOW HARD?
Installing extensions is just a matter of a couple of mouse clicks.

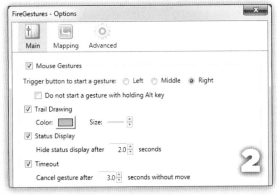

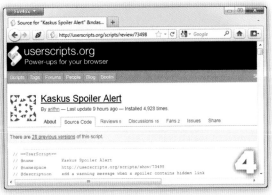

Introducing Google Chrome

If you're unsure whether to stick with Internet Explorer or jump ship to its major rival Firefox, there's a third option that's worth a try. Google Chrome is a web browser that's designed and supported by Google itself, the undisputed king of web searches and the operator of a whole range of popular online services, including GMail, Google Maps, Google Docs and Google Calendar. Like Firefox, Chrome is available from the Windows 7 browser ballot, or you can install it yourself from www.google.com/chrome.

You may question whether the world really needs a third browser, but Chrome has a decent following – some reports put its share of the browser market at around 20% and climbing. And if you want to use Google's online services, it makes sense to access them via that company's own browser, to be certain of getting the best performance. When Chrome emerged in 2008, it was the fastest browser on the block for this type of use, leaving its rivals far behind in the benchmarks.

Today, Chrome can no longer claim that crown. In the online SunSpider benchmark, the latest version of Chrome proved a smidgen slower than Firefox or IE9, completing the tests in 339ms against its competitors' scores of 327ms and 303ms respectively. That's still a good score, though, and Chrome feels very fast in everyday use.

KEEPING IT SIMPLE When Chrome first came out, web browsers tended to be cluttered with lots of buttons and bars: if you've used an older version of Internet Explorer or Firefox you'll know what we mean. Chrome introduced the minimal look, and other browsers have since followed suit. Compare IE9 or the latest version of Firefox and Chrome's influence is obvious.

A MIX OF FEATURES Chrome may not be the fastest browser, nor the cleanest, but its particular blend of features has a lot going for it. Like IE9, it uses a single bar – dubbed the "Omnibox" – for both addresses and search terms. Like, Firefox it supports downloadable Themes and Extensions, so you can make the browser look and act just how you want. "Incognito mode" does the same job as Private Browsing, ensuring no-one can follow your tracks online.

One way in which Chrome is distinctive is that it comes with the Adobe Flash Player built in. This enables you to play games and watch online videos without needing to install the Flash plug-in separately.

And Chrome's update mechanism is much more active than its rivals'. It's constantly checking for updates and downloading patches (see box, opposite), so it's less vulnerable to hacker attacks than other browsers.

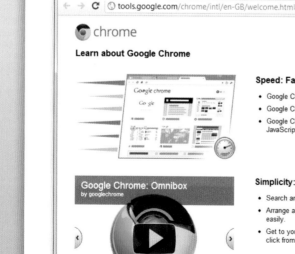

Google Chrome is the original minimal browser: as the developer says, it's designed to maximise speed and simplicity.

HOW TO...
MASTER GOOGLE CHROME

① OPENING A NEW TAB When you open a new tab in Chrome (by pressing <Ctrl+T>) you'll see a set of little thumbnails of all your most frequently visited sites (just like in IE9). Along the bottom you'll also see a list of tabs you've recently closed, so you can get back to a recently visited page quickly. Hover over one of the thumbnails and you'll see a frame appear containing two icons. One of them is a pin icon, which lets you keep a particular site always in that place (if you don't like where it is, simply drag it elsewhere before clicking on the pin). You'll also see a close icon, which removes the site from this page, Finally, along the top you'll see a bookmark bar. Drag any site here and you'll always be able to access it from this page, even if you don't visit it very often.

② INSTALLING EXTENSIONS The idea of adding extensions to your web browser was originally introduced by Firefox; but Chrome has jumped on board and there are now well over a thousand freely installable extensions to choose from. With these you can have your email automatically checked, speed up page loading, download multiple files with a single click and much more. Many of these extensions were actually written by the Google Chrome team, so you can be confident that they're safe and reliable. To browse the whole library visit http://chrome.google.com/extensions.

③ WEB PAGE TRANSLATION Google Chrome has the great advantage of being able to draw on Google's other services to offer extra features withouth bloating the browser itself. Web page translation is a perfect example of this. When you visit a site that's not written in your native language, Chrome will automatically detect it and put up a blue box offering to translate the page for you. If you click Translate, the page is fed through the Google Translate service and seamlessly fed back to your browser. It's not always a perfect translation, but it's effortless to use and can be very handy for getting the gist of a page. In other browsers, to get a feature like this you'd need to install a specialist add-on.

④ CONSTANT UPDATES All web browsers need to be regularly updated: the browser, after all, is your first line of defence against any malware lurking out there on the web. Google Chrome is unusually conscientious about this. Rather than inviting you to download a new version every few weeks or months, Chrome is constantly patching and updating itself in the background, to ensure you always have up-to-the-minute security and features. If that sounds like a drain on resources, don't worry: the process is so efficient you won't even notice it happening – though you may notice new features becoming available from time to time.

HOW LONG?
Downloading and installing Chrome takes just a few moments.

HOW HARD?
As with any browser, the basics are a breeze, but you'll need to use Chrome for a day or two before you're au fait with its ins and outs.

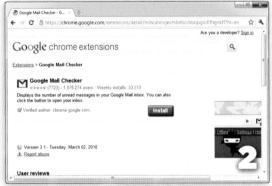

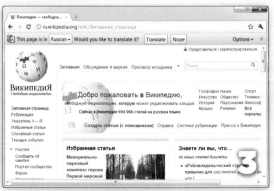

IF THE MAINSTREAM BROWSERS DON'T FEEL RIGHT TO YOU, THERE'S NO NEED TO FOLLOW THE HERD – TRY ONE OF THESE MORE ESOTERIC ALTERNATIVES.

Alternative web browsers

Between them, Internet Explorer, Firefox and Chrome make up more than 90% of the browsers in use today. But they aren't your only choices: the Windows 7 browser ballot will also offer you several lesser-known alternatives (see opposite). There's no harm in giving one of these a try – they all work in fundamentally the same way, and if you don't get on with one you can always uninstall it.

WHAT TO LOOK FOR If you're trying out a new browser, there are a few things to consider. The first is performance – you don't want a browser that chugs along when you're checking your email or looking up an address. We've already referred to the SunSpider benchmark, which compares the speeds of different web browsers. You can put any browser to the test by visiting http://webkit.org/perf/sunspider/sunspider.html and following the on-screen instructions.

SunSpider scores are specific to the PC on which the test is run, so you can't meaningfully compare your results to ours, or to anyone else's. But if you test two or more browsers on the same computer, any difference in performance will be exposed. SunSpider only checks how quickly a browser can run web applications such as Google Docs: it can't analyse more touchy-feely issues, such as how quickly a browser responds when you click a button. That's something you'll have to gauge for yourself.

WEB STANDARDS You've probably noticed that some websites look slightly different in different browsers. That's not normally deliberate: web page code is complex, and browsers sometimes render it wrongly. Ideally, you want a browser that makes as few mistakes as possible.

Enter Acid3, a benchmark designed to catch out web browsers with 100 samples of obscure and tricky code. You can run it for yourself by visiting http://acid3.acidtests.org. Wait for the page to load and you'll see a brief animation that builds up to a final score out of 100, showing how many tests were completed correctly.

When subjected to the Acid3 test, Internet Explorer 9 scores a creditable 95%, but Firefox 4 beats it with 97% and the latest version of Google Chrome takes the prize with a flawless 100% score. That doesn't guarantee that all sites will look perfect in Google Chrome, however – sometimes it's the web designer who's made the mistake!

OTHER FEATURES Many alternative browsers offer speed and rendering accuracy that's similar to the "big three", so your decision may well come down to the user interface and features. This is a matter of personal taste: some people prefer their browser to be as simple as possible. Others enjoy the extra bells and whistles offered by alternative browsers – some of which we look at in the box opposite.

Tip

Browser benchmarks such as the Acid3 test (see main text) are a useful comparison tool but a rather blunt instrument. What really matters is that your browser works well for the pages you visit, offers the features you want, and feels responsive. The best test is your own experience, so it makes sense to try a few browsers before settling on the one you'll use every day. Some people keep two or more regular browsers, using each for different purposes, such as general surfing and managing a website.

Apple's Safari browser is most commonly seen on Apple's own computers and mobile devices, but it's available for the PC as well. One of its characteristic features is the Top Sites view. Plenty of browsers show a grid of frequently visited sites, but Safari does it with that unmistakeable Apple shine.

Opera

The Opera browser has been around for years, and is now up to version 11. Originally, its selling points were its unrivalled speed and simplicity, but these days it's been overtaken by other browsers. The latest version of Opera (11 at the time of writing) took longer than any of the mainstream browsers to complete the SunSpider speed test. It was a close run thing, though: practically speaking, Opera's total time of 342ms was identical to Google Chrome's 339ms.

Opera's front-end also looks comparatively busy compared to the latest version of Internet Explorer, Firefox and Chrome, with a fair number of buttons dotted around the place. Look more closely and you'll find Opera also has a host of extra features hidden under the bonnet. For starters there's a whole email program tucked away inside the browser, along with native support for mouse gestures. An extension framework lets you add new features and controls, just as you can with Firefox and Chrome.

Opera even includes support for "widgets", miniature information displays and controls similar to Windows 7 Gadgets (see p40). We're not sure why you'd want these in your browser, but the option's there.

Clearly, Opera is a browser for those who want everything but the kitchen sink. If you fancy giving it a try, you can download it for free from www.opera.com.

Apple Safari

The Safari web browser (pictured opposite) has long been included with Apple Macintosh computers, iPhones and iPads, but it's also available as a free download for Windows.

Unusually for Apple, the interface isn't exactly clean, with more buttons and links than the likes of IE9. But there are plenty of nice aesthetic touches elsewhere, including the Top Sites view (pictured to the left) which adds a sheen of glamour to the pedestrian business of choosing a web page to visit. The History view is similar: it uses Apple's "Cover Flow" interface, familiar from the iPod and iTunes, to whizz you through the pages you've previously viewed against a shiny black backdrop.

Happily, Apple knows when to be low-key. When you want to focus on reading an online article, you can enable Safari's Reader mode, which dims the interface, along with any distracting adverts and other web page items.

Safari also brings all the expected browser features. Those include a smart address bar that you can use to search for previously visited sites, and support for extensions so you can add features that the browser lacks.

Safari isn't the fastest browser. It took 469ms to complete our SunSpider tests, a little way behind the rest of the pack. But its web page rendering is impeccable, scoring a perfect 100% in the taxing Acid3 test – the same as Chrome, which is perhaps no surprise as the two browsers use the same rendering engine.

Like all of these browsers, Safari is available from the Windows 7 browser ballot; or you can get it as a free download from www.apple.com/safari.

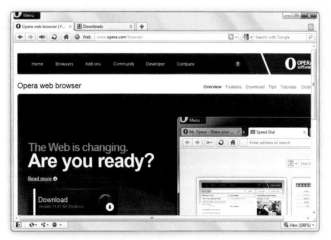

Opera has lost its lead over other browsers in areas such as speed, but it has plenty of features and can be further enhanced and customised with widgets and extensions.

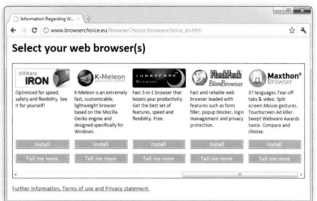

The front page of the browser ballot shows all the most popular choices, but scroll to the right and you'll see a whole host of alternative browsers you've probably never heard of before.

Online benchmarks such as SunSpider and Acid3 can tell you how fast a browser works, and how accurately it renders web pages according to the current industry standards – but they don't tell the whole usability story.

... and the rest

That's five browsers, but we're not done: the Windows 7 browser ballot offers a further seven choices of browser. You might not notice them at first, though, as – as if to emphasise that they're not for everyone – they're hidden away off the edge of the main window, and you have to scroll sideways to find them. (If the browser ballot doesn't appear on your computer, you can access it at www.browserchoice.eu.)

There's nothing exactly wrong with these other browsers. Many of them are customised versions of more mainstream browsers, so they use fast and stable code.

The customisations, however, may not be to everyone's taste. Maxthon Browser, for example, is festooned with buttons and options: we suspect only real control freaks would choose this over Internet Explorer, which it's based on.

Another option is SRWare Iron, a spin-off of Google Chrome with all features that could potentially compromise your privacy removed. Flock, also based on Chrome, comes with built-in additions for accessing numerous social sites including Facebook, Twitter and Flickr.

The most ambitious browser is Lunascape, which includes the browsing engines from Internet Explorer, Firefox and Chrome, for you to switch between as you choose.

You can click the "Tell me more" button below any of these browsers to learn more about them – but for most users, we suspect sticking with one of the "big three" browsers is the best path to a stress-free online existence.

Setting up a wireless network

Broadband internet is very common these days, so there's a good chance you already have a Wi-Fi router in your home. If you don't, this could be a good time to acquire one, so you can enjoy wireless internet access anywhere in your house. If you do already own a router, it's worth making sure it's configured to give you the best performance and security.

The specifics of setting up a router vary from model to model: you'll need to check the manufacturer's instructions for precise details on how to connect to the router from your PC and change its settings. In general, you can normally log in by visiting http://192.168.1.1 in your browser.

CHOOSE A PASSWORD Your router will have an administration password – by default a preset password that's given in the manual (either "admin" or nothing at all are two favourites). Change it as soon as possible. Standard passwords are common knowledge among hackers, and you don't want strangers to be able to change your settings.

CHOOSE AN SSID The SSID (Service Set Identifier) is the name that your wireless network shows to the world. It will probably start off as something like "Default Network", or the name of the router's manufacturer. Change this

to something more distinctive to minimise the risk of confusion with your neighbours' Wi-Fi routers, but don't use your name or address in your network name: this just makes life easier for tech-savvy thieves.

SET UP SECURITY To avoid any passer-by connecting, your router will offer various security systems. Your best bet is WPA2-PSK, which stands for Wi-Fi Protected Access 2 with a Pre-Shared Key (your router may call it WPA2 Personal, or just WPA2). It's very secure and works with smartphones, Wi-Fi printers, games consoles and other wireless devices. If some of your kit doesn't support WPA2, standard WPA should still deter casual hackers, but WEP, the least secure option, is much less effective protection.

Once you enable WPA2, you'll be asked to choose a password. It should be more than eight characters long; it should be memorable to you, but impossible to guess.

PICK A PROTOCOL Ensure your router is set to use the fastest Wi-Fi protocol your PC supports (see Tip, left). This may not speed up web browsing, as even a fast connection is slower than your network. But a higher protocol can make a big difference when transferring files within your home, and may improve Wi-Fi reception too.

Tip

Wireless networking uses four standard protocols – all referred to as "802.11" followed by a letter. 802.11a was designed for business back in 1999, and you're unlikely to run into it today. 802.11b is more common but comparatively slow; 802.11g is faster, and the fastest protocol is 802.11n. You may also see "draft-n" devices that were produced while 802.11n was still officially under development – these are compatible with real 802.11n hardware, though they may not be as fast. Most modern laptops can connect to any 802.11b, g or n network, and most routers can use several protocols at once, acting as a go-between so computers using different protocols can communicate with each other.

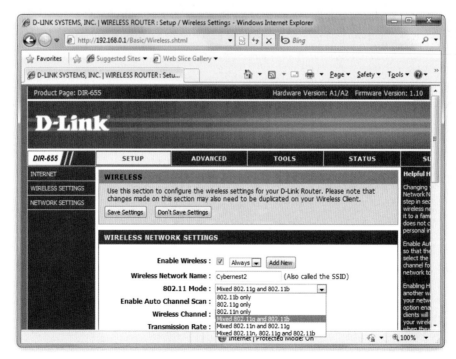

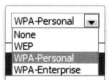

Today's wireless routers generally come with easy setup wizards. There shouldn't be many tasks to complete, but among the most important are setting an admin password, to prevent other users changing your settings, and applying encryption-based security, such as WPA2 (aka WPA-Personal), to ensure unauthorised users can't access your network or intercept your data traffic.

HOW TO...
CONNECT TO A WI-FI NETWORK

① ENABLE WI-FI Obvious, but easy to overlook. Many laptops have a Wi-Fi switch (so that you can turn off wireless networking in a public place or simply to increase battery life), while some use a key combination – typically the Fn key plus the key marked with an antenna. There's usually an indicator light.

② PICK YOUR NETWORK Left-click on the wireless icon in the Windows System Tray and you'll see a list of networks in range. At home, look for the name you gave your router. At a public hotspot, there should be a network with the name of the advertised Wi-Fi provider; if in doubt, ask. A yellow warning symbol next to a network means it's unprotected, so you can connect but your data won't be encrypted as it travels over the airwaves, so it could be intercepted by snoopers. This is common with public Wi-Fi hotspots.

③ MAKE THE CONNECTION When you click on a network name, you'll see an option to connect to that network automatically. Enable this and, in future, Windows will connect to that network whenever it's in range. You can enable this for any number of different networks; if more than one is in range at a given time, Windows will choose the most recently used, or you can go to "Open Network and Sharing Center" at the bottom of the network list and select "Manage wireless networks" to choose which networks take precedence.

When you click "Connect to join a protected network", you'll be asked to enter a security key. If you're attempting to connect to your own router, this will be the passphrase you chose during the setup process (see "Set up security", left). If it's someone else's network, you'll need to ask for the password before you can connect.

Note that when you tell Windows to automatically connect to a network, it will also remember that network's passphrase, and provide it whenever it needs to connect. That's a convenience, but it could also be a security risk: if you let someone else use your network temporarily, in theory they could reconnect to it later without your knowledge. If you think your passphrase could be abused, change it.

④ CHOOSE A NETWORK LOCATION Once connected, you'll be asked whether this is a Home, Work or Public network. If you tell Windows you're at home or work, you'll be able to share files and printers with other computers on the same network. Choose home and you'll also be able to join a HomeGroup (see p98). If it's a public network, those types of connection will be automatically blocked to prevent strangers from accessing your files. As Windows suggests, don't choose Home or Work for "public places such as coffee shops or airports".

HOW LONG?
If your PC and the router are working normally, it's quick to get them talking.

HOW HARD?
A few clicks and it's done. If you can't see a network, first check your Wi-Fi on/off switch, then try moving closer to the router.

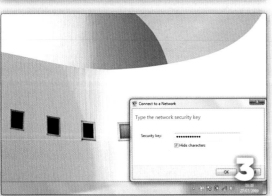

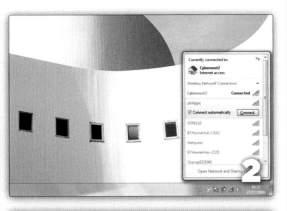

FAQ

Q: Will I be able to access my homegroup when away from home?

A: HomeGroup only works within your home network, not over the internet. For a laptop that regularly returns home, you could use offline files; for computers that are permanently on separate networks, you could try Windows Live Mesh (see p80) or a similar service.

Q: Is there any disadvantage to making files available offline?

A: It consumes some space on your hard disk, and with a large amount of data it may be slow to sync. But you can reduce your power consumption by switching off additional computers when not in use, so that's a benefit.

Introducing HomeGroup

If you have more than one computer, it's very useful to be able to share files and resources between them. Windows 7's brand-new HomeGroup feature makes it effortless to set this up. Perhaps you have a desktop and a laptop, or several members of your family each have their own PC. No matter how your computers are distributed, it's likely they're all connected to the same router (see p96). This means not only can they all access the internet, but they can also share files with each other. So you don't need to keep multiple copies of your data on multiple PCs, and everyone can get at files on your main PC without interrupting you. If one of your computers is connected to a printer, you can share that, too, so other users can print to it from their own PCs. You can even play music and videos from one PC on another.

If you're an experienced Windows user, you might be thinking this all sounds rather familiar. And you're right: these abilities aren't new to Windows 7. File and printer sharing is a well-established technology, although it's only really become commonplace in the past few years as home networks with multiple PCs have become the norm.

But setting up file sharing has always been a tricky business, requiring you to understand user accounts, permissions and workgroups. Windows 7 makes it much easier with a new system called HomeGroup.

GROUP THERAPY Simply put, a homegroup is a collection of computers that can access the files in one another's Libraries (we discussed Libraries in chapter 3). You can set up a homegroup with a few clicks from any computer in your home running Windows 7. Once it's created, other PCs connected to the same network can join by entering a password. You can set this yourself, or you can have a secure code automatically generated by Windows.

The beauty of HomeGroup is that, unlike previous Windows file-sharing systems, at no point do you need to know the name or network address of any of the computers. Nor do you have to worry about the various user accounts and permissions of different members of your family. You can see just how straightforward the process is in our tutorial on p88.

Once your homegroup is up and running, you'll see it appear in the Windows Explorer navigation pane, with a list of all the other computers in your homegroup that are online. Simply click into one and you'll be able to access its Libraries as if they were your own. You can even incorporate files from your homegroup into your own Library.

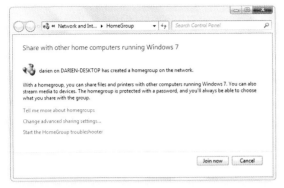

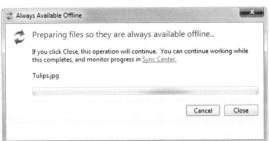

Windows 7's HomeGroup makes it easy to get all your computers sharing files. By making files "always available offline", you can even access files on a PC that isn't currently switched on. Spooky.

Of course, this could raise some concerns about the security of your personal files, so there are a few points we should make clear. You don't have to share all your Libraries: on each computer, you can choose which of your Pictures, Videos, Music or Documents Libraries to share. By default, Documents is disabled, so you can let other family members listen to Dire Straits' "Private Investigations" without giving them the ability to snoop on your financial records. You can also manually mark specific files or folders as private to prevent anyone else accessing them.

And as an extra level of security, when you first set up a homegroup, all the folders you share will be read-only to other users in the group – so you don't need to worry about anyone accidentally deleting or corrupting your files. Nor will the kids be able to fill your hard disk with temporary files and unwanted downloads. But if you do want to enable other users to edit a particular file, or let them add files to one of your folders, that's easy to set up, as we'll show you over the page.

KNOW YOUR LIMITS HomeGroup is designed to be as simple as possible. That's its strength, but it means it isn't very versatile. When you share files and folders using the HomeGroup system, your sharing settings affect everybody in the group. If you want to create a more complex sharing system – for example, you want to give your partner access to your Documents Library without extending it to your kids – you'll need to go back to the old, slightly more complicated way of sharing folders.

Another important limitation of HomeGroup is that it works only with PCs running Windows 7. If some of the computers in your household are still using Windows XP or Vista, they won't be able to join your homegroup. Nor

STREAM MUSIC AND MOVIES It's very convenient to be able to use HomeGroup to give others access to your Music and Video Libraries. But there may be hundreds or even thousands of files in these folders, so it can be a pain for users to find what they're looking for in Windows Explorer. Happily, there's a better way: when you set up a homegroup, you'll be given the option to enable media streaming. If you do so, other members of your homegroup will be able to use Windows Media Player to browse your music, video and photo collections, just as if they were sitting at your PC. They can even listen to songs and watch videos without having to copy the files onto their own PC first. For more information on media streaming, see p114.

can you use HomeGroup to share files with anyone using an Apple Macintosh or a Linux-based computer. In all these cases, you'll need to use traditional file sharing to let other computers access your files and folders. We'll show you how at the end of this chapter.

GO OFFLINE The bane of any file-sharing arrangement is finding that the PC containing the files you want to access is switched off. Even Windows 7 can't talk to a system that's powered down. The good news is that there's a workaround: while browsing files or folders that reside on a different PC, you can tell Windows to make them available "offline". After you do this, you'll find that, magically, you can access them even when the other computer isn't available.

Of course, there's a trick to it. When you make a file from another machine available offline, Windows creates a hidden copy of it on your own hard disk. Later, if it can't access the file over the network, it shows you this local copy instead. It all happens transparently. The other user might change the file, of course, but Windows synchronises its copy with the original whenever it can – and files won't get changed on the other PC while it's turned off. So for most purposes it's just like working with the actual file. For more on offline files, see our guide to Sync Center on p140.

HOW LONG?
The great thing about HomeGroup is that you can set it up in seconds.

HOW HARD?
This has deliberately been kept simple – the most difficult step is entering the password.

HOW TO...
SET UP A HOMEGROUP

There are just four simple steps to HomeGroup heaven, making it easy to share files and resources among all the Windows 7 PCs and laptops in your house.

① HEAD HOME As we've explained on the previous page, HomeGroup makes the painfully difficult task of sharing files over a home network more bearable. However, there's one complication: Windows 7 won't let you create or join a homegroup unless the network you're connected to is designated as a Home network, as opposed to Work or Public. To change that, go to the Network and Sharing Center. Under "View your active networks", click to change the location to Home.

② GROUP PRESSURE Once you're on a Home network, a dialog box will appear extolling the virtues of HomeGroup and prompting you to start setting one up. You can choose what type of files you want to share, and whether or not to stream music and video to all the other PCs in your homegroup.

③ INVITE ONLY After a short pause, a window will appear in which a password will fade elegantly into view. You'll notice the password is long and random. You can write it down or, preferably, copy and paste it into a new text document. On the positive side, it's very secure. The annoying part is that there's no facility for transferring the key to a USB flash drive that you can simply plug into other computers; you have to type it in.

④ TIME SHARE With the homegroup set up, you can join it from any other Windows 7 PC on the network by clicking the HomeGroup entry in the left-hand pane of any Windows Explorer window.

When the Join HomeGroup box opens, enter the password you wrote down, select which of the documents you want to share on this computer, and that's all there is to it. (You can leave the group at any time from the HomeGroup settings window.) This PC can now also share devices plugged into your main computer; most obviously, an external hard disk or a printer. Handy if you need to print something from your laptop.

By default, a homegroup shares everything under the banner of Documents, Music, Pictures or Video, depending on which options you select when you create or join it. To exclude a folder or file, go to the top menu bar (known as the Command bar) and click "Share with"; then, to make this item private, select Nobody.

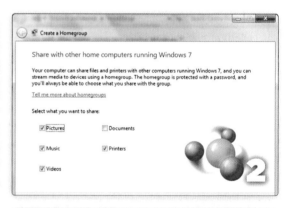

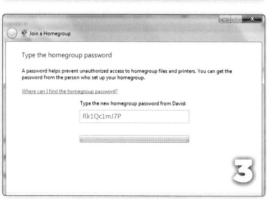

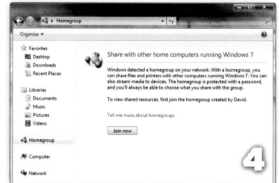

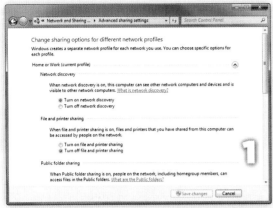

HOW LONG?
Five minutes should be enough to create the necessary user accounts and set up sharing.

HOW HARD?
It can be a little fiddly, but the principles are simple once you understand them.

HOW TO...
SHARE FILES MANUALLY

HomeGroup makes it simple to share, but if you want more security or flexibility, you can share any file or folder on your system with specific users. Here's how.

(1) CHECK SHARING SETTINGS Open the Network and Sharing Center, click "Change advanced sharing settings". In the window that opens, scroll down and ensure password-protected sharing is on. Also check that the top two items, "Network discovery" and "File and printer sharing", are on, to ensure other computers can find your shared items. Then click "Save changes".

(2) CREATE USER ACCOUNTS Password-protected sharing requires users to log in to your PC before they can access shared items. So you need to create a Windows user account (see chapter 3) on your PC for each person. You can simplify things by having, say, one account called Kids and giving the password to all your children. But if you want to let your eldest child access more shared items than the others, he or she will need their own account.

(3) SELECT WHAT TO SHARE To share a folder, left-click on it in a Windows Explorer window and, in the bar at the top, click "Share with". If your computer is connected to a homegroup, you'll see options

to share with either the group or specific people. Select the latter to set up password-protected access. If there's no homegroup, choose Advanced sharing settings.

(4) SELECT WHO TO SHARE WITH A panel will appear showing who has access to the file or folder you've selected. Your name will already be there; if you click OK now, the file or folder will be accessible from other PCs on your network by entering your personal username and password. To give access to another user, click the dropdown arrow next to the Add button, select their username and click Add. You can click below Permission Level to choose whether each user has full read/write access or whether they're only able to read the file.

Anyone on your network should now be able to see your PC under Network in Windows Explorer. To access it, they'll be asked to log in, and when they do so they'll see the folders you chose to share with them.

For security, Windows 7 won't let people log on to your PC over the network if their user account has no password. Make sure you create a password when you set up each account, and that it isn't blank.

IN THIS CHAPTER

7

Windows 7 entertains

ENTERTAINMENT

All work and no play would make Windows a very dull place, but Microsoft's latest is also designed to please. In the Home Premium, Professional and Ultimate editions, you'll discover the latest version of Windows Media Center. Partnered with a TV tuner, this is the key to turning any PC or laptop into a fully featured cutting-edge home entertainment system. Whether

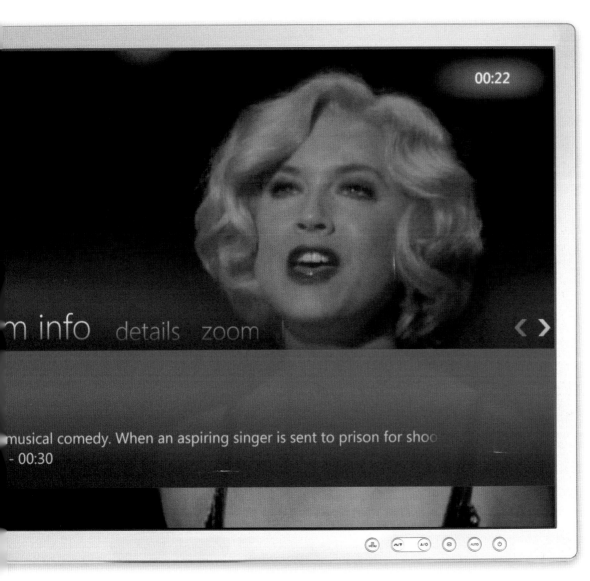

00:22

m info   details   zoom   ‹ ›

musical comedy. When an aspiring singer is sent to prison for shoo
- 00:30

IN WINDOWS 7

watching and recording TV, enjoying DVD movies or listening to your favourite music, it's the place to come for playing and managing all your digital media. In this chapter, we delve into Media Center and show how to get it up and running with minimum hassle. We also sing the praises of Media Player 12, check out iTunes and explain how to stream your music.

IT'S YOUR DIGITAL GATEWAY TO MUSIC AND VIDEO. WINDOWS 7 BRINGS THE MOST CAPABLE VERSION OF WINDOWS MEDIA PLAYER YET.

Introducing Media Player 12

On the face of it, Media Player 12 doesn't look like a big upgrade to version 11, which came bundled with Vista. The interface has been tweaked, but to little benefit; the large buttons for Now Playing, Rip, Sync and so on are gone, and a new line-up of tabs occupies the right-hand side. Hoped-for features such as Blu-ray playback are still missing.

Yet it's a smarter and more streamlined application, better focused on playing media and moving it between devices. The main window acts as a permanent Library view, no longer segregating content into music, video, pictures and TV, and you can use the left pane to flick between media types. Click Music to select by Artist, Album or Genre; if you'd rather go by Year or Composer, just right-click on Music, then pick Customize Navigation Pane.

The views, heavy on cover art, make it easy to find what you're looking for, and covers are stacked in Artist, Genre and Year views; double-click a stack to show a list. The Search bar, near the top, works brilliantly, narrowing down results as you type.

Those tabs on the right let you make drag-and-drop playlists for listening, burning to disc, or syncing with a portable media device. You can still hide the panel if you want, but the tabs help avoid losing it altogether.

IN SYNC Synchronising content to an MP3 or media player is even easier: just connect it, open the Sync tab and click Start Sync. For more control, click the Menu button below the Sync tab, select "Set up sync", and choose which playlists

to synchronise. Alternatively, clear them all and just drag songs, albums or videos manually onto the list.

You can switch from the Library view to Now Playing using the button to the far right of the playback controls. If you want visualisations (graphics that follow the music), right-click in the window, choose Visualizations and browse the extensive list. Right-clicking also enables you to alter EQ, add enhancements or view the current playlist. To return to the Library view, click the button at the top right.

VIDEO STAR Windows Media Player 12 can play more types of video than previous versions. DivX, XviD and H.264 files are fully supported, as is the AVCHD format used by most HD camcorders. Even Apple's MOV format is supported, although this and M4V may still refuse to play.

Media Player 12 really comes into its own when you want to share your media around a home network. If you keep a library on your laptop but want to play tracks on a media PC hooked up to your TV, first enable an option on the PC: go to the new Stream dropdown, between Organize and Create Playlist, and choose "Allow remote control of my Player", then "Allow remote control on this network".

The Stream menu contains one more gem. Select "Allow Internet access to home media", and you can stream audio, video and images from your home system to another Windows 7 PC. Both PCs and your user accounts must be linked to a Windows Live ID, and you'll need to download a small applet to create the link. See p114 for more.

Tip

Want a quick preview of the track you're about to play? Hover over it with the mouse pointer, then click on the Preview button in the box that appears. The Skip link handily skips 15 seconds further into the track, making light work of browsing longer pieces.

Windows Media Player 12 may look simple, but under the hood are some sophisticated features, including advanced network support. If you have Media Extenders – whether music-streaming devices, an Xbox 360 games console or a networked media player – you can now highlight an item in your Library within Media Center, right-click on it and select "Play to". Choose a device and the file plays on it. See p118.

HOW TO...
RIP A CD TO YOUR HARD DISK

(1) INSERT A DISC When you insert a music CD, two new buttons, Rip CD and Rip settings, appear to the right of Media Player's "Create playlist" button. To copy and encode all the tracks at the default settings, just click Rip CD. To select or deselect tracks, click the checkboxes to the left of the track names.

(2) CHOOSE YOUR TRACKS Media Player automatically tries to download the CD's cover art and track listings from the internet. If the album art or track information is incorrect, right-click on the cover art and select Find Album Info. Media Player 12 compares the CD data against Microsoft's database, and comes back with a list of possible matches. Run through the results until you find the correct details. Click Next, then Finish.

(3) SELECT A FORMAT To see more options before going ahead and ripping the tracks, click the "Rip settings" button. The key options are Format and Audio Quality. For Format, MP3 is still the most widely compatible with different computers, programs and devices, but Microsoft's own WMA and WMA Pro formats can create better-sounding tracks with lower file sizes. Of these, WMA Pro is the most effective, but also the less widely supported by MP3 players. WMA Lossless and WAV Lossless are designed for creating a premium-quality archive of your

music; the files will sound as good as the original CD, but they'll be large, so you won't be able to fit as many on the average MP3 player, if it's capable of playing them in the first place. In short, it's horses for courses, so make sure you back the right one before continuing with the ripping process.

Digital audio always involves trading off quality against file size. Choose 192Kbits/sec WMA/WMA Pro or 320Kbits/sec MP3 if you want the very best sound, have the speakers or headphones to do it justice, and don't care how big your files are; or go for 128Kbits/sec if packing more music into a smaller amount of memory – perhaps on an MP3 player – is your primary concern. Now, click the Rip CD button and copy the tracks from the CD to your hard disk in your chosen format.

(4) OVER-PROTECTIVE The first time you rip an audio CD, Windows 7 will ask whether you want to copy protect your music. This means the files will play only on your PC (not other computers) and on compatible secure devices. There's absolutely no benefit to this. Choose the "Do not add copy protection to your music" option and tick the box next to the disclaimer. There's no downside to doing so, and it will save you frustration later on when you can't copy tracks to other devices. Remember, of course, not to share copies illegally.

HOW LONG?
Exact timings will vary, but ripping a CD in Windows is several times faster than listening to it.

HOW HARD?
Ripping is effortless; checking track names and fiddling with audio formats are optional.

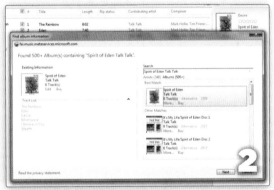

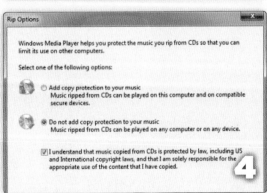

APPLE ITUNES IS A FULLY FEATURED ALTERNATIVE TO WINDOWS MEDIA PLAYER – THOUGH IT'S EARNT A LOVE-IT-OR-HATE-IT REPUTATION.

Introducing Apple iTunes

As we've described, Windows Media Player is a powerful and user-friendly application for managing and enjoying your media library. But many people use an alternative – one that's made by Microsoft's arch-rival, Apple.

It's likely you've already heard of iTunes, as it's used on many millions of computers around the world. Part of that success is down to its tight integration with Apple's hugely successful iPod, iPhone and iPad hardware. If you buy one of these devices, iTunes is the only software that will allow you to transfer media to it, so an awful lot of people are pretty much forced to use it. But even among those without an investment in Apple gadgets, iTunes is a popular choice, thanks to its ease of use and a wide range of convenient features.

GETTING STARTED If you want to give iTunes a try, simply download the installer from www.apple.com/itunes. Follow the prompts to install it, and when asked, allow it to import your music library. iTunes likes to do things its own way, so if you've previously set up playlists or star ratings in Windows Media Player, these won't be imported. Your album art might not be stored in an iTunes-compatible way, but iTunes will try to automatically fix this. Similarly, iTunes doesn't support Microsoft's WMA music format, but if any

of your songs are in this format, iTunes will offer to create copies in its preferred AAC format.

With all these restrictions, iTunes may sound like a duff deal, but once you're up and running these foibles will quickly be forgotten – and the program has plenty of other charms to compensate. Chief among them is the user interface, which many people find more intuitive than Windows Media Player. Just click on a category or resource in the left-hand pane to make it appear in the main window; then you can either browse or type into the search box to find individual items. If you prefer, you can go to the View menu and select Apple's Cover Flow interface, which lets you picks songs by flicking through a gallery of album art.

EXTRA FEATURES Though iTunes is easy to pick up and use, there are all sorts of neat features tucked away beneath the surface – as we demonstrate in the box to the right.

One example is Genius, a tool that automatically mixes your music based on which songs go well together. For example, start playing "Hotel California" and Genius will cue up a whole playlist of rock songs, allowing you to shred away on the air guitar for as long as you like without Jay-Z butting in and killing the mood. In a similar vein, iTunes DJ automatically produces an endless playlist – so you can set it

Tip

If you like the extra features that iTunes offers over Windows Media Player – but don't like its idiosyncrasies and the way it's locked to Apple hardware – there's a third alternative worth considering. It's called Songbird, and it's free to download and use. You'll find more about Songbird, and many other great free applications, on pp82-85.

The main iTunes interface presents a lot of information, but it's easy to find your way around thanks to its clean layout and logical controls.

going at a party, then leave it to take care of the music while you enjoy yourself. Songs can be removed from the list, added or reshuffled at any time. iTunes DJ works well with iTunes' Home Sharing feature, which allows you to stream music from any other computer on your home network without any need for fiddly configuration.

A TREAT IN STORE iTunes' little touches are nice, but what really sets Apple's offering apart from Windows Media Player is the iTunes Store. Microsoft's application is a great way to organise songs and videos that are already on your PC, but it doesn't offer any way to obtain new material – its capabilities are limited to importing CDs you already own.

iTunes comes with the largest online shop in the world, built right into the front-end. At the time of writing, there are more than 13 million songs available to download, from artists ranging from the Beatles to the Black Eyed Peas. Songs typically cost 99p each for an instant download in high-quality AAC format. Whole albums are available at a discounted rate. It's the easiest way to buy music, and on its own it's a compelling argument for iTunes.

The iTunes store isn't limited to music either: it offers an extensive library of films and TV programmes to download. You can download podcasts too – episodic spoken-word "broadcasts" which you can store on a portable player and listen to at any time. Podcasts are normally free to download, and they cover a huge range of topics: for example, if you're interested in technology, check out the *PC Pro* podcast by opening the iTunes Store, browsing to the podcast section and entering the title.

APPS THE WAY TO DO IT iTunes also plays host to Apple's App Store. If you use an iPod touch, an iPhone or an iPad, this is how you acquire new software to run on your device. The range of apps on offer is superb, ranging from games to information resources, photographic tools and even a gateway to the Amazon Kindle store, so you can download and read books on your device. The App Store is a huge success: between its launch in 2008 and the start of 2011, it served up more than 10 billion apps, both free and paid-for.

Impressive stuff – but if you don't have an Apple device to run such programs on, the App Store is no use to you. Those with Android Phones can use the free Android Market app instead, and if you're using a Windows Phone 7 Device you can download new apps via the Windows Marketplace (see p16).

WHAT'S THE CATCH? If you're thinking of switching to iTunes, we've a few caveats. Unlike Windows Media Player, iTunes isn't a general purpose video player. It's very choosy about file formats, and if it doesn't like a particular file it simply refuses to play it. It's also very choosy about mobile devices: it won't copy songs or videos to a non-Apple player.

Finally, it's worth restating that iTunes likes to do things in its own way. Once you set up iTunes ratings, playlists and album art for your songs, you can't easily move those settings back to Windows Media Player if you subsequently decide iTunes isn't for you.

ITUNES' GREATEST HITS

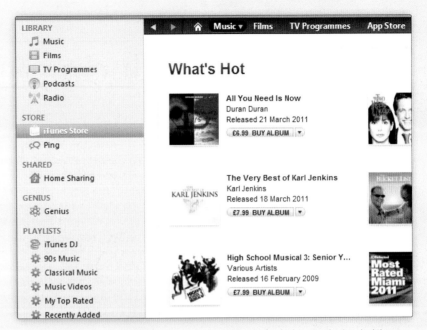

There are other online music and video stores, but iTunes has by far the largest selection. And the songs you download don't use DRM, so you don't have to worry about being unable to play them in the future when technology advances. Some of the downloads on the iTunes store are exclusive, meaning you can't even buy them in shops. And because Apple has a record of your iTunes account, if disaster strikes and your media player or hard disk fails, you can simply download your purchases again.

Apple's Ping service adds a social networking aspect to iTunes. You can use it to share your favourite artists with other Ping users, join in discussions and get the latest news about what your musical idols are up to. The clever part is that Ping integrates right into the iTunes player, so it can analyse your library to work out which artists you like, then show you relevant news and information as you listen to them.

iTunes DJ is a boon for any host, automatically cueing up songs from your library for as long as the party keeps jumping. If your guests have iPads or iPhones, the iTunes Remote App allows them to browse your music library on their own devices, and add their own choices of songs to the playlist. You can specify how much freedom they have to browse, and whether song choices must be put to the vote. Why waste money on a professional DJ when your guests can do the work?

ADD A TV TUNER TO YOUR PC AND YOU CAN TRANSFORM IT INTO YOUR FAMILY'S PRIMARY SOURCE OF ENTERTAINMENT, THANKS TO MEDIA CENTER.

Introducing Media Center

Windows Media Center has come a long way since its inception back in 2002, and in Windows 7 it's matured into a key attraction. At a quick glance, it might look similar to previous versions, but look closer and it's both easier to use and more powerful than ever before.

FRIENDLY FACE Media Center's simple, friendly interface gives you access to TV, music, movies and photos at the touch of a button. If you're looking at the pretty screenshots and wondering where all the clutter and convoluted file menus have gone, well, you won't find any. Media Center has been designed to be intuitive and straightforward, whether you're using it at a desk with a keyboard and mouse or from the comfort of your sofa with a compatible Media Center remote control (see Tip, left). It's even more usable than in previous versions, with neat additions such as the new desktop widget giving rapid access to recently recorded TV shows at the press of a button.

Even if you forego a dedicated remote, it's also easier to navigate via mouse and keyboard, with Windows 7 bringing welcome improvements to the user interface throughout. A timeline at the foot of the screen lets you skip back and forth through video files, or even time-shifted TV programmes, and previously neglected or hidden-away features have been refined and made easier to access.

HD OR NOT HD Windows 7 Media Center has an MPEG2 video decoder built in, so it will play DVD movies right off the bat. With the assistance of a TV tuner it can also receive analogue, digital and – for the first time – satellite TV broadcasts.

What's more, Media Center in Windows 7 has built-in support for DivX, XviD and the H.264 video format, which paves the way for receiving high-definition TV. You can do this by installing a satellite dish and a DVB-S or S2 satellite TV tuner card to tune into Freesat's free-to-air services. Or, you can invest in a DVB-T2 tuner and enjoy high-definition television through your regular aerial, courtesy of the Freeview HD service.

RAY OF HOPE One mild disappointment is that support for Blu-ray is absent. If you have a Blu-ray drive and want to play HD movies, you'll have to budget for extra software, such as ArcSoft's TotalMedia Theatre or CyberLink's PowerDVD software. Both cost extra, but integrate seamlessly into Media Center's menu, so you can just pop in the disc and watch.

If you're wondering why you should choose Media Center over the more straightforward charms of a Sky+ box or hard-disk based PVR, then turn to p110, where we go into more detail about Media Center's considerable range of TV-related abilities.

 Tip

If you're looking to integrate a Media Center PC into your lounge, make life easier with a dedicated Media Center remote control and USB infrared receiver, available together for about £20. Dedicated shortcut buttons give rapid access to your media and put all of Media Center's functions within easy reach. Press the My Photos button, for example, and even if it wasn't already up and running, Media Center bounds into life and takes you straight to your photo library.

Welcome to Windows Media Center

The best way to experience TV on your PC.

Continue

HOW TO...
NAVIGATE MEDIA CENTER

① MAIN MENU Media Center's main menu is simplicity itself, split into six main headings: Extras, Pictures+Videos, Music, Movies, TV and Tasks. Scroll up or down to the category you want, then left and right to select from the available options. If at any point you want to return to the main menu, you can toggle back and forth by clicking the green button at the top left of the screen or, if you're using a remote, by pressing the actual green button. This doesn't interrupt the playback of TV, video files or music; audio continues to play in the background, and thanks to a nifty transparency effect, video is still visible behind the menu.

② MUSIC As long as all your music is stored in your Windows 7 Music Library, Media Center will automatically present it as a quilt of CD covers that stretches across the screen. It's possible to sort your music according to a range of criteria, such as album, artist, genre, composer and year of release – or you can just start typing a keyword to instantly find the music you're looking for. If you don't see your music, go to Tasks | Settings | Media Libraries, and manually add the directories where your music is located. These can be on local or network drives, so it doesn't matter where you store your music; it could even be on a home server, or a NAS (network attached storage) device elsewhere on your home network.

③ VIDEO/PICTURE Just like the Music option, the picture and video libraries tile your display with little thumbnails of your media files. Videos can be ordered by name and date taken – a handy option for camcorder users – while pictures can be sorted by name, date taken, embedded tags or their star rating (manually applied by you in Windows). You can now edit your pictures, too. Right-click an image (or press the Info button on your remote), select Picture Details and you can access basic editing tasks such as rotating and cropping, enhancing contrast or removing red-eye, as well as printing out images quickly. Any changes you make are saved to the original image file, though, so be careful before accidentally ruining your precious photos.

④ TV The TV menu provides access to TV shows you've recorded, the TV guide, and live TV. You can also search Media Center's TV listings. If you like a particular actor, for example, you can find every upcoming film or TV programme that they'll be starring in. There have been plenty of other improvements here, too. Hit the up cursor – either on your keyboard or on your remote control – while watching TV and the new Mini Guide appears. This lets you browse through a reduced version of the TV guide without obscuring too much of the programme in the background.

HOW LONG?
Give yourself 20 minutes to fully explore Media Center's features.

HOW HARD?
Media Center is designed to be intuitive, and it is.

FAQ

Q: Are there alternatives to Media Center?

A: A Sky+, Sky HD or Virgin V+ HD box may seem a simpler option than setting up a Media Center system. Products such as the Wyplay Wyplayer, Popcorn Hour A110 and Western Digital WDTV bypass the need for a PC entirely. And services such as BBC iPlayer and 4OD let you catch up with missed TV shows without the need for any extra hardware or software (see p116).

Yet Windows Media Center is more versatile than any of these alternatives. It can be upgraded, by adding extra TV tuners, Blu-ray drives or multiple hard disks. And its reach can be expanded via Microsoft's Xbox 360 console or other Media Center Extenders, easily delivering live and recorded TV, videos, photos and music to a whole house over your network. Once you press the green button, you won't look back.

WHO NEEDS A SEPARATE, NON-UPGRADABLE PERSONAL VIDEO RECORDER WHEN YOUR CUSTOMISABLE PC CAN DO THE SAME JOB EVEN BETTER?

Watching and recording TV

No-one likes sitting down to relax at the end of a long day only to find there's nothing on TV. Get to grips with Media Center's comprehensive TV guide, movie listings, recording functions and video-on-demand features and you can be sure there's always something worth watching.

CENTER OF ATTENTION Windows 7 Media Center includes a TV guide showing what's on now and next at a glance. It stays up to date by downloading 15 days of advance listings every day, so you never need to miss a thing. Want to record a single programme? Press the record button once. Want to record the whole series? Press it again.

If you'd like to know more about a programme, you can bring up the information overlay. This provides a synopsis and, if you're the sort of person who tends to miss things, lets you know when it will be repeated. You can also use the search feature to find programmes you want to watch by title, keyword, category, actor or director.

At the foot of this page you'll see one of Media Center's neatest features: the Movie Guide. This presents forthcoming movies on TV as a browsable grid of covers. You can see what films are on now or next, select a movie genre to search for, or just list all the films showing in the next 15 days. You need never miss a good film again.

TUNER SANDWICH A basic TV tuner can cost as little as £30, so it's eminently affordable to turn your PC into a lounge-friendly PVR (personal video recorder) – and, as our guide opposite shows, it's easy too. If you get more ambitious you can add extra tuners later. Previous versions of Media Center only supported two analogue or digital tuners at once, but Windows 7 has moved with the times. As well as supporting analogue, digital, satellite and cable tuners, it ups the ante by supporting up to four of each. Pair two twin-tuner TV cards together and (as long as your PC can keep up) you can record programmes on up to three channels at once while channel-hopping live TV on the fourth tuner. The possibilities are almost endless.

ON-DEMAND DELIGHTS Even if you can't find a broadcast show that excites you, Media Center can keep you entertained with a range of on-demand shows. Scroll to the top of the TV guide and you'll find the MSN Video Player, offering a great range of classic British comedies, dramas and documentaries. They're all available to watch for free at the click of a button – all you need is an internet connection.

Sky subscribers can also make use of the Sky Player application built into Media Center, giving access to exclusive Sky content on any Windows 7 PC.

HOW TO...
ADD A TV TUNER

① CHOOSE A TUNER Whether you're installing your first TV tuner in a PC or adding a second, it's a pretty simple process. Windows 7 allows you to choose analogue, digital, satellite or cable TV tuners – up to four of each simultaneously. The UK is progressively switching to digital TV, so it's best to avoid analogue-only tuners. Instead, spend a little more on a dual digital tuner which will allow you to record one channel while channel-surfing freely with the other – or record two channels at once while watching one of your recorded TV shows. As long as your chosen device has the Media Center logo on the box, suitable drivers should be included.

You can run satellite tuners and digital tuners side by side (in any combination), but apart from a few new HD channels on Freesat, many of the channels will be identical. At the time of writing, Freeview HD is just taking off: it remains to be seen whether it will carry much distinctive content. We wouldn't recommend a cable (DVB-C) tuner yet: the UK setup process is incredibly finicky.

② LOAD THE DRIVERS If you don't have a driver disc to hand, download the appropriate drivers from the manufacturer's website. Don't worry if there aren't any specific Windows 7 drivers, as Vista-certified drivers should work fine. Be sure to follow the installation instructions: usually it's necessary to install the drivers and then install the TV tuner afterwards. If it's a USB device, that's a simple case of plugging it in; with an internal card you'll need to open up your PC's case – follow the manufacturer's instructions carefully.

If you can't find your driver disc or any suitable drivers on the internet, you can try installing the tuner anyway: Windows Update will search for driver files online, and you might well be lucky. Once the tuner is successfully installed, fire up Media Center and go to Tasks | Settings | TV | Set Up TV Signal.

③ FIND TV CHANNELS Once the setup process is in motion, Media Center leads you through a simple wizard. You'll need to enter your postcode and select your nearest transmitter, so you can download the appropriate TV listings, and then Media Center will start scanning for channels. Make sure your aerial is connected, then go for a cup of tea while scanning completes.

④ TROUBLESHOOT If you're using a Freeview tuner, Media Center should pick up close to 100 TV and radio services. If any expected channels are missing, you might be struggling with a weak signal. Try a signal booster between the TV aerial and the tuner, and see if it helps. If so, go back to the end of step 2 and run through the TV signal wizard again to get all the channels.

HOW LONG?
You may want to spend some time choosing your kit, but it shouldn't take long to set up.

HOW HARD?
Dead easy with a USB tuner; with a PCI Express card, you'll need to open the PC's case.

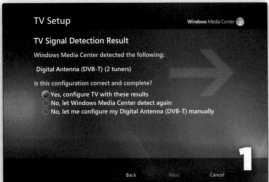

WINDOWS 7 IS GREAT FOR GAMING – ALTHOUGH WE'RE NOT BOWLED OVER BY THE SELECTION THAT COMES BUNDLED WITH THE OPERATING SYSTEM.

Playing games in Windows 7

More or less everyone who buys Windows 7 in the UK gets a selection of bundled games. Only those who buy a netbook with Starter edition miss out – and even they're not left completely in the cold. Windows 7 Starter includes several old favourites such as Minesweeper, Hearts and Solitaire, which have hooked millions with their simple gameplay.

The other editions get some meatier games, including Chess Titans and Mahjong Titans. Chess offers ten levels, a 3D chessboard and the ability to save a game in progress to continue later. It's also possible to choose the materials your chess pieces and board are made of and tweak graphical options to make sure Chess Titans will run on your PC, no matter how modest its specification. There's no option to record games so that you can learn from them, though – nor do you get any sort of rating to see how you match up to the rest of the world.

Mahjong Titans offers a more polished experience. The classic tile-matching game can be played using six different styles of board and, thanks to impressive 3D graphics and plenty of sound effects, it's the best Mahjong we've played. Plenty of customisation is available: you can pick which tile set and background you use, and save your game so you can come back to it later if you're interrupted.

Younger users are catered for by Purble Place, a suite of three games specially designed for children, set in a colourful world full of sound effects and cute animation. The first game, Purble Pairs, is a simple tile-matching game with three levels of difficulty. The second, Comfy Cakes, is a fun cake-making challenge. The third, Purble Shop, is a guessing game featuring a cute potato-head-style character.

Finally, there's a selection of internet games too: you can play Backgammon, Checkers or Spades against your online friends, although there's no way to play them locally against your own PC.

These games are a jolly enough way to pass the time; but if you've upgraded from Windows Vista you'll find the selection disappointingly familiar. There's nothing here that wasn't included in the previous version of Windows.

ALL IN ONE All Windows 7's default games can be accessed through the Games Explorer, a simple window that gathers together all your installed games for easy access and updating. It also shows any third-party games you install, keeping all your titles in one place. Double-click on the icon that promises "More games from Microsoft" and you'll be taken to a web page featuring various additional mini-games that integrate with Windows Live Messenger, allowing you to pit your skills against your friends online.

FAQ

Q: I've heard that Windows 7 includes DirectX 11 for games. What does this mean?

A: DirectX is Microsoft's system that makes it easy for developers to write fast, graphically sophisticated games. DirectX 11 is the most advanced version yet. It makes it easier than ever for developers to make full use of modern processor chips, and to make objects look more realistic. To get the benefit you'll need a modern graphics card, so older PCs might not qualify.

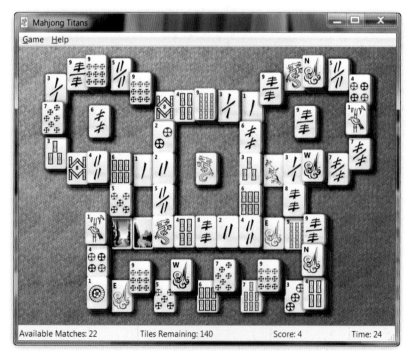

Windows 7's games collection is fun but oddly familiar to Vista users.

How to find more games

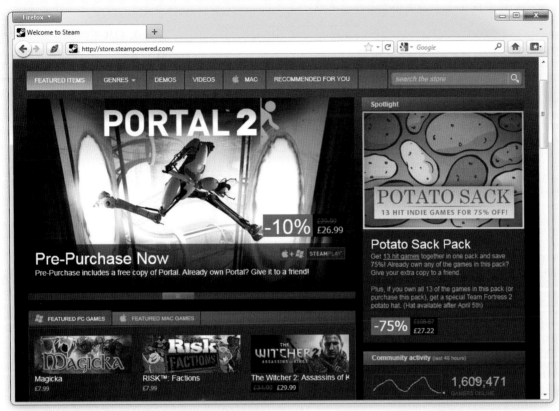

Steam is one of the most popular ways to get new games: its huge catalogue has something for everyone. It includes games from a wide range of different publishers, so if you've heard of a game, chances are it will be available to download on Steam.

If the games bundled with Windows 7 aren't enough to keep you entertained, there's a whole world of additional games out there to enjoy.

GAMING IN YOUR BROWSER Many games can be played in your web browser, so no installation is required and you can pit your scores against those of the best gamers on the web. One of the best known websites for online games is www.popcap.com, where you'll find a host of fun action and puzzle games including Bejeweled and Plants vs Zombies. If you find that you crave more depth than these online diversions can offer, there are also expanded versions to download and run on your own PC, normally for a small fee.

There's also a thriving industry in online casino games, including poker, blackjack and roulette. Be warned, you can lose money on these sites, but if you're a card shark you can make a profit against real opponents.

ADDICTIVE DOWNLOADS Looking for a more substantial challenge? You can find it on one of the web's many gaming download sites. The biggest and most popular site is Steam (www.steampowered.com). It offers a huge archive of games of all genres, from adventures to sporting simulators. There's also a good collection of massively multiplayer games on offer, such as EverQuest and Guild Wars, where you team

up online with other players – or compete with them – to complete quests. Some games are free, but big names tend to require online payment; there are often demo versions to download, so you can try before you buy. And since all games on Steam download direct to your desktop, you can be playing in minutes. Purchases are linked to your personal Steam account, so if you buy a new computer in future you can easily download your games again and keep on playing. There are regular sales and price promotions, and many games run on the Mac as well as the PC, so it's a great site for everyone from casual gamers to joystick fiends.

BLOCKBUSTERS Some of the most successful games these days are first-person action and adventure games that give you a vast, immersive 3D world to explore. Recent examples include Red Dead Redemption, Crysis 2 and the Grand Theft Auto series. These games can take months or years to complete entirely, and they're so big that they're not always offered as downloads: you may have to go to a shop (or an online retailer) and buy the DVD.

Be warned that such games can make big demands of your hardware: to experience them at their best, your PC will need a powerful graphics card. On a humble laptop or a low-end desktop system, the graphics are likely to appear chunky and jerky, spoiling the effect.

Tip

Many action games are available for the Xbox 360 and PlayStation 3 games consoles as well as for the PC. Most gamers agree that, all things being equal, your home computer is the best platform to play on. One big reason for this is that using a mouse and keyboard to control your character gives you greater flexibility than a console gamepad. But if your computer isn't powerful enough to run these games with all their graphical effects enabled, it may make sense to reserve 3D games for the console in the front room, as the cinematic visual experience is part of the fun.

TAKE A LITTLE TIME TO DIG INTO THE FEATURES OF THE NEW WINDOWS MEDIA PLAYER AND YOU'LL BE SHOCKED BY JUST HOW MUCH YOU CAN DO.

Streaming music and video

We've already seen how you can enjoy your music, movies, TV and photos on your computer using the new features in Windows 7's Media Player 12 and Media Center. You can even display media from your PC on your widescreen TV. But there's another way to enjoy your favourite content without having a noisy computer in the lounge. It's called media streaming, and allows your Windows 7 PC to serve up movies, recorded TV and music to a multitude of devices over your home network – or even across the internet.

Imagine being able to play the album you downloaded from Amazon or iTunes last night on your internet radio in the kitchen, without having to move your laptop or burn a disc. If you travel, you could even watch a programme you recorded on your PC in the UK in a hotel room in the US. That's the sort of thing Windows 7's streaming features make possible.

EASY AS PIE Streaming video and music in Windows 7 is much easier to use than it was in any previous version of Windows. Fire up Media Player and you'll see it's one of the three main menu items at the top of the screen. To enable it, turn on streaming in the Stream dropdown menu, then select the third of the three options in that menu: "Automatically allow devices to play my media" (it's selected by default). It's as simple as that. Now connected devices that support UPnP media servers (or any device bearing the DLNA logo) will be able to share and play all the media

that Windows Media Player 12 makes available over a local network. On the opposite page, we investigate how to stream your content over the internet too.

PLUG AND PLAY Windows 7 uses UPnP (Universal Plug and Play) media server technology to make its media library available to third-party devices, so when buying a streamer, look for the UPnP logo. Windows 7 also complies with DLNA (the Digital Living Network Alliance standard), which makes these products extremely easy to set up.

DLNA media streamers, such as the WD TV Live Hub, bring another of Windows 7's new features into play: the ability to remote-control connected devices from your PC. It's called "Play to". Rather than simply letting devices pull video or audio from your computer, this allows you to send content actively to them. With a DLNA Digital Media Renderer (DMR) device connected to your network, you can right-click a file – or several files – in Windows Media Player 12, select "Play to", and pick from the list of connected devices. (See this in action on p104.)

The great thing about this feature is that it isn't just limited to music and video streamers. All sorts of products support the DLNA standard and can be used in a similar way. With a DLNA-compliant digital photo frame, for instance, you can send a photo from your computer at any time. With a digital radio, you can send tracks from your PC and even adjust the volume remotely.

Tip

If you're looking to buy a media-streaming device and want to take advantage of Windows 7's advanced features, make sure your new box is DLNA-compliant. This is usually indicated by a logo on the packaging, or you can check the DLNA website at www.dlna.org

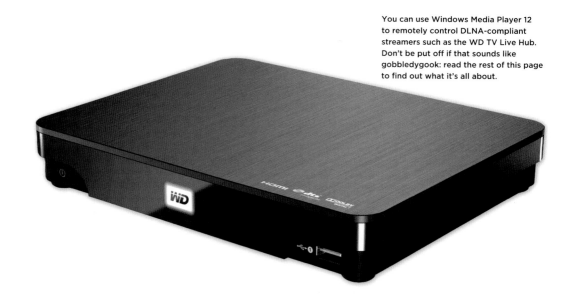

You can use Windows Media Player 12 to remotely control DLNA-compliant streamers such as the WD TV Live Hub. Don't be put off if that sounds like gobbledygook: read the rest of this page to find out what it's all about.

HOW TO...
SET UP INTERNET STREAMING

While you were looking through the Stream menu (see opposite page), you may have noticed a couple of other options. These are the new additions to Windows 7's toolbox of media-streaming features: internet streaming and remote control.

The more exciting of the two is the former, which allows you to share media, not only around your home network but also over the internet. This creates the opportunity to listen to your music from anywhere without having to duplicate a massive collection of MP3 files, and also to watch home movies or even TV shows recorded using Media Center.

It works by linking the media collection stored on your PC to a Windows Live ID. As we'll see in this tutorial, it isn't a complicated process. Once you follow these four steps, you'll be able to access your music and movies wherever you are. And that also means you won't have to remember to load up the MP3 player before you go off on your travels.

 ACCESS ALL AREAS Fire up Windows Media Player and click the Stream option at the top left. Enable "Allow Internet access to home media". You'll need to link your Windows Live ID to Media Player before you can do anything else, so in the next window choose the option to "Link an online ID".

 SHOW YOUR ID A window should now appear prompting you to choose an online ID provider. Click "Add an online ID provider", then choose Windows Live on the following web page. This will take you to the page for the Windows Live Sign-in Assistant program; download and install this, taking care to follow the instructions correctly.

Now go back to the "Link online IDs" box, which should still be open; if not, press the Windows key and type "link online IDs", then press Return to launch the item when found. Click the link labelled "Link online ID", and in the next box enter your Windows Live username and password and hit Sign in.

JOIN THE ASSOCIATION Windows 7 will take a few seconds to associate your ID with Windows Media Player. Once this is done, click OK, then in the Internet Home Media Access dialog box select the "Allow Internet access to home media" option and, finally, click OK once more.

ANOTHER LINK IN THE CHAIN To link your second computer to the first, simply repeat these steps. The first computer's media library will now appear in the Other Libraries list in the left-hand pane of this PC's Windows Media Player 12 window, and vice versa.

HOW LONG?
Barring complications, you could be ready to go in ten minutes.

HOW HARD?
There are a couple of obstacles, but anyone who can use a Windows Live ID can get this done.

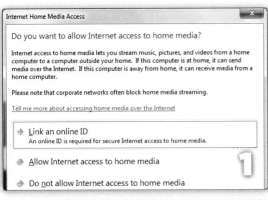

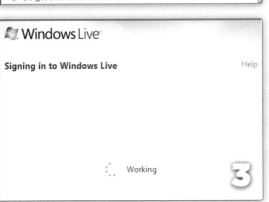

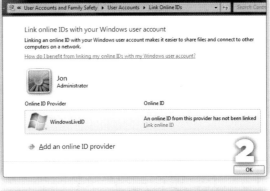

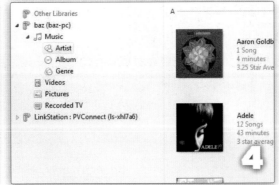

AS IF DVDS AND DOWNLOADABLE MOVIES WEREN'T ENOUGH, A WINDOWS 7 PC CAN ALSO BE YOUR GATEWAY TO A WORLD OF ONLINE TV CONTENT.

Watching TV on the internet

In this chapter we've discussed numerous ways you can use Windows 7 to enjoy movies and TV shows, including playing video files in Windows Media Player, downloading movies in iTunes and watching live TV in Media Center. There's one more way to enjoy your favourite programmes in Windows 7, and that's to stream them over the internet.

Strictly speaking, this isn't a feature of Windows 7. You can view streaming TV on more or less any computer that's attached to the internet. Some services even work on tablets, mobile phones and games consoles. For our purposes, though, we'll focus on Windows 7.

STREAMING SERVICES The best-known internet TV service is BBC iPlayer (www.bbc.co.uk/iplayer). At the iPlayer website you can click to watch almost any programme that's been recently broadcast on the BBC, right there in your browser (you can listen to BBC radio programmes too). It makes missing your favourite show a thing of the past, and it's all paid for by your television licence fee so there are no adverts and you won't have to dig out your credit card. See the box (right) for a guide to iPlayer's handy features.

BBC iPlayer comes with a few caveats. For laptop and netbook users, watching on your computer screen can be a cramped experience. And programmes generally vanish from the site after a week or so, so if you were hoping to use iPlayer to catch up with a series that's halfway through, you're out of luck.

Although iPlayer covers only BBC broadcasts, there are several other services out there that provide content from other channels. ITV, Channel 4 and Channel 5 programmes can be found via the ITV Player (www.itv.com/itvplayer), 4oD (www.channel4.com/programmes/4od) and Demand5 (www.channel5.com/demand5) services. They work similarly to BBC iPlayer, but they don't offer all the same features. And these are commercial services, so you'll have to put up with the odd advert – just like real TV.

GOGGLE BOXES If you want to watch online programmes on your front room TV, one option is to set up a PC in your front room and use your browser in parallel with Windows Media Center (see p108). There are also iPlayer viewers built into the Wii and PlayStation 3 games consoles.

Alternatively, you can invest in a dedicated set-top box, such as the Apple TV or the Boxee box. These devices connect your TV to the internet and let you download films, TV shows, YouTube clips and other media with the click of a remote – although whether they're more convenient to use than your Windows 7 PC is open to question.

Tip

Internet TV is great, but with each of the major channels operating its own website it can be hard to keep up. The website www.seesaw.com aggregates programmes from multiple services, so you can search and stream multiple channels at once. There's also a range of content that you can access for a fee, including a huge range of sitcoms and dramas.

4oD – Channel 4's On Demand streaming service – is one of several free sites that let you catch up with TV programmes you've missed. You don't even need to remember to set the video recorder any more.

HOW TO...
WATCH TV WITH BBC IPLAYER

1 GET WITH THE PROGRAMME If you just want to watch a recent show in your browser, using iPlayer is simplicity itself. First, go to www.bbc.co.uk/iplayer and locate the programme you're interested in. The website organises shows by category, by channel and by schedule, as well as offering an A to Z listing, so it's easy to find what you're looking for. Once you've found the programme, click on its title or thumbnail and you'll be taken to the viewing page. Press the Play button and you're away. Along the bottom right of the video window you'll see a series of icons: if there's an "S", you can click this to enable subtitles. The other icons control the volume; switch to a larger video size; move the video into a pop-out window; and switch iPlayer to a full-screen view.

2 PLAYING FAVOURITES Over time, you may find that you repeatedly come back to a particular show. iPlayer will learn from this, and will start putting that programme (and others like it) in the "For You" section of the home page. You can also tell iPlayer which shows are your favourites. To set a favourite, simply click the star icon next to a show's thumbnail, or on its viewing page. Next time you visit iPlayer, click the TV or Radio Favourites link and your programmes will be presented along the top of the window. To remove a programme from your favourites, click the star again.

3 LET'S BE FRIENDS If you let it, BBC iPlayer can share your viewing habits with others, and can present recommendations for other shows you might like from friends and family. Sign up using the Friends link on the main iPlayer home page and you'll receive your very own iPlayer page, where you can tell the world which shows you like. BBC iPlayer can also connect to your Facebook and Twitter accounts: it won't post anything to those services, but it will use them to find out which of your friends are already using iPlayer, so you can share programme recommendations with them.

4 DESKTOP DOWNLOADS The iPlayer website is a fantastic resource, but naturally you need an internet connection to access it. With the iPlayer Desktop application, you can save programmes to watch when you're offline. It's a free download from the iPlayer website, and once it's installed you can click the Download link next to almost any programme on the iPlayer site to save it for later (some programmes, such as sporting events, can't be downloaded, sadly). Programmes marked as favourites are downloaded automatically. You get 30 days to watch downloaded programmes, after which they quietly disappear. iPlayer Desktop is great for travellers, and it can also come in handy if you suffer from a stuttering internet connection that makes streaming unsatisfactory.

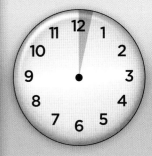

HOW LONG?
How long does it take to visit a website and click a few buttons?

HOW HARD?
There's nothing difficult about it, but as usual the more advanced features of iPlayer and other services involve a slight learning curve.

THANKS TO WINDOWS 7, IT'S EASY TO PLAY PHOTO SLIDESHOWS, LISTEN TO
MUSIC AND WATCH RECORDED TV WITH YOUR MICROSOFT GAMES CONSOLE.

Using an Xbox with Windows 7

Millions of homes have an Xbox 360 console tucked under the living room television or in a teenager's bedroom. What many of them might not realise is that the console can be connected to a Windows 7 PC, turning it into a home entertainment centre as well as a fine games machine.

That's because the Xbox 360 is one of the devices that Microsoft calls a Media Center Extender. This means you can use it to enjoy all the features of Windows Media Center – photo slideshows, music, live and recorded TV – as if you were sitting in front of your PC. It's particularly useful if you connect your Xbox console to a large HDTV set, because you can enjoy all the media stored on your PC on a far bigger screen. Conversely, if you have a Media Center PC connected to your living room TV, you can now watch all the shows on its hard disk from another room.

Another little-known fact is that you can stream BBC iPlayer shows downloaded on your PC to the Xbox. This, coupled with the Xbox 360's Sky Player service, essentially turns your console into a TV-on-demand box.

JOIN UP Both your Windows 7 PC and Xbox will need to be connected to your home network. To stream live or recorded TV, you'll need a strong wireless connection – or, even better, an Ethernet cable – to your router, especially if you want to watch high-definition (HD) content. The last thing you want is for your TV programmes to stutter at crucial moments! If your wireless connection isn't good enough (see opposite page) and you can't physically cable your devices, consider HomePlug Powerline adapters, which use your mains electricity circuits to transmit data.

It's worth noting that some antivirus programs can be overly fussy when you attempt to connect a Windows 7 PC to an Xbox 360. Keep an eye out for any pop-ups from your security software during the setup procedure, which might seek your permission to allow the console to connect. If you can't make the two devices see one another, check your security software's website for any special instructions on connecting an Xbox 360, such as opening firewall ports.

TAKE CONTROL Microsoft offers dedicated Media Center remote controls for the Xbox 360, offering a host of advanced playback controls, but don't think you have to spend extra. The standard Xbox 360 controller is perfectly adequate for operating the Media Center features. This works the other way too: both wired and wireless Xbox 360 controllers can be used directly with your PC (the wireless version requires an extra USB dongle), which saves you investing in gaming joypads if you already have an Xbox.

Tip

◁ To watch BBC iPlayer shows on your Xbox 360, you need to download the special Windows Media Player files to your PC, not the standard iPlayer downloads. Save them in the Videos folder on your PC and they should appear in the Xbox's video menu once downloaded. See pp116-7 for more information on iPlayer and similar services.

With an Xbox 360, you have a great way to play content from your PC on your TV, without having to copy any files or shell out for any extra hardware or software.

HOW TO...
USE AN XBOX AS A MEDIA PLAYER

① PREPARE YOUR EQUIPMENT Switch on your PC and your Xbox 360 and make sure both are connected to your router, either via a wired or wireless connection. If you have an Xbox Live account, you should see a pop-up message saying you're logged in to it, assuming your internet connection is working. Alternatively, check you're online using the Test Live Connection facility in the setup menus. If your PC is connecting wirelessly, hover over the Wi-Fi symbol at the bottom right of the screen and check that the signal strength is either good or, preferably, excellent. If it's any weaker, try moving the PC closer to the router, or the Xbox may struggle to stream content from it successfully.

② CONNECT TO MEDIA CENTER On your Xbox 360, go to the My Xbox menu and scroll right until you reach the Media Center option. Click on this and click "Create a New Connection", and on the next screen write down the eight-digit code that's shown. Now click Continue. Your Xbox will tell you to visit www.xbox.com/setup on your PC and download some software. You can ignore this – it's completely unnecessary with Windows 7. Back on your PC, all you need to is open Media Center, select Tasks and Add Extender. You'll now be asked to enter the code you were given earlier. The PC should now connect to the Xbox console.

③ CHECK SIGNAL STRENGTH If the wireless signal between your PC and the Xbox is weak, you may see a screen that helps you improve it. A sliding scale reveals whether your connection is strong enough for standard-definition television (SDTV) or high-definition streams (HDTV). If the connection is weak, try moving your Xbox or your PC closer to the router. Make sure no other devices on the network – such as mobile phones or network storage devices – are operating while you perform these tests. If the connection is still too weak, check you have the latest drivers for the wireless card in your PC: these can greatly improve the connection. If all else fails, you may have to resort to cables or an alternative such as HomePlug networking.

④ START USING MEDIA CENTER Your Xbox should now be showing the same Media Center screen you see on the PC. The first time you use Media Center on the Xbox, performance can be sluggish as the console scours through all your photos, videos and music. Don't worry, it soon settles down. And don't fret about all those files filling up your Xbox's hard drive: the content stays on your PC while the Xbox streams it over the network. This does mean the PC has to be turned on, but you can use it to do other things at the same time. Just avoid intensive tasks such as video editing or 3D games.

HOW LONG?
Ten minutes should do it, unless you have to rejig things to get a Wi-Fi signal.

HOW HARD?
Easier than any game you'll play on the Xbox 360.

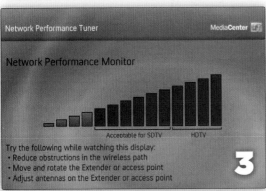

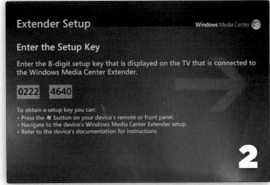

IN THIS CHAPTER

8
Staying safe

STAYING SAFE IN

Windows 7 is the most secure Windows operating system yet, but that doesn't mean you can be complacent. Whether it's children let loose on vital files, malicious code invading your system or pure and simple hardware failure, a computer is always under threat. Luckily, there's a wealth of options to keep things running. You can use Security Essentials – or

All Control Panel Items ▸ Action Center   ▼ ↵   *Search Control Panel*   🔎

Review recent messages and resolve problems

Action Center has detected one or more issues for you to review.

Security   ⌄

Virus protection (Important)   [Find a program online]
Windows did not find antivirus software on this computer.
Turn off messages about virus protection

Maintenance   ⌄

If you don't see your problem listed, try one of these:

Troubleshooting   Recovery
Find and fix problems   Restore your computer to an
                                             earlier time

WINDOWS 7

one of its many rivals – to hold back viruses, while the
built-in firewall keeps hackers out. Windows Backup
goes from strength to strength, and User Account
Control is a useful way of keeping your PC safe from
both accidental and intentional changes. So Windows
7 is pretty safe out of the box – and in this chapter
we'll look at ways to make it even more secure.

CHILDREN CAN GET INTO ALL SORTS OF TROUBLE USING A PC. WINDOWS 7 GIVES YOU WAYS TO LIMIT THE DAMAGE TO THEMSELVES AND THE COMPUTER.

Introducing Parental Controls

Allowing your kids on the home PC is a crucial part of their education these days, but give any inexperienced user unfettered access and you're asking for trouble. Windows XP started the ball rolling by allowing multiple restricted accounts, and Vista introduced the concept of parental controls for individual users, building in features such as internet security and web filtering. In Windows 7, web filtering is now part of the optional Windows Live Family Safety application, which we look at on p124.

There are two main facets to Parental Controls: time limits and controlling access to applications. It all hinges on having multiple limited Standard user accounts as well as a full-blown Administrator account, as we explained on p44. Once you have at least one Standard account, and a password-protected Administrator account, you can start restricting what users can do. By default, a Standard user can't make changes that affect other accounts, so they can't erase your spreadsheets or crucial system files.

Parental Controls goes much further. You can restrict which games a user can play by setting a maximum age rating. Windows matches games you've installed against the ratings issued by the British Board of Film Classification (BBFC) and Pan European Game Information (PEGI) – 12, 15, 18 and so on. Alternatively, you can allow a certain age certificate, but bar particular games if they include content you find objectionable. For instance, you could allow games rated up to 15, but not if they include violence. You can also opt to block any game that doesn't have an official rating.

Finally, you can select individual games and say whether your children can or can't play them. Clicking the "Block or Allow specific games" link presents you with a list of the games currently installed: click Always Allow or Always Block. Similar controls are available for allowing or prohibiting users from accessing certain applications.

GRANTING ACCESS If a child attempts to launch a game or application that you've blocked, they'll get the opportunity to send you a message requesting permission to run it (or you can type in your password there and then).

Parental controls are just the start, though. We recommend you download Microsoft's Windows Live Family Safety application – it's free, gives much more control over what children can and can't do, and, as we show overleaf, it's also very easy to implement.

Tip

It should go without saying that when it comes to kids and PCs there's no substitute for direct involvement. Parental Controls and web filtering can help to limit access to unsuitable material, but it's wise to minimise the time a child can use a PC without human supervision. And check that your Administrator account is password-protected, and that your kids don't know the password. Without this, all your work setting up Parental Controls will be for nothing.

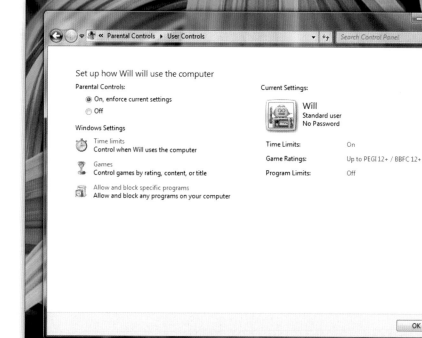

To control what your kids get up to on your PC, it makes sense to set up an individual account for each of them, especially if they're of different ages.

HOW TO...
SET UP PARENTAL CONTROLS

 TIME LIMITS This is where you set when and for how long a child (that is, a specified Standard user account that a child will be logging in as) can use a PC. The blue squares represent the hours during which this user account will be inaccessible. You can choose specific times for each day of the week, so you could allow an hour every school-day evening and then a few hours more during the weekend, blocking off the PC after bedtime and in the morning. To change a schedule, once you've dragged the mouse over a block of hours, simply repeat the process to revert them to free hours. By default, a new user account is free all the time.

CLASSIFIED INFORMATION Click on Games in the main Parental Controls panel and you can choose which games each user will be allowed to load, based on their content ratings. The first question is whether a user is allowed to play any games at all; if they are, your next task is to set which age ratings they can access. Remember, an age certificate is just the beginning – different games have different reasons for being awarded certain certificates. Windows 7 acknowledges this, and you can block games that have certain attributes, such as violence, bad language or sexual content. Keep track of the option at the top, which allows you to block games that don't come with a rating.

 EXCEPTIONS You can override the settings you made in step 2 by clicking "Block or Allow specific games". This presents you with a list of all the games currently installed on your system. Here, it doesn't matter what age or content restrictions you may already have set up: if you click Always Allow, this user will be able to load the specified game. The games that come supplied with Windows 7 are a tame bunch, and none is rated unsuitable for anyone over the age of three, but this is a good place to experiment with your settings.

BLOCKING APPLICATIONS It's unlikely that you have many applications (as opposed to games or documents) on your PC that you wouldn't want a child to access, but by clicking Block and Allow specific programs, and then choosing the second option, you can see a list of those available and choose which to prohibit. You might want to block high-end apps such as Microsoft Excel as part of protecting your work content, or restrict programs that access the internet, such as web browsers, while allowing common applications such as Microsoft Word and essentials such as virus scanners. In the unlikely event that an application you want to block isn't in the list, click Browse at the foot of the screen and navigate to the program's application file (the file that its shortcut in the Start menu points to) to block it.

HOW LONG?
Five minutes; longer for lots of users or if you want to set up a complex barrage of controls.

HOW HARD?
Easy. And if you do get stuck, you can always ask a teenager to help. No, hang on a minute...

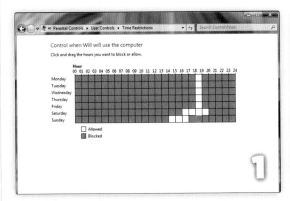

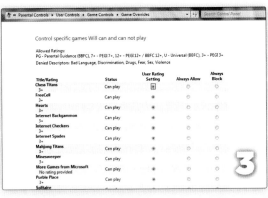

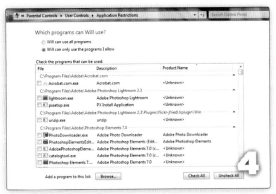

THERE'S SOME DODGY STUFF ON THE INTERNET, BUT WINDOWS 7'S VERSATILE FILTERING AND MONITORING SYSTEM HELPS KEEP IT AWAY FROM YOUR KIDS.

Windows Live Family Safety

Parental Controls help you ensure your kids don't spend their whole lives glued to the screen, but when they are online there's a chance they could stumble across dodgy content or unsavoury characters. Enter Family Safety, one of Microsoft's Windows 7 Live Essentials (see chapter 5).

It works using Windows Live IDs, so you'll need a free Hotmail or Live account for yourself, as a parent, and one for each child. Once Family Safety is installed, your child simply needs to sign in using the Family Safety applet in the Windows System Tray – either on your PC or their own – and they're protected.

WEB FILTERING Family Safety has three main modules, all configured through the Family Safety website. Web Filtering governs what children can see in the browser. The most restrictive setting blocks all websites except a shortlist of "child-friendly" sites. For older kids, basic filtering opens up most of the web but excludes known pornographic or violent sites, plus pages related to hacking. You can use a custom filter to block other types of page or individual sites.

Since Web Filtering works at the operating system level, kids can't get around it by switching to a new web browser. And it's versatile: if a child finds a site they want to access is blocked, you can enable it immediately by entering your parent password. If you're not around, the child can click a button to have an access request emailed to you, to review and respond to at a later point (or instantly).

ACTIVITY REPORTING The Activity Reporting module shows you which websites each user has visited. You can view details of every page to see exactly what your child has been browsing – or check which sites they've attempted to access but found blocked. If you see a blocked site which is in fact appropriate, you can enable it from here.

Activity Reporting also shows you which programs other than web browsers have been accessing the internet, so it can help you ensure no unwanted communications or data are flowing into or out of your home. You may want to warn your kids if you plan to make regular use of these feature, though: nobody likes being spied upon.

CONTACT MANAGEMENT The third major module is Contact Management. This lets you restrict the email addresses and online personalities with which your child can communicate. While we don't subscribe to the view that the internet is a terrible place full of terrible people, young children using email could get into some confusing situations. Again, if a child finds someone they want to contact is blocked, they need only click a button: you'll receive an access request, which you can approve or deny.

Note that one limitation of Windows Live Family Safety's Contact Management is that it works only with Microsoft services, such as Messenger and Hotmail. If your child uses a different system, such as Google's Gmail, Family Safety can't help you.

Tip

Windows Live Family Safety covers the basics, but some third-party alternatives offer more advanced features. For example, the free Norton Online Family service (http://onlinefamily.norton.com) can monitor children's use of social networking sites, so they can't be lured into inappropriate conversations or give away personal information. There are dozens of options to choose from, so if Family Safety doesn't set your mind at rest, shop around for a package that does.

Family Safety will say no to resources it thinks aren't suitable for kids, but the final decision lies with you. If you're not on the spot to override the block with your password, your child can opt to send you an automated email that you can respond to online to give or deny permission instantly.

HOW TO...
PROTECT YOUR CHILD ONLINE

① INSTALL WINDOWS LIVE ESSENTIALS The Windows Live Family Safety tool is one of the Windows Live Essentials, so you'll need to install it via the Live Essentials installer. You can access this either from your PC or via Microsoft's Windows Live Essentials homepage – see chapter 5 for more information. Once Family Safety is installed, you'll find it in your Start menu under Windows Live. Run it, and the first thing you need to do is sign in as a parent. If you don't have a free Microsoft Hotmail or Live account, you can create one right now.

Once that's done, you'll be ready to configure the software. However, for Family Safety to be useful, you'll also need to create Windows Live IDs for your children. You can do this easily on the Family Safety website; click the link to visit it. Note that Family Safety can only protect a PC it's directly installed on, so if your children use their own computers to access the internet, you'll need to install it on thoise PCs as well as your own.

② CONFIGURE FAMILY SAFETY At the Family Safety website, you can set up web filtering, activity reporting and contact management for each of your children by clicking on the relevant tabs down the left-hand side of the Family Safety website. You'll need to be logged in as a parent to do this. Remember to hit Save after making any changes to the settings.

③ MONITOR THE KIDS Your child now simply needs to log in to the Family Safety client, on whichever PC they're using, and they're free to browse the web without supervision. If you've enabled Activity Reporting, you can later check which sites they've been visiting – and which particular pages within those sites – simply by returning to the Family Safety website, logging in (as yourself) and clicking on Activity Reporting in the left-hand bar. You can filter the access log by date, to make it easier to see the most recent activity, or you can narrow it down by computer or user account.

You'll also see a separate tab for Other Activity. It's worth checking this, as your child could be using software that isn't fully protected by Family Safety. Apart from the risk of exposure to unsuitable content, they could be illegally sharing files (for which you could be held liable), or might even be unwittingly hosting some type of networked malware.

④ MANAGE REQUESTS You can manage your child's access requests from the same page. Click on Requests and you'll see full details of blocked web pages and contacts that your child wants to access. There's a simple dropdown menu that you can use to approve a page or a contact for everyone, or just for that child. Or, of course, you can say no.

HOW LONG?
Ten minutes using the standard settings; longer to set up your own lists of contacts and websites.

HOW HARD?
The Family Safety web interface is clear and simple to use, once you understand the way it works.

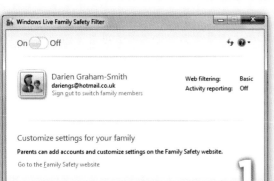

THE ACTION CENTER IS SO HIDDEN AWAY YOU COULD BE FORGIVEN FOR IGNORING IT, BUT IT'S AN EXCELLENT SOURCE OF INFORMATION ON SECURITY.

Introducing the Action Center

Computers are complicated things, and they need a certain degree of maintenance to stay in shape. Unfortunately, we're not all computer experts, and it's not always obvious when something's amiss.

Happily, Windows 7 anticipates this problem. The Action Center automatically keeps track of a range of potential vulnerabilities or problems with your PC – and when there's something you ought to do it gives you clear, non-intrusive advice.

WATCHING BRIEF Think of the Action Center as a watchdog, rather than a valet. It won't fix system problems for you, nor will it automatically scan your system for viruses. It will, however, warn you if it thinks a problem might be arising, and it will advise you to install antivirus software if you haven't done so. It monitors the state of the Windows Firewall (see opposite), User Account Control (p128) and Windows Update (p136), and will also keep an eye on your backup settings.

At the bottom of the Action Center window you'll find two additional useful links: Troubleshooting and Recovery. Troubleshooting brings up a list of common steps you can take to get your PC healthy again, while Recovery gives you a gateway to System Restore, which we cover on p166. If you're unsure what's gone wrong, you can also view an archive of messages Action Center has already displayed to help you track down the problem.

GETTING THE MESSAGE Action Center appears in your system tray (next to the clock) as a white flag. When it has a warning to convey, a red "X" icon appears in front of the flag. Click it and you'll see the message, along with a link to open the main Action Center interface.

No-one likes being nagged, though, and sometimes Action Center might complain about something that isn't really a problem. For example, if your data backups are handled by a third-party application, you won't want to receive warnings that Windows Backup isn't running (see p134). You can fix this by opening the Action Center window, clicking Change Action Center settings and unticking the relevant box.

Don't disable warnings willy-nilly though: Action Center's alerts could be the only warning you get of serious problems, such as virus infections or backup failures.

Tip

If you right-click on the Action Center flag (which sits in the System Tray area of the Taskbar at the foot of the screen, near the clock), you can troubleshoot a problem there and then. Unlike in previous versions of Windows, the troubleshooting tool actually works.

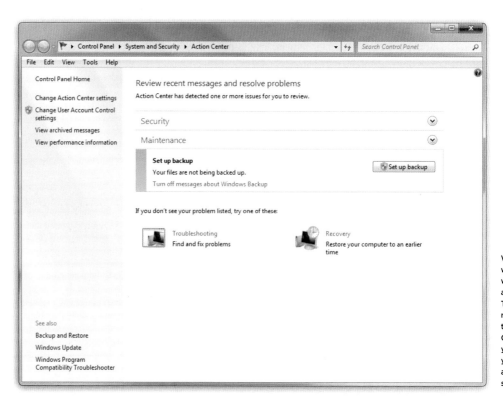

When a small white flag with a red "X" appears in your Taskbar, it's a message from the Action Center telling you to check your security and backup status.

HOW TO...
CONFIGURE WINDOWS FIREWALL

A firewall is a software service that prevents unwanted people and programs from connecting to your PC over the internet. It can also prevent untrusted programs on your PC from opening outbound connections, which can help stop the spread of malware. Every security suite on the market comes with its own firewall (see p132) – some are designed to be simple and friendly, while others are much more complex, and are intended for internet experts. For a typical desktop computer, the firewall that's built into Windows 7 is more than adequate. Here's how to ensure it's set up correctly.

 WHERE ARE YOU? When you connect to a new network, you're asked to define it as a Home, Work or Public location. Windows Firewall is more relaxed if you're at home or at work, as you're less likely to be sharing a network with nefarious characters than you might be at an internet café. Either way, you're told when an application tries to access the internet.

 FIREWALL CONTROLS Access the Windows Firewall controls by opening Control Panel and entering "firewall" in the Search box. To change an application's internet access, click "Allow a program or feature through Windows Firewall". This opens a list of all the apps that have accessed the internet through your system. If you want to alter any settings you may need to click "Change settings", You can then adjust your options. For instance, you might want to make an app available on a public network, or block one altogether. It would make sense to clear both the Private and Public checkboxes, but instead you should use the Remove button below

ALERT! Clicking "Change notification settings" doesn't just affect how often Windows Firewall alerts you; you can also set how paranoid the firewall is. "Block all incoming connections, including those in the list of allowed programs" means your internet access is effectively shut off. At the other extreme you can switch off Windows Firewall altogether using the radio button at the bottom. You'll then be inundated with warnings (although you can disable them) until you turn it back on.

MORE DETAIL Experts can click on "Advanced settings" to filter connections by application or network domain. From here you can also view and edit connection rules in far greater detail. For example, you can allow a connection only if it's secure, and you can define precisely what you mean by secure. And you can selectively grant network access to applications depending on which user is logged in. If that sounds complex, don't worry – for most users this level of control isn't necessary.

HOW LONG?
Most people will be happy leaving Firewall as it stands. Fiddling with it still shouldn't take long.

HOW HARD?
If you adjust settings, be sure you know what you're doing – it's easy to make mistakes.

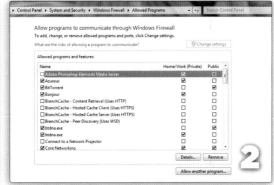

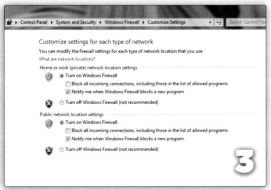

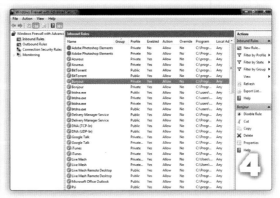

8
Staying safe

Introducing User Account Control

User Account Control – UAC for short – doesn't really have much to do with user accounts, but it's everything to do with control. In Windows 7, when a user or a program wants to make changes to your system, a UAC requester appears, requiring an Administrator to authorise the change.

That may not sound like a big deal, but in terms of security it's a huge improvement over Windows XP. In that operating system, programs had free reign to do what they wanted to your system settings, without your permission and often without your knowledge. This led to all sorts of unwanted software and customisations ending up on Windows XP systems, and provided an avenue for malware to sneak under the radar. In principle, User Account Control should prevent all of that.

Unfortunately, when UAC was first introduced in Windows Vista it popped up far too often, nagging users to confirm even trivial actions such as changing the date. Understandably, many people simply turned it off – leaving themselves just as vulnerable as they had been under Windows XP. The unfortunate souls who couldn't figure out how to kill it had to make do with swearing at it every time it appeared.

BETTER BY DESIGN After that experience, Microsoft could hardly have been blamed for removing User Account Control from Windows 7. But rather than give up, Microsoft set out to fix the problem. Windows 7 still uses UAC, but it's an improved version that's considerably more user friendly than what went before.

The most obvious improvement to UAC in Windows 7 is how rarely you see it. In your first few days with the new operating system you'll probably run into it half a dozen times, as you install applications and customise your desktop, but after that it quietens down. In everyday use you'll rarely see a Windows 7 UAC requester without a good reason.

If you need to make UAC settings more or less strict, this is also far easier to configure in Windows 7 than it was in Vista – as we demonstrate in the box to the right.

In fairness, Microsoft can't claim all the credit for toning down the UAC nagging. Since Windows Vista was launched in 2007, software developers have had several years to learn how to take account of UAC, and to write their programs in ways that don't cause it to pop up unnecessarily.

Tip

Don't let other users of your main PC have Administrator accounts. Making Administrator-level changes is far too easy, and you run the risk of others rendering your PC unusable. Give them Standard accounts instead – most people won't notice the difference, and UAC will prompt them to ask an Administrator when necessary.

Whenever you initiate an operation that could harm Windows – or a malicious program tries the same thing without your knowledge – the User Account Control dialog will appear to check that you really want the operation to be carried out. You can only proceed by entering an Administrator password.

TAKING ACCOUNT At first glance, UAC may seem like a rather weak sort of protection – just a requester with Yes and No buttons, which does very little to prevent you from accidentally making disastrous changes.

If you think that, however, it's only because you're running Windows as an Administrator. These privileged types see simple Yes and No options in their UAC requesters. When a user logged in with a Standard account tries to do something that's protected by UAC – such as installing a new application, or changing important Windows settings – they'll see a requester like the one to the right, prompting them to enter an Administrator password. Without this password, the operation can't be completed.

As we explained on p44, it's good practice with Windows to have all the users of your PC – including yourself – log in with Standard accounts. This makes it far easier to control your users: you can't, for instance, apply Parental Controls to an Administrator account, since by definition an Administrator can do whatever they like. And when you use a Standard account yourself, it's harder for you to make system-level changes by accident – though, thanks to the way UAC works, you can still change settings if you wish to, simply by maintaining a separate Administrator accound and providing its password when required. Using a Standard account also means that if you leave your PC accidentally logged in, other users can't come along and take advantage.

LIFE WITHOUT UAC If you regularly carry out tasks that provoke UAC warning boxes, and you find the intrusions annoying, you can turn them off. We certainly don't recommend this, but it's easy enough to do. Simply open Control Panel, run the User Accounts utility and click on Change User Account Control Settings. Then drag the slide bar down to its lowest position and click OK, at which point the screen will dim one last time and you'll be asked if you really, really want to do such a thing. If your PC has only recently booted, your new settings may take effect immediately; normally, though, you'll have to restart your PC to be rid of UAC.

Without UAC, you can still use the different privileges of Administrator and Standard accounts to protect your system, ensuring other users log in with Standard accounts and doing so yourself whenever you know you won't need to change system settings or install software. But you'll lose the extra security of UAC when running as Administrator. And Standard users – including you, when you're logged in as such – have it worse. When they try to carry out a task that's normally protected by UAC, they won't be prompted to provide a password: instead they'll just see a message saying they "must be a computer administrator" to perform this task. They (or you) will have to save their work, log out and log back in as an Administrator.

Depending on how you use your PC, this could prove to be more hassle than putting up with UAC in the first place. It really isn't such a bad system after all.

Windows 7's UAC shows four different types of prompt depending on what an application or user is trying to do. They have fairly self-explanatory logos: the quartered shield, reminiscent of a Windows logo, indicates that a function within Windows is trying to start. A question mark indicates an application that isn't part of Windows but has a valid digital signature. An orange shield with an exclamation mark means an unknown program is trying to run, and you should check where it came from. A red shield with a white cross (not shown) tells a Standard user they can't proceed without Administrator access.

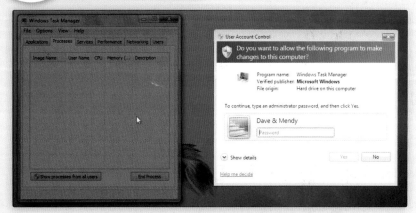

Other users may not be too keen on someone else (you) being in charge of their accounts and applications, but it's in their interest. When a user on a Standard account tries to access someone else's files, run a protected application or make a change to the system, they'll see this screen. At this point, you – the crucial person who knows the Administrator password – will need to authorise the action.

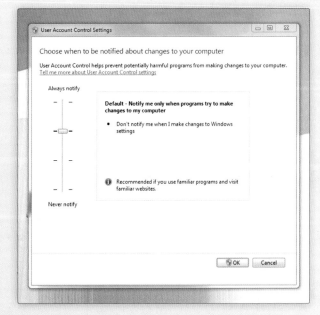

UAC in Windows 7 is quite well behaved on its default settings, but you can make it more or less strict depending on how worried you are. To change it, click the Start button and type "uac", then click on Change User Account Control Settings. On the slider, the higher the bar, the more UAC will appear. The top setting notifies you whenever you or an application make a significant change. The second setting alerts you only when an application makes a change. A lower setting doesn't dim the screen and stop you working, and the final option turns UAC off – after questioning your sanity.

8

Staying safe

 INSTALLING MICROSOFT'S FREE SECURITY SOFTWARE CAN KEEP YOUR WINDOWS 7 PC – AND YOUR PRECIOUS DATA – SAFE FROM VIRUS INFECTION.

Protecting your PC from viruses

Computer viruses are a fact of life. Even Windows 7, with its many security enhancements, isn't immune. On these pages we'll fill you in on the virus threat, and show you how to protect yourself with Microsoft's free security software. Overleaf, on p132, we look at some of the alternatives and explain why you might want to use them.

WHAT IS MALWARE? We hear a lot about computer viruses, but strictly speaking, the big problem these days isn't viruses but other types of unwanted software. So when we're talking about keeping your computer safe, it's clearer to say we're fighting "malware" – a general term for all kinds of malicious software.

Malware can get onto your PC in lots of different ways. The most common way to get infected is by downloading a file from the internet that claims to be a fun game or a useful utility. But when you run it, it infects your system. Congratulations: you've just been tricked by a trojan (named after the Trojan Horse of legend).

Some clever hackers are even able to create web pages that automatically install malware on your PC as soon as you visit the site – this is called a "drive by download." To encourage you to go to these sites, they might send links to your email address, or advertise them on popular websites such as Facebook or Twitter.

Even if you take care to avoid visiting unknown websites, you're still at risk, because the cleverest hackers have been known to break into well-respected websites and plant their own code there – turning the most reputable websites into malware hazards.

A final category of malware you should be aware of is "worms" – programs that can connect directly to your PC over the internet and infect you from afar.

WHAT'S THE RISK? There are millions of different malware programs out there, and they do many different things. Some are just experiments, written by students for fun to see how many computers they can infect. Others have more sinister purposes. Much of today's active malware is designed to harvest online bank details and send them back to the author, who can then use them to transfer money out of your account. A typical way to do this is by silently recording your keystrokes on the keyboard, or by closely monitoring the websites you visit.

In truth, the actual odds of being infected by this type of malware are fairly low. But if you do get struck, there's a lot at stake – and because most malware is designed to be all but invisible, you may not realise you're being spied on until it's too late. Clearly you can't afford to be complacent about the risks.

Tip

Some people avoid running security software because they believe it will slow down their system. But as we reveal on p132, most modern security packages are extremely lightweight, consuming only a small amount of memory and placing a tiny load on your computer's CPU. It makes far more sense to live with this minor imposition than to leave yourself vulnerable to malware attacks.

Microsoft's free Windows Security Essentials can scour your system and eliminate any trace of malware before it ruins your day.

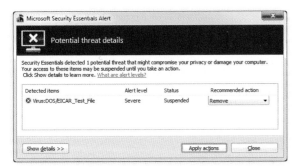

If Security Essentials detects a file it considers a threat, it will immediately block access to it and ask you what to do. You can remove the file from your system, have it quarantined for further investigation or – in the rare case of a false positive – trust it.

HOW CAN YOU PROTECT YOURSELF? Hackers are constantly looking for new vulnerabilities in Windows, so the first step to protecting yourself is to let Windows Update install new security enhancements as they become available (see p136).

You should also pay attention to User Account Control requests (see p128). If UAC pops up unexpectedly, warning you that a program is trying to change your system settings, that's a strong hint that something dodgy is going on. As a matter of course you should deny UAC requests unless you know what caused them.

By far the most effective approach, however, is to install a dedicated security package (often referred to as "antivirus" software, though it will protect you against all kinds of malware). Such software works by forensically examining every file that's opened on your system, comparing it to a vast database of known malware, and automatically blocking it if a match is found. If there's a program that hasn't been recognised but is nevertheless operating in a suspicious way – recording your keystrokes, for example – it will again be blocked.

All this checking has a small impact on performance, but there's no substitute for the protection it provides against online nasties. As a second level of defence, most security software will also perform periodic scans of your hard disk, to ensure that even the files you aren't running don't contain any sort of digital infection.

THE BARE ESSENTIALS There are many different security packages on the market, but a good starting point is Microsoft's Security Essentials package, which provides basic malware protection for free. It isn't installed with Windows 7, but it's available as an "Optional Update" via Windows Update – to get it you might need to open Windows Update and tick the box. Alternatively, you can download it directly from www.microsoft.com/en-us/secuity_essentials.

Once Security Essentials is installed, its malware databases will automatically update each time Windows Update runs, ensuring that Security Essentials is fully up-to-date and able to protect you against the latest malware threats. See the box to the right for a guide to Security Essentials' main features.

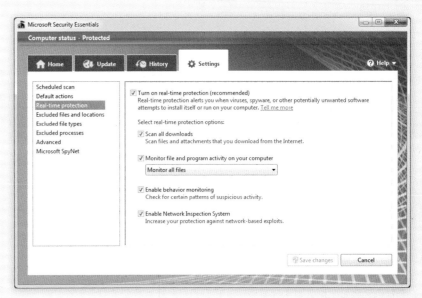

SECURITY ESSENTIALS

Microsoft Security Essentials is a basic tool, but it's still quite configurable. Under the Settings tab you'll find a host of options, divided into categories in the left-hand pane. Under Scheduled scan you can choose how often Security Essentials should conduct a sweep of your whole hard disk for malware. "Default actions" lets you choose what to do when threats are found, based on their severity – for example, you might want to remove confirmed serious threats on sight. As we show above, the next category lets you control Security Essentials' "real-time" protection, and the options below that let you specify if a particular file, folder or program should be excluded from the scan – useful if you run into a false positive. Finally, you can choose to submit information about the threats found on your system to Microsoft's SpyNet intelligence network, and help Security Essentials become even smarter.

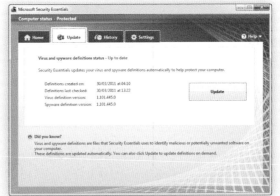

It's important to keep your security software updated, as new types of malware emerge every day. Security Essentials gets its updates via Windows Update, which means most of us will never have to think about it. However, if you've disabled automatic Windows Updates, your security database is in danger of falling behind. You can click on the Update tab to check when Security Essentials was last updated, and launch an immediate update by clicking on the big button at the right.

Security Essentials integrates into Windows' menus, making it effortless to scan a file or folder you don't trust. Simply select the files you want to check with the left mouse button, then right-click and select "Scan with Microsoft Security Essentials...". The main Security Essentials interface will open and show you the program's progress as it checks each file in turn. If it finds anything suspicious, a warning requester will open and let you choose what to do – unless you've already set a default action in the Settings tab, in which case it will be carried out immediately.

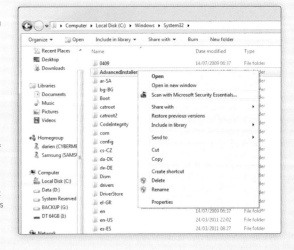

8
Staying safe

Other security software

Security Essentials does a decent job of keeping you safe, and sticking with the Microsoft brand promises a certain peace of mind. But if you're looking for more features, or a different approach to security, there's a huge range of third-party alternatives, both free and paid-for.

FREE SECURITY SOFTWARE There are several independent antivirus packages that are free to use for as long as you like. One popular choice is AVG Anti-Virus Free, which you can download from http://free.avg.com. It offers similar malware detection capabilities to Security Essentials, with a few extra features. Our favourite is the web browser plug-in, which adds security warnings to web searches so you can spot dangerous sites before you click to visit them.

Other options include Avast! (www.avast.com) and Avira AntiVir Personal (www.avira.com/free). Both are lightweight scanners that shouldn't slow your PC down.

There's no catch as such with these free packages, but you will normally have to put up with a certain degree of in-program advertising: their publishers make their money by persuading free software users to upgrade to paid-for packages. Avira AntiVir is particularly intrusive, popping up an advertisement every day to "remind" you that Avira also offers commercial security software.

PAID-FOR PACKAGES If you're willing to pay, you can get a more sophisticated antivirus package. Such packages typically scan the files on your PC whenever your computer is idle, and they're normally updated more often than free programs, allowing them to detect more types of threat as soon as they're discovered.

For more comprehensive protection, consider a complete internet security suite – an integrated software bundle that combines virus protection with a host of additional features. Typically a suite will include a souped-up firewall and parental controls to replace the standard Windows 7 components, plus tools to help you keep your passwords secure. Some packages also include a backup module for keeping your files safe.

When it comes to choosing your package, you're spoilt for choice. One user-friendly range of security software is Trend Micro's Titanium series (http://uk.trendmicro.com). Those who want a few more buttons to press might like to check out the ranges offered by Norton (http://uk.norton.com) or BitDefender (www.bitdefender.co.uk). These are just some well-known names: there are dozens of alternatives. Magazines such as *PC Pro* or *Computer Shopper* test such packages against real viruses, so check out the reviews to help you choose.

A full internet security suite does offer benefits over Microsoft's free offering, with better support, faster virus updates and added features (such as superior parental controls) for good measure.

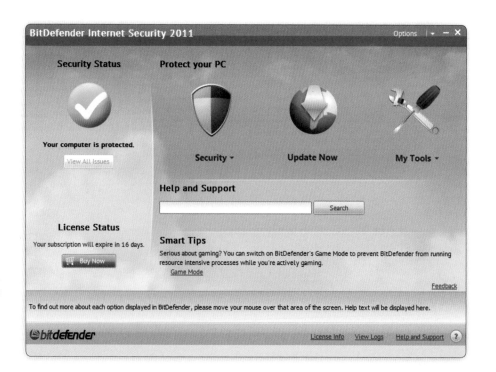

With APC Back-UPS, your digital life goes on...

APC Legendary Reliability

even when the power goes off.

Preserve what's most important to you.

Reliable power backup for 24/7 availability

Whether DVRing your favorite show, updating your Facebook® status, or playing a live networked game, you depend on your home electronics every day, all day. That's why APC by Schneider Electric™ has designed battery backup solutions that protect the constant availability and connectivity you expect...and depend on.

Peace-of-mind protection on two levels

When the power goes out, our popular Back-UPS™ units go to work. They instantly switch your home technologies to emergency power, allowing you to work through brief power outages or safely shut down your systems so you won't lose valuable files—such as digital photos and media libraries. They also feature surge outlets to guard your electronics and data from 'dirty' power and damaging power surges—even lightning. So you get two levels of protection in every APC Back-UPS unit!

Energy-saving insurance for what matters most

Our Back-UPS units protect your home office, digital living and home media applications, notebook computers, DVRs, and gaming application. And since we now offer energy-efficient models that reduce electricity costs through unique power-saving outlets, you can realize true energy savings regardless of the applications you're backing up. Throughout your home, the APC Back-UPS is the cost-saving insurance you need to stay up and running and reliably safeguarded from both unpredictable power and wasteful energy drains.

Keep your electronics up and your energy use down!

ES Series

The ever-popular ES models are priced affordably yet provide enough extended runtime to allow you to work through short and medium power outages. Some power-saving models have been designed to actively reduce energy costs.

The energy-efficient ES Series

The new ES boasts innovative power-saving outlets, which automatically shut off power to unused devices when your electronics are turned off or asleep, eliminating wasteful electricity drains.

BE700G-UK
- 8 Outlets • 405 Watts / 700 VA
- Up to 80 minutes runtime
- Telephone/Network Protection

BE550G-UK
- 8 Outlets • 330 Watts / 550 VA
- Up to 55 minutes runtime
- Telephone/Network Protection

Register today and get a chance to WIN an iPad™!

Visit www.apc.com/promo **Key Code** 87809t • **Call** 0845 0805034 • **Fax** 0118 903 7840

by Schneider Electric

8

Staying safe

WINDOWS 7'S BACKUP AND RESTORE CENTER IS MICROSOFT'S MOST ADVANCED SO FAR, BUT BEWARE OF LIMITATIONS IN THE HOME PREMIUM VERSION.

Setting up Windows Backup

We all have files we couldn't bear to lose, from work documents to photo albums, music collections to TV shows. Windows 7 has a powerful Backup and Restore utility built in for precisely this reason, and all you need to run it is a spare hard disk, network drive, blank DVD or memory stick.

If you've used Vista's Backup tool or third-party software such as Acronis True Image (www.acronis.co.uk), you'll be familiar with how it works. The wizard-based utility takes copies of your chosen files – although, disappointingly, not system or program files – and compresses them all into one smaller file, then stores this in an external location.

When you need to retrieve files, the wizard allows you to browse through them and restore them to your hard disk. You also have the advanced option of browsing and restoring backup sets from any other Windows 7 PC, giving you a useful way to manage backups across several systems.

SET UP AND FORGET When you create a new backup task, Backup and Restore will either attempt to choose your backup files automatically or save and compress every file you select. Whenever the same task is run again, it will only add new or edited files, saving time and disk space. The

original file and folder structure is retained, which is vital for organised files such as a music collection.

Backup and Restore includes a comprehensive scheduler, so you can leave it to run automatically. It can be set to run monthly, weekly or even daily. If your PC is off at the specified time, the backup will run as soon as you log back on, and it runs in the background so as not to disrupt your work. Backup and Restore also includes options for managing the storage of backup sets, so you can delete old backups as well as setting the system to only store the most recent full backup if you're short on hard disk space.

TOTAL PROTECTION Users of Windows 7 Home Premium have a slightly limited version of Backup and Restore, but the Professional and Ultimate editions include an extra option that elevates it to a genuine all-purpose backup tool. It's the ability to image your entire hard disk, so should the worst happen you can boot from the install DVD and restore your system onto a new hard disk exactly as it was when it was imaged. It's a good idea to add this option to your backups every so often as a safety net, and it's enabled by default the first time you set up a backup task.

Tip

Third-party backup software will generally add more features and flexibility, especially if you have Windows 7 Home Premium with its more basic functions. Acronis True Image Home 2011, for instance, adds continuous protection for your data and can even migrate all your data and programs from one installation of Windows to another.

Tip

Backup and Restore also gives you the option to create a System Repair Disc. While not quite as comprehensive as a full system image, this DVD will at least allow you to boot in case of emergency, and includes all the Windows recovery tools you'll need to rescue your vital files. See p170 for more details.

This is the drive to which you're going to back up. Make sure you have enough free space for all your files. If there isn't enough room, click **Manage space** to free some up.

Windows 7 makes it simple to **restore** all your backed-up files or specific ones you need to retrieve.

Creating a **system repair disc** gives you an extra line of defence: should things go horribly wrong, you can use it to restore your PC to a working state.

You can see the time of your **last backup** and if it failed, along with the next scheduled backup time and its contents.

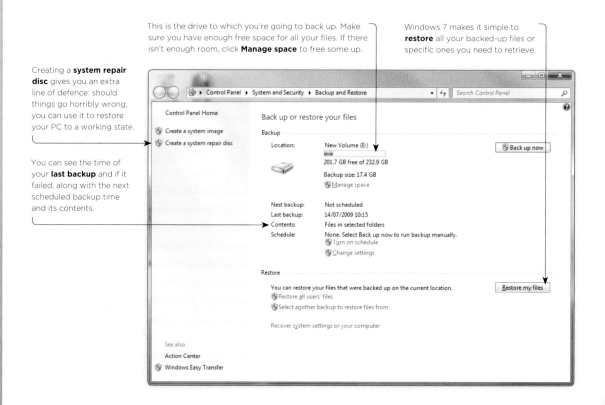

HOW TO...
BACK UP TO AN EXTERNAL DRIVE

 RUN BACKUP AND RESTORE To begin the process of setting up your backup, open the Start menu, go to All Programs | Maintenance, and click on Backup and Restore. In the window that appears, select "Set up backup". You'll be offered a choice of all the storage devices connected to your computer – internal and external hard disks, DVD drives, USB flash memory drives – as well as a button to choose a network location to back up to if you prefer. We'll choose an external hard disk. Windows will offer to select the files to back up, but you're better off ticking the option to pick your own.

CHOOSE YOUR FILES Backup and Restore cleverly makes use of Windows 7's new Libraries, allowing you to quickly back up files of a particular type. You'll want to choose your Music, Pictures and Video libraries as well as the other key user account elements, such as Documents and Favorites. (If you have the patience, you should ideally set up separate backup tasks for your media and for your documents, and have them run at different intervals depending on their importance.) Then, if need be, browse through your main hard disk and add any other folders you'd like to protect. Finally, users running the Professional or Ultimate editions of Windows 7 can choose whether to add a full system image to the backup task.

 SCHEDULE THE TASK Your new backup task will run immediately once it's set up, but you should also schedule it to run daily, weekly or monthly, so that you always have a safe copy of your important files. Before you save your backup task and exit, click "Change schedule". Then choose a day of the week as appropriate, and pick an hour of the day from the dropdown list. Whenever this time is reached, the backup task will automatically begin in the background, so you can continue working undisturbed. If your PC is off at the time, it will run next time you log on. Now that you've scheduled the task, click "Save settings and run backup" to begin your first backup. It may take anywhere from a few minutes to several hours, depending on the amount of data involved.

 RESTORE YOUR FILES If you ever lose any files, it's now easy to restore them. Open Backup and Restore and choose the Restore option at the bottom. It should show any recent backups, or give you the option to locate one stored elsewhere. Restore the entire backup set (or full disk image), or browse through the files you've previously saved to choose which needs to be restored. Then start the restore process and sit back and wait for your vital files to find their way back to where they should be: safe on your hard disk.

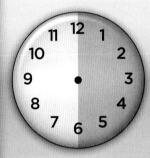

HOW LONG?
Half-an-hour to several hours, depending on the amount of data.

HOW HARD?
It's easy – the wizard takes you through the whole process.

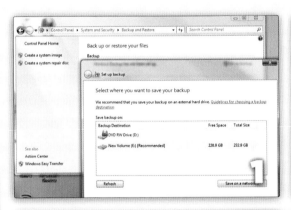

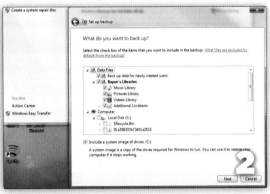

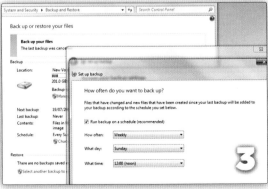

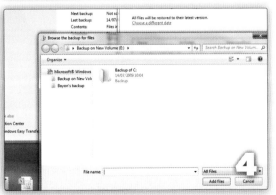

8

Staying safe

IT'S IMPORTANT TO MAKE SURE YOUR SYSTEM HAS ALL THE LATEST SECURITY ENHANCEMENTS AND DRIVERS. WINDOWS UPDATE MAKES IT A BREEZE.

Introducing Windows Update

Once upon a time, installing an operating system was a one-off job: you might run for years with the same system files. These days, computing moves much faster. Microsoft is constantly rolling out improvements, and Windows Update is your gateway to those often important system patches.

WHY DO YOU NEED UPDATES? The main reasons to keep your PC up to date are stability and security. An operating system as huge and complex as Windows 7 is bound to encounter occasional problems with combinations of hardware and software, and that's before you consider the cybercriminals actively seeking ways to break Windows 7's security so they can take over your computer (see p130).

Windows Update lets Microsoft fix a problem and push out the fix right away, so users always have the most stable and secure system possible. Keep an eye on the updates as they arrive and you'll see a regular stream of security enhancements. In fact, some of the most damaging malware infections of the past few years have exploited weaknesses that, for Windows Update users, had already been fixed.

As a welcome side-effect, Windows Update can improve performance by making sure you have the latest versions of the correct drivers for all your hardware. Alongside the critical fixes, it will also deliver "recommended" updates such as new Help files or upgraded device drivers.

AUTOMATIC INSTALLATION When you start Windows 7 for the first time, you're prompted to configure updates. The default is to download and install key updates automatically. This is a great idea from the point of view of keeping your PC up to date, but sometimes after an update is installed Windows needs to be restarted, which can be inconvenient. So you may prefer to let Windows download updates, but hold off installing them until a time of your choosing. Or you can avoid checking for updates altogether. If you take one of these paths, Action Center will warn you that you're not as safe as you could be. Carry out your own regular checks or you'll be vulnerable to emerging security risks.

If you install Microsoft Office or other Microsoft applications, you'll also be given the option to turn Windows Update into a more general Microsoft Update centre. It's worth doing this: Office, too, could be exploited by crooks to gain access to your information unless you keep your security patches up to date.

Tip

Windows is far from being the only piece of software that can benefit from regular updates. You'll find many non-Microsoft products, such as Mozilla Firefox and Apple iTunes, have their own built-in updaters. Use them regularly to ensure everything on your system is running with maximum security and efficiency.

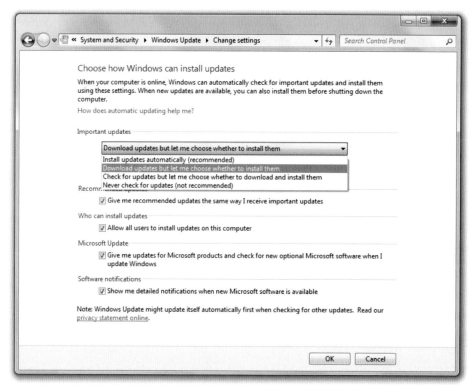

Windows Update can be set to wait for your say-so before installing updates, but it's safest to let it apply patches automatically as soon as they're available.

IN THIS CHAPTER

9
Laptop computing

WINDOWS 7 ON

Laptops are now selling faster than desktop PCs, and Microsoft has stuffed Windows 7 full of features that make it easier to use on the move. In this chapter, we'll take you through some of the key enhancements that have been designed with laptops in mind, including 3G dongle support – which can allow you to surf almost anywhere, even if you don't have access to a wireless

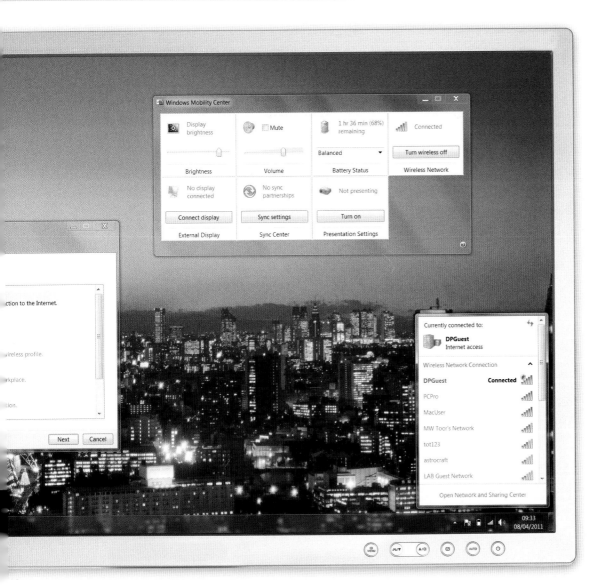

YOUR LAPTOP

internet hotspot – and Windows 7's Tablet PC features. We've also come up with some top tips to extend your battery life, from simple power-management tweaks to more advanced options that could dramatically increase your time between mains sockets. If you want to get the most out of your laptop in Windows 7, the following pages are essential reading.

Laptop computing

IF YOU WANT TO WORK WITH FILES ON A NETWORK OR STORED ON ADDITIONAL DEVICES, WINDOWS 7'S SYNC CENTER IS YOUR FAITHFUL FRIEND.

Introducing Sync Center

The Sync Center is the one-stop destination for keeping all your files up to date on all your computers and devices. After all, with the potential for hundreds of gigabytes of data to be scattered everywhere on your home network and on mobile devices such as smartphones, it isn't practical to keep everything in sync manually.

Sync Center comes to the rescue, ensuring two or more versions of the same file stored in different locations are matched with each other. If you add, delete or modify a file on one computer or device, Sync Center can mirror this on the same file in the other locations that you choose to sync with, whenever you choose to sync.

HOW IT WORKS The most common type of synchronisation will be for mobile phones (see opposite) and files on your network – or, if you own one, a network-attached storage (NAS) device that connects to your router. If you set up a homegroup (see p98), this makes it easy to keep files synchronised between your various PCs.

The simplest way to set up a new sync is to browse to a folder on your network and right-click on it. Then choose the "Always available offline" option. Windows 7 will churn through all the documents in that folder before telling you that it's finished and the files are ready. We suggest you

then create a shortcut to that folder by dragging it to the Favorites category in the left-hand panel of the Explorer window; this makes it much easier to find.

When you start a sync, Windows 7 compares the same files in different locations, determines if any have changed (including files that have been added or deleted), and works out which version of each file to keep, then copies that file to the other locations you selected. It's seamless.

By default, as you'd expect, Sync Center keeps the most up-to-date version of a file and overwrites the older versions with this. If the same file has been modified in two different locations, you have what's known as a "conflict". Sync Center won't try to guess which is the "right" version, but will ask you which version you want to keep and which you want to update.

WHAT YOU CAN SYNC You can sync any type of file, including music and photos from an MP3 player, photos from a digital camera, and contact or calendar information if your mobile phone supports Sync Center.

Not all devices support it, and unfortunately, the only way in which to find out is to plug in your device, install any software that came with it, and see if it then appears in the list of new sync partnerships within Sync Center.

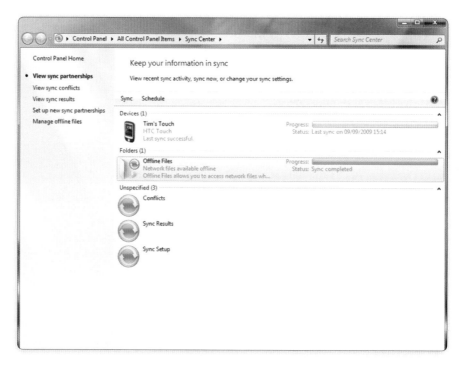

Windows 7's Sync Center automatically keeps selected files and folders up to date between multiple storage locations and devices. It's especially handy with portable devices, although only those based on Microsoft's own mobile operating systems get the full benefit.

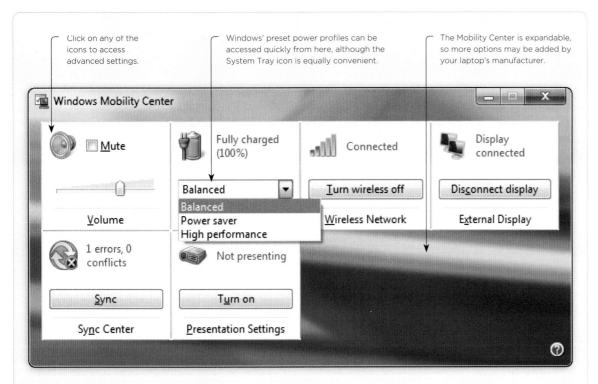

Click on any of the icons to access advanced settings.

Windows' preset power profiles can be accessed quickly from here, although the System Tray icon is equally convenient.

The Mobility Center is expandable, so more options may be added by your laptop's manufacturer.

Introducing
Windows Mobility Center

You can control all your laptop's vital functions, such as brightness and power, in Mobility Center – but it's a collection of shortcuts rather than a proper feature.

Only available on a laptop or Tablet PC, Windows 7's Mobility Center is a central hub for tweaking the most common mobile settings. It's a small window with a variety of tiled options, most of them familiar. To get advanced options for each tile, just click the icon in the top-left corner and you'll be taken straight to the relevant Control Panel page.

SIMPLE OPTIONS The first box adjusts the system volume, and also offers a checkbox to mute the speaker. This is of limited worth, as it's simpler and quicker to click the speaker icon in the System Tray, or indeed use the hardware controls or keyboard shortcuts that are likely to be on your laptop. A similar System Tray shortcut handles power options, but if you prefer to use the Mobility Center there's a useful quick-select box that allows you to choose the preset Power Saver or High Performance modes, rather than the default Balanced.

You can enable or disable your wireless connection from the next tile, and it displays the usual five bars to let you know the signal strength. Clicking the bars takes you to the pop-up window that normally appears when you click on the network icon on the taskbar, so you can connect to any available networks, or open the more comprehensive Network and Sharing Center. Again,

however, we'd question the point of this when you can just click on the Taskbar.

When not on the move, many laptop users prefer to connect to a home or office monitor. With Mobility Center running, plug a display into a vacant video port and click the "Connect display" button. You'll be given the option to duplicate or extend the display or use the monitor alone (switching off the laptop's screen). Tablet users get an extra option to change the orientation from landscape to portrait.

ADVANCED OPTIONS The final two standard tiles may be less familiar. The first is a link to the Sync Center (see opposite). Windows 7 users can use this to keep files up to date between their PC or laptop and other mobile devices; in the Professional and Ultimate editions you can also sync PCs, laptops and devices across a network.

The final tile lets you turn on the extremely handy Presentation mode, which changes the power settings to disable the screensaver, adjust the system volume and switch the current display background to something more appropriate. The system will always stay awake, and system notifications are turned off. These settings can be tweaked by clicking the icon. The only disappointment is that there isn't an option to temporarily hide all your desktop icons, from the standard Windows installation in Windows 7.

FAQ

Q: How do I access the Mobility Center?

A: You can open the Mobility Center in several ways: click on the power icon in the System Tray, then select Mobility Center from the resulting menu; go to the Control Panel and click on "Adjust commonly used mobility settings"; type "mobility" into the Search box; or, quickest of all, hold down the Windows key and press X.

ALMOST EVERY LAPTOP COMES WITH WI-FI, BUT ONLY A 3G MODEM LETS YOU ACCESS THE INTERNET WHEN YOU'RE NEITHER AT HOME OR IN A HOTSPOT.

Using 3G in Windows 7

Walk into PC World or the Carphone Warehouse and you'll be blitzed by offers for 3G mobile broadband. This is a different proposition to Wi-Fi: that technology allows you to connect to your router when you're at home, and to public hotspots such as those in coffee shops. 3G data is more versatile. It gives you internet access more or less everywhere, using the same networks as mobile phones – indeed it's provided by mobile phone providers such as O2 and Vodafone. It's charged like a mobile phone too, with either a monthly or pay-as-you-go contract. The connection is made with a small USB stick, or "dongle", that plugs into your laptop and contains a network SIM card and receiver.

3G DONGLE SOFTWARE Plug your dongle into one of your laptop's USB ports and Windows 7 will invite you to launch the dongle software. The first time you do this the dongle will automatically configure itself; then you'll see all the tools the manufacturer has provided for configuring and monitoring your 3G connection. Typically, you can customise and monitor your connection, check the speed that it's running at, and see how long you've been connected and how much of your monthly data allowance you've used up. A more detailed breakdown is often available, so you can see exactly where you're using up the most megabytes. There will be dozens of advanced settings, too, from updating and connection options to extra services such as text messaging.

MANAGING 3G IN WINDOWS Most users won't need to tinker with the advanced options, and often it's faster to manage your 3G connection using Windows 7's built-in network connections manager instead. To do this, click the wireless internet icon in your Taskbar and click on your mobile operator's network when it appears. If it fails to show, you can click the Network and Sharing Center link, which displays your internet connection and also gives you access to numerous other connection management tools.

To explore more settings, right-click your 3G connection and click Properties, or select the Manage Network Connections link to open a menu containing all of your connections: Windows 7 now groups them together, whether they be wireless internet, 3G or a wired network. Once your dongle has been installed, its security settings can also be handled by the Windows 7 Network and Sharing Center, so you won't need specialist software to get online.

SLOW CONNECTIONS 3G reception is widely available in urban areas, but you can expect slower speeds outside of the cities. Even when you have a strong signal, your mobile internet service will almost certainly be slower than your home connection – the whizzy 3G speeds you'll see advertised are just a theoretical maximum. When you're out and about you'll be lucky to hit half the promised speed. Unfortunately that's just something you'll have to live with.

Tip

3G can be excellent value these days, but compare tariffs carefully and read all the small print. All "pay monthly" deals place a limit on the amount of data you can transfer, with automatic charges for every megabyte beyond this. And think twice before using your 3G dongle when abroad: "roaming" charges can very quickly add up to tens or even hundreds of pounds for what may seem fairly light usage.

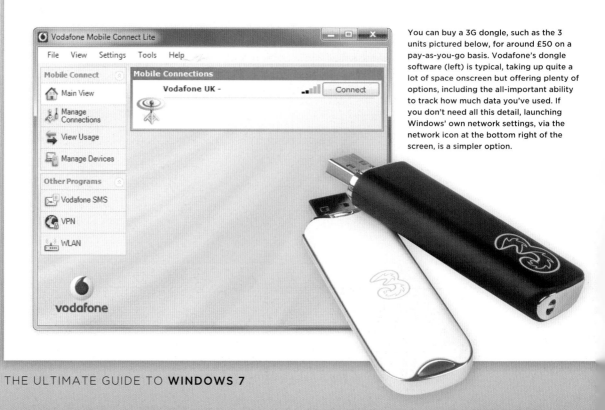

You can buy a 3G dongle, such as the 3 units pictured below, for around £50 on a pay-as-you-go basis. Vodafone's dongle software (left) is typical, taking up quite a lot of space onscreen but offering plenty of options, including the all-important ability to track how much data you've used. If you don't need all this detail, launching Windows' own network settings, via the network icon at the bottom right of the screen, is a simpler option.

9

Laptop computing

Extend your battery life

Windows 7 offers a trio of power plans that can help to either maximise your laptop's performance or conserve power, depending on which is important to you. When the Power Saver plan is selected, for instance, your screen is dimmed, the processor is reined in, and other unnecessary services are halted to help your battery last longer. The High Performance plan goes to the opposite extreme, letting all components do their utmost regardless of power usage.

For most people, the Balanced plan strikes the right, well, balance – upping processor power if need be, but reducing it to a low level when it isn't being pushed. To switch between these plans, simply click on the battery symbol at the bottom right of the Taskbar. You'll initially be presented with the two choices of Balanced or Power Saver. Clicking "More power options" shows others – although you may still need to click on the small downward arrow next to "Show additional plans" to reveal the High Performance option and any custom plans you add.

TWEAK ADVANCED SETTINGS The three default power plans also have further options, giving you more control over your PC's power usage: click "Change plan settings" to access these. At their simplest, these control when the display is switched off and when the computer goes into Sleep mode, but clicking "Change advanced power settings" opens up a new world of tweakery. The list of variables is vast: you can turn off your hard disk after a certain period of inactivity, for instance, or selectively suspend USB ports that aren't being used to stop them draining a trickle of power. You can also tweak your processor, specifying minimum and maximum levels of CPU activity, so that when you don't need all of your system's capability you can throttle down the chip to prevent it draining excessive battery power.

Many of these options can be set to different levels depending on whether your laptop is plugged in or running on the battery, so there's no need to limit your computer's performance when you're on the mains.

REDUCE SCREEN BRIGHTNESS Whether your laptop is a tiny 8in netbook or a mammoth 17in desktop replacement model, a screen running at full brightness is a huge power drain. Turning down the brightness a few notches is one of the most efficient ways to instantly increase your battery life. It's easy to do: most laptops have shortcut buttons on the keyboard to raise and lower brightness, and Windows 7's power management screen has a slider for this.

Tip

A useful setting, found on the Power Options homepage, is "Choose what closing the lid does". This should normally be Sleep, as closing the lid is the instinctive action when you've finished working; when you open it an hour or a day later, it will spring back to life without having run down the battery. However, if you like to listen to music tracks with the lid shut, for example, you'll want to change this to Nothing.

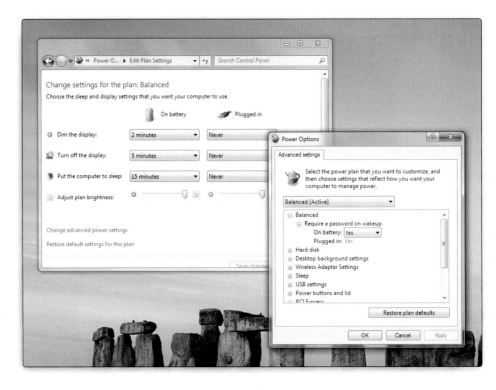

Windows 7 provides three default power plans; you can customise these, for example, to vary how your laptop behaves depending on whether it's plugged in or on battery power. You can also create your own power plan from scratch: go to Create a Power Plan in Control Panel to add a custom plan.

SPRING CLEANING If you're more confident messing around with your computer, it pays to do some laptop housekeeping every so often, because keeping your system clean and tidy can actually help to conserve battery power.

More often than not, unscrewing the bottom of your machine (see, we said you'd need to be confident) will reveal the fan that keeps your processor and graphics chip cool, and some further careful screw removal will let you pry the fan itself away from its mounting. This will allow you to gently clean dust away from the fan and its vents (usually on the side of the machine), which will improve your computer's efficiency and make it use less energy. A dusty PC will need to drive its fan harder because of the hotter, more claustrophobic conditions created inside its case.

DISABLE WIRELESS AND BLUETOOTH The wireless transmitters and receivers inside your laptop draw plenty of power, and if you're not online, they're sitting there draining the battery for no benefit. Some laptops include a hardware switch for turning Wi-Fi on and off, while others use a shortcut key (such as <Fn+F8>). If you know you won't be using wireless networking any time soon, however, you can disable them altogether.

To do this, you'll need to access the Device Manager: a tool that lists, and helps you interact with, all the hardware installed in your PC. To find it, simply open the Start menu and type "device manager" into the search box, then press Return when it appears at the top of the list. When it opens, navigate to the Network Adapters submenu and open that: it shows your laptop's wireless card, Ethernet adapter and any 3G or Bluetooth radio components you may have. Right-click the wireless icon and select Disable to turn off the device and stop it using energy. When you need to use it, just go back and enable it again.

TURN OFF UNNECCESARY SERVICES Your computer loads dozens of services and applications when it's booted up, but how many of them do you use? If you have ten icons sitting in the System Tray but never interact with any of them, the chances are that you have applications and services running that you don't need. Every one of these wastes additional processing power.

To halt applications that you don't need, type "msconfig" into the Windows 7 search box to open the System Configuration menu. The Services tab lists the dozens of small applications that run in the background of your machine: tick the Hide All Microsoft Services box, then disable any others that you don't need. The Startup tab lists all the applications that load when your laptop boots, so simply untick those that are unnecessary. It's easy to reverse this – you just need to go back into System Configuration and re-tick the boxes.

KEEP YOUR SYSTEM ORGANISED It may seem trivial, but keeping your PC organised and its hard disk defragmented can make it run more efficiently, which has an effect on both processing power and battery life. Windows 7's disk

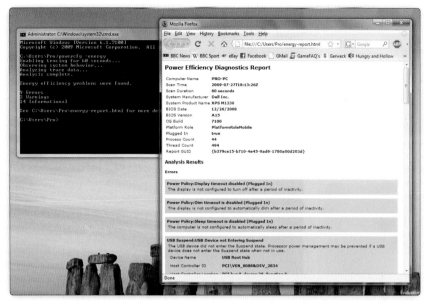

Although it's a bit geeky to use, Powercfg can find extra ways to reduce power consumption.

Turning off devices you won't be using ensures they're not drawing battery power unnecessarily.

Windows loads dozens of small apps whenever your laptop starts up. Removing those that aren't essential can reduce the load on the CPU and thus save energy.

defragmenting tool reorganises files on your hard disk to make them easier for the system to find and faster to access. Type "defragmenter" into the search box to find this tool, then open it and select "Analyze disk" to see if your hard disk could benefit from a little spring cleaning. If you do opt to defragment, this time-consuming operation will be performed in the background, so you don't need to stop working while it's tidying up your PC – although, ironically, it will use up the battery faster while in progress.

Third-party software can also be useful in the fight against clutter. Applications such as the *PC Pro* award-winning CCleaner (www.ccleaner.com) will scan your system for redundant Windows Registry entries, cluttered caches and memory dumps, then hunt down and delete the offending items. The result? A laptop that spends less time churning through pointless files and more time being useful, meaning that you can do more work while expending less energy – and for longer, too.

DELVE A LITTLE DEEPER If you're comfortable using the command prompt, a little-known tool called Powercfg could help pinpoint areas where your battery is using up power unnecessarily. To use this, load the Command Prompt by typing "cmd" into the Windows 7 search box and clicking the first item that appears. When it's loaded, type "powercfg -energy" (with the minus sign, but without the quotation marks) into the box and press Return. The software will run for 60 seconds and then generate a report, which is saved into the root folder of the active user account.

This detailed breakdown of your laptop's energy usage should highlight dozens of ways in which you could trim your power consumption and increase your battery life, as long as you're prepared to get into the nitty-gritty of adjusting various settings. It may be a last resort but, if you're trying to extract every possible second from your battery, it could provide the extra boost you need.

9

Laptop computing

The Tablet PC advantage

Tip

If you'll excuse the pun, this is a TIP tip. On the Touch Interface Panel, go to Tools | Options to tweak the interface. You can choose where the panel docks, to ensure it doesn't block any icons or programs you need; select the thickness of ink and the length of the pause before entering characters; and change the strikethrough gesture from the new "scratch out" back to the old-style Z pattern.

Think of a tablet and you probably think of Apple's iPad – or one of its many imitators. These are handy devices, to be sure, but they're typically limited to running simple, cut-down applications. Windows 7 includes extensive Tablet PC features, so you can run the full operating system, and real Windows applications, on a handheld device.

We've mentioned Windows 7's touchscreen capabilities elsewhere, but that's just one aspect of its tablet support. If your notebook or tablet came with a stylus, you can use the Tablet Input Panel, or TIP, to enter text. It's been trained to analyse your handwriting for more efficient text entry with, hopefully, fewer mistakes – and it learns more about your writing as time goes on. See p61 and the box opposite for more on entering text in this way. When not in use, the TIP docks unobtrusively at the side of the screen.

The stylus can also take the place of the mouse – just tap on the icon or menu you want to select or open. Hover the stylus over the desktop and a dot appears to show exactly where it's located; tap an item and a small ripple appears, with a right-click producing a stronger circle.

These functions are built into the core of Windows 7, so you won't even need Aero to use them – handy if you're running a stripped-down edition that doesn't include the Aero effects, or you've disabled them to help a slow PC cope.

WHAT'S NEW The TIP was first introduced in Windows Vista, and in Windows 7 it's largely unchanged. However, it should now recognise more styles of handwriting, and a new Smart Correction feature makes correcting mistakes far easier than in the previous version of Windows.

Elsewhere, it's possible to enter a URL and then visit that web page, and new visual effects make the on-screen keyboard simpler to use. Predictive text can suggest which word or phrase comes next in your sentence, and mathematical equations can now also be input.

FLICKS AND GESTURES Gestures are more advanced stylus functions that can replicate key presses and other often-used commands. Gestures can be used instead of tab, backspace and spacebar, for instance. A quick flick can scroll a web page up or down, or even copy and paste. These functions can be customised in the Pen and Input Devices section of the Control Panel, which also lists many other gestures. Flicks can be set to one of eight directions and several sensitivity levels, and a practice mode is available.

Also worth investigating are Sticky Notes and Windows Journal: the former creates small notes on your desktop, and the latter is for longer jottings. Journal files can be converted to regular text and are fully searchable.

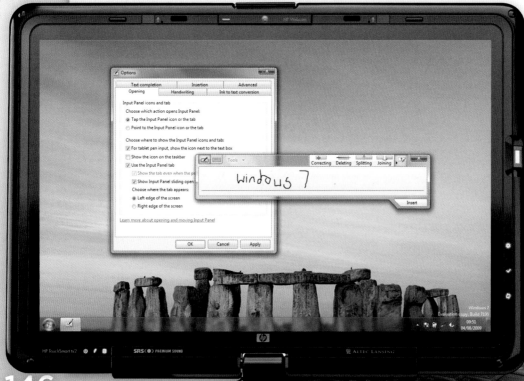

Touchscreen laptops, such as HP's TouchSmart series, offer completely new ways to interact with your computer – and Windows 7 is ready to take full advantage. But you don't have to own a touchscreen to use some of Windows 7's touch-based features. Add a graphics tablet (from a company such as Wacom) to any PC and you can use the same flicks and gestures as if you were working directly on the screen.

HOW TO...
USE HANDWRITING RECOGNITION

The Tablet Input Panel may not immediately impress, but it can be quickly trained to recognise your style of handwriting – and, like at school, it's simply a case of copying out words and letters with your pen.

① START TRAINING Go to Start | All Programs | Accessories | Tablet PC and open the Tablet PC Input Panel. Rather than beginning to write, go to the Tools menu and choose Personalise Handwriting Recognition to begin training Windows 7. Later you can teach it to recognise specific errors, or switch on automatic learning to have it analyse your scrawl as you write, but it's best to start with "Teach the recognizer your handwriting style". You'll be asked whether you'd like to enter full sentences or letters, and led through options that take advantage of Windows 7's improved training and recognition algorithms.

② EASY AS A, B, C The wizard will guide you through eight screens that cover a range of commonly used letters, numbers and characters. The first deals with digits, the second punctuation, and so on. Simply input your letters into the yellow boxes below the characters, working your way through each stage and letting Windows learn your writing style. Unlike with handwriting recognition systems of the past, you're not expected to write in a special way; stick to your usual script and let the software get the hang of it. Once you've filled in every stage, you'll be returned to the main screen.

③ JOINED-UP THINKING Now you've trained the system to recognise individual characters, it's time to move on to full sentences. Choose the relevant options and you'll be presented with a similar interface, but with randomly selected sentences to copy rather than letters and numbers. Again, you should write the words exactly how you would on paper. There are 50 sentences to complete, but you can exit at any time and the training database will still be updated.

④ TROUBLESHOOTING The final option can target specific problems, such as words or letters that Windows 7 frequently misreads when you write them. If you know which word or particular character is proving problematic, you can type it and then write it four times to allow the system to store it in its database. Alternatively, some written shapes may be interpreted to be several different characters – for example, "0", "o" and "O". Once this stage is complete, you should notice an immediate improvement in the accuracy of recognition, but make sure automatic learning is activated to help the system refine its database as time goes on.

HOW LONG?
Ten minutes for basic training, but up to an hour to refine the system.

HOW HARD?
Training is a no-brainer – you just have to copy out text from the screen.

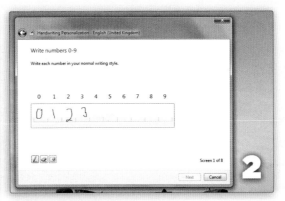

9

Laptop computing

Introducing BitLocker To Go

BitLocker is an encryption system, included in the Ultimate and Enterprise editions of Windows 7, that's designed to protect your entire hard disk from prying eyes. If you're using BitLocker and your laptop is stolen, no-one can access any of the data on its hard disk without the correct password. Even if the drive is removed from the laptop, it will still be unreadable. When BitLocker was first introduced in Windows Vista it had one major limitation: it only worked with fixed system disks, doing nothing to protect confidential data stored on portable hard disks and USB flash drives. In Windows 7, that security gap has been plugged with a new feature called BitLocker To Go.

BitLocker To Go is a godsend for security-conscious companies. System administrators can now stipulate that USB flash drives can only be used once BitLocker encryption has been enabled. Local authority departments throughout the land should take note. A potential benefit for users is that this offers a responsible alternative to banning USB drives altogether, which can be highly inconvenient.

PASSWORD PLEASE Encrypting a drive using BitLocker To Go is simple (see opposite), but think carefully when choosing your BitLocker To Go password. When someone is trying to break into the data on the drive (and that's the eventuality that all this fuss is about in the first place), the strength of the password becomes hugely important: much more so than with, say, a webmail account, where people are locked out after three wrong attempts. If someone

has nabbed your drive, they can leave cracking software running 24 hours a day doing a brute-force attack on your password – that is, trying every combination of letters and numbers – until they hit the right one. The longer and more complicated the password, the less likely they are to succeed.

BitLocker To Go is perfectly happy with spaces in its password, so you can use phrases. A nonsensical phrase is a good idea, since it's long, unique and easy to remember. "I made 12 biscuits, and watched EastEnders!", for example, is a phrase that no human being has probably ever uttered before (so it won't be in hackers' dictionaries) but is easy to memorise once you've thought of it.

Never use proverbs or film quotes, since they'll be cracked in a jiffy. It has to be something you've made up, ideally containing numbers as well as characters such as exclamation marks or question marks. When you set up

FAQ

Q: Will BitLocker To Go take ages? And will it slow down my PC?

A: In our tests, from hitting Start on an empty 1GB drive to the drive being ready took just over 11 minutes. Once a flash drive is encrypted you can use it transparently, dragging and dropping as normal; Windows handles the encryption in the background. On a modern PC we found performance was largely unaffected when using BitLocker. On a five-year-old Core 2 Duo PC, write speed was 11% slower and read speed 5% slower. You'd only notice a difference when transferring huge files.

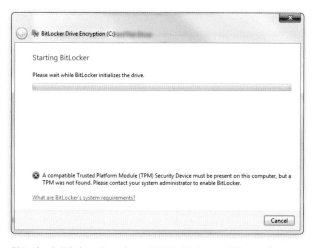

BitLocker in Windows 7 requires a TPM 1.2 chip in your PC before it can encrypt system drives, but you don't need it to use BitLocker To Go.

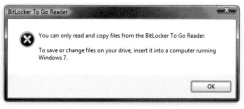

The BitLocker To Go Reader enables access to a drive (with the password); it's offered when the drive is connected if AutoPlay is on. Users can read files but can't write to the drive.

BitLocker To Go on a flash drive, it will stipulate a password of at least eight characters and won't allow anything shorter – we'd recommend a password at least double that length.

THE RECOVERY KEY Once you've entered a password, Windows will generate a recovery key and offer to save it to a text file and print it. The key itself is a 48-character string that you can use to unencrypt the drive without the password if it's ever forgotten. Remember that BitLocker uses strong encryption, so if you do forget the password, the recovery key is your only chance of ever getting your data back. If there's any chance at all you'll forget the password, make sure the key is both saved to a file and printed. Don't carry the printout with the drive.

EASY ACCESS Once your USB drive is encrypted, there's a neat feature you can make use of. If you head to Control Panel | System and Security | BitLocker Drive Encryption, you'll see that the encrypted drive appears with a padlock icon, and there's an option to Manage BitLocker. Click it and, among the obvious options like changing the password, there's also the option to "Automatically unlock the drive on this computer". Click this, and your system will remember the password, allowing you to use the flash drive with this PC (and only this one) without having to enter the password every time you plug it in. So you can use the drive as if it wasn't encrypted, but if it goes astray your data is safe.

VISTA AND XP Although BitLocker To Go is Windows 7-only, you can still access encrypted drives on other Windows PCs, including any edition of Vista or XP. When Windows 7 converts a disk, it creates an unencrypted area on the drive containing a program called the BitLocker To Go Reader. Double-click this (or choose it from the AutoPlay menu) and you'll be prompted to enter the password for the drive. This opens a window showing the drive's contents. You can then view and copy contents from it, but you can't write files back to it, or edit existing files on the disk.

FULL-STRENGTH BITLOCKER We've concentrated on BitLocker To Go here, but what about encrypting your whole system drive using BitLocker? First, go to Control Panel | System and Security | BitLocker Drive Encryption. The resulting window shows every drive on the system; just click Turn on BitLocker to prepare the drive as required.

Note that your PC must have a TPM 1.2 (trusted platform module) on its motherboard for this to work. These are now common on business laptops, but rare in consumer models. Fortunately, you don't need it for BitLocker To Go.

HOW TO...
USE BITLOCKER TO GO

 TURN ON BITLOCKER Connect the drive you want to encrypt, and open the Computer view. Right-click on the drive and select "Turn on BitLocker". The BitLocker wizard starts up, and after a brief pause you'll be asked to enter the password you want to use. Ensure this is a strong password, for the reasons we explain on the opposite page – but make it one you can remember.

 SAVE THE RECOVERY KEY Once you've entered a password, the wizard will offer to save and/or print the recovery key file. Do both. The recovery key is your only alternative to the password should you ever forget it; without either, your data is lost forever. Before the drive can be protected, the whole structure has to be encrypted. This process takes roughly ten minutes for every gigabyte of capacity on the drive, so before you start, make sure you won't need to access anything from it in a hurry.

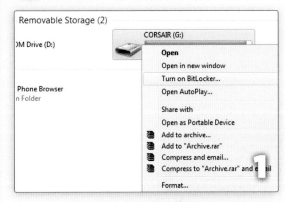

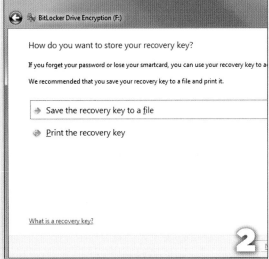

FINISH UP Once the encryption process has begun, pay attention to the warning in the progress box and don't remove the drive without pausing. We'd also be on the safe side and avoid trying to copy any files to or from it either. When the process is complete, the drive will work as before, but all the files it contains will be automatically encrypted as they're written to it. If you take the drive out, when you re-insert it you'll see a dialog box asking for the password. As soon as you enter it, you're away again.

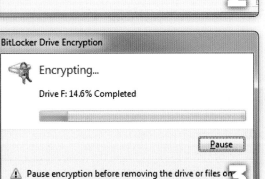

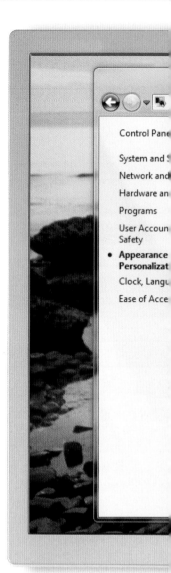

10
Fine-tune Windows 7

FINE-TUNING W

Windows 7 is designed to be easy to use right out of the box, but there are a huge number of ways to tweak the operating system and make it work exactly how you want. In this chapter we look at the Control Panel, which allows you to customise features as diverse as the appearance of your screen, your security settings, your hardware drivers and the way your PC connects to a

ol Panel ▸ Appearance and Personalization ▸   ▾ | 🔍 | Search Control Panel

mily

Region

Personalization
Change the theme | Change desktop background | Change window glass colors
Change sound effects | Change screen saver

Display
Make text and other items larger or smaller | Adjust screen resolution
Connect to a projector | Connect to an external display

Desktop Gadgets
Add gadgets to the desktop | Get more gadgets online | Uninstall a gadget
Restore desktop gadgets installed with Windows

Taskbar and Start Menu
Customize the Start menu | Customize icons on the taskbar
Change the picture on the Start menu

Ease of Access Center
Accommodate low vision | Use screen reader | Turn on easy access keys
Turn High Contrast on or off

Folder Options
Specify single- or double-click to open | Show hidden files and folders

Fonts
Preview, delete, or show and hide fonts | Change Font Settings | Adjust ClearType text

NDOWS 7

network. We examine how to measure performance: is
everything in your system running as well as it should,
and how can you keep it fast and responsive? Finally,
we explore the latest accessibility options, including
High Contrast and the Magnifier. It's all designed to
make sure anyone – young or old, novice or expert –
can get the very best from Windows.

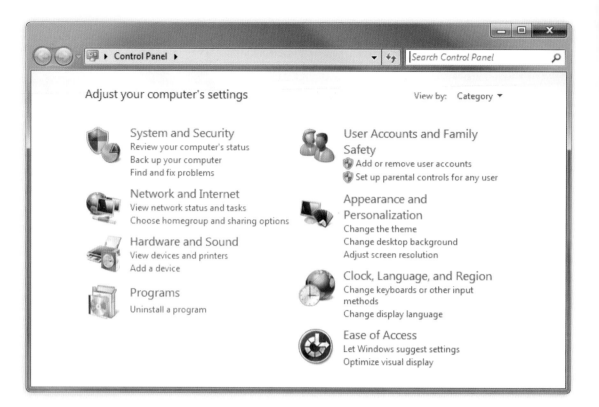

Mastering the Control Panel

The Windows 7 Control Panel lets you adjust hundreds of aspects of your computer's behaviour and appearance. This isn't just a feature for die-hard tweakers: even if you're a novice, you're sure to find settings and options here that will help you make your PC behave just how you want. You'll find a link to the Control Panel in the right-hand pane of the Start menu, or you can simply navigate to Computer in Windows Explorer and click Open Control Panel in the bar along the top of the window.

The default Control Panel view is divided into eight main categories of settings, which we'll discuss below. Beneath each heading are links to some of the most useful tasks.

When you click on a category, the headings move over into the left-hand pane, while the main window shows the various configuration options for the category you chose. These appear in the same format, with shortcuts underneath that link directly to common tasks. The actual categories are a bit loose, so some settings appear under more than one: Power Options, for example, can be found under both System and Security and Hardware and Sound.

You can also access all of Control Panel's features by clicking the dropdown menu and switching from the Category view to one of the icon-based views. Many options can also be accessed from the relevant places within the Windows interface, and anything you can find in the Control Panel can be located with Windows Search (see box, right). Consider the Control Panel simply a handy central repository where you can find all your settings in one place.

A full explanation of all of the settings availble in the Control Panel would fill a book in itself, but here's an overview of the categories.

SYSTEM AND SECURITY This category includes the tools that let you check or change details about the day-to-day functioning of your PC – for example, if you want to know how much memory it has, or modify your Windows Update settings, this is the place to start. You can launch tools such as System Restore or the hard disk defragmenter from here, and configure BitLocker encryption if it's included in your edition of Windows 7.

NETWORK AND INTERNET From here you can access the Network and Sharing Center, which holds all the options you need to check your network settings and configure your home network and internet connection. You can set up HomeGroup (see chapter 6), and change various settings relating to your web browser.

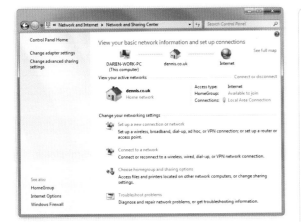

The Network and Internet category takes you to the Network and Sharing Center, where you can alter all of Windows 7's settings that relate to your network and internet connection.

System and Security contains the core settings that govern how your Windows PC works, including how long it waits before going to sleep, when it backs up your files, and how Windows protects you from malware. You can also sort out your hard disk here.

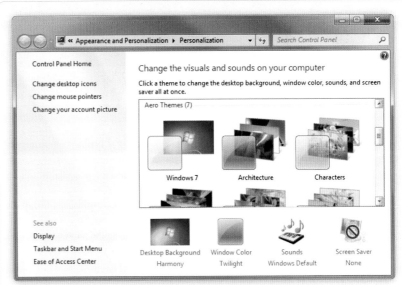

ALTERNATIVE ROUTES Control Panel shows your system settings all in one place, but in everyday use you won't need to visit it often, because most options can be accessed directly from the relevant part of Windows 7. For example, if you want to tweak your desktop, right-click on the background: the menu that opens will contain direct links to Screen resolution, Gadgets and Personalization. If you want to configure your Taskbar, right-click on it and select Properties. The same thing works with the Start button and numerous other elements of Windows.

If you want to tweak your network settings, right-click the networking icon in the System Tray at the bottom right of the screen. From here, you can open the Network and Sharing Center and take control of everything to do with networking.

When you're in a hurry, you can use Windows Search to jump straight to the setting you want. Either use the Search box at the top right of the main Control Panel window, or just open the Start menu and search from there. If you do this, your results will be divided into sections, one of which relates to Control Panel.

For example, if you type "display" you'll see a shortcut to the main Display Properties page, followed by shortcuts to relevant configuration tasks. All the main Control Panel windows, and many of the most common settings, can be accessed in this way, so you can find the setting you want simply by typing one or two words.

HARDWARE AND SOUND Here you can change the way your hardware works: for example, you can set up multiple monitors and manage printers, MP3 players and other peripherals. You can also set what happens when you insert removable media such as a DVD or a flash drive.

PROGRAMS If you want to uninstall a program, or tell Windows to open a particular program when you double-click a certain type of file, this is the place. You can also add or remove Windows components and Gadgets (see p40).

USER ACCOUNTS AND FAMILY SAFETY This is where you create and modify user accounts , and configure file and folder sharing over your home network (see p98). You can also access Windows 7's Parental Controls and manage any passwords that Windows has memorised.

APPEARANCE AND PERSONALIZATION This heading brings together various settings that affect the way you interact with your computer. Links to Display and Gadgets reappear here, and you can customise how the Windows Taskbar and Start menu behave. You can also set Ease of Access options (say, to make text larger for anyone with impaired vision), along with cosmetic settings such as those that control your desktop wallpaper, screensaver and system fonts.

CLOCK, LANGUAGE AND REGION This is one of the most self-explanatory categories. You can set the date, and tell Windows which time zone you're based in. You can also change regional settings, such as your keyboard layout, the format you use for dates and times, and the language in which you prefer to read system messages.

EASE OF ACCESS This final category reveals the same Ease of Access settings that are found in the Appearance and Personalization category, plus speech-recognition options, so you can set up Windows 7 to be controlled without using a mouse or keyboard.

THERE ARE BENEFITS TO USING SLEEP RATHER THAN SHUTTING DOWN FULLY, AND YOU CAN SAVE POWER BY ENSURING YOUR PC SLEEPS WHEN NOT IN USE.

Shutdown and sleep

The most obvious way to switch off Windows is to use the "Shut down" button to the bottom-right of the Start menu. On most systems you can also instigate a shutdown by simply pressing the power button. If you hold it down for five seconds you'll force an immediate shutdown, but be warned you'll lose all your unsaved data.

Click on the arrow to the right of the "Shut down" button and you'll see more options for closing down your Windows session. "Switch user" and "Log off" will both take you back to the logon screen so a different person can use your PC — the difference being that "Log off" closes down all your programs first, while "Switch user" leaves them running so you can switch back to your own desktop later. "Lock" hides your Windows desktop so it can't be accessed without your password. "Hibernate", meanwhile, saves the current state to your hard disk and shuts down.

SLEEP MODE It's the bottom option – "Sleep" – that's the most interesting. When you send your computer to sleep, it remains switched on but suspends all programs and cuts the power to most of its components to almost zero. It also powers down the hard disk and any fans in your computer, and sends a "sleep" message to your monitor, causing the screen to go blank. A sleeping computer looks very much like it's switched off.

The big difference is that, when you start up again, you don't need to wait for Windows to reload. Your operating system is already there – in a suspended state – ready to spring back to life in a few seconds as soon as you move the mouse, press a key or do something else to let your PC know you want to use it. Clearly, most of the time, sleep is more convenient than a full shutdown.

One warning about sleep mode: although the computer may appear to be switched off, there's still power running through its circuits. If you install or remove a hardware component – such as a new graphics card or a RAM module – while the computer's asleep, you could damage it. Always make sure your PC is fully switched off before you open the case: we suggest you unplug it from the mains to be absolutely certain, and if it's a laptop you should remove the battery too.

Windows 7 can automatically put your PC to sleep if it detects you're not using it (see opposite), so you get the convenience of a PC that's always available for use while drawing much less power than if you simply left it switched on all the time. A system that draws 200W from the mains when fully powered-up is likely to consume only a few watts in sleep mode – barely more than if it was switched off altogether. That's good for the planet, and for your electricity bills.

Tip

If you get into the habit of always using Sleep, rather than powering down, it's easy to go for days and even weeks without needing to restart Windows. That's great, but sometimes when you install a new application or a Windows Update, the installation can't complete until you reboot. In such cases, you should let the system restart as soon as you get a chance — if the latest updates aren't fully installed, the security and stability of your system could be at risk.

You don't have to make do with Windows 7's default power settings. You can change what pressing the power button does, for instance, and if you're worried that others may use your PC while you're away then force it to require a password when it wakes from Sleep mode.

HOW TO...
SET POWER OPTIONS

Windows 7's default settings will send your computer to sleep after 30 minutes — but you can customise numerous settings, and even set up your own bespoke power plans to make your PC behave exactly as you want in different circumstances.

(1) **POWER OPTIONS** You'll find Power Options in the Control Panel, under "System and Security". In the left-hand pane are some simple options to adjust settings such as when the display is turned off, and how long the computer will sit idle before going to sleep. The main pane is dedicated to power plans. You'll see two pre-configured plans listed, named "Balanced" and "Power saver". A third plan, "High performance", is hidden by default. Your PC manufacturer may have included additional plans too. You can customise these plans to suit your preferences, but we suggest you create a new plan for your personal settings. To do so, click "Create a power plan" in the left-hand pane.

(2) **CHOOSE A TEMPLATE** Windows will ask you which of the existing power plans you want to use as the basis for your new plan. This is just to save you time — whichever option you pick, you'll be able to tweak all its settings later. The "Power saver" plan is designed to keep electricity consumption low at the expense of speed. "Balanced" lets your computer run at full speed when it

needs to. "High performance" keeps full processor power available all the time.

(3) **SET BASIC OPTIONS** On the next page, you can set how long Windows waits before turning off the monitor and putting the computer to sleep. Choose these intervals and click "Create" to start using your new plan. You'll now see your new power plan listed in the main Power Options window. If your priorities change at a later date, you can always come back to this page and switch back to one of the predefined plans — or create more plans of your own.

(4) **SET ADVANCED OPTIONS** You can take more control over your power settings. Click on the "Change plan settings" link to the right of your new power plan, then click "Change advanced power settings". The window that opens lets you configure many additional settings, such as how long Windows should wait before spinning down the hard disk, and whether Windows should sleep or shut down when you press the power button. Some of these settings require a certain degree of technical understanding: if you're not sure what a setting does, click on the "?" icon in the top-right of the window to open Windows Help. This should help you decide whether or not to change a particular setting.

HOW LONG?
If this is the first time you've configured power options, allow 15 minutes.

HOW HARD?
It's easy to change settings, but some of the options available to you are quite technical.

Tip

When a laptop PC is in sleep mode, it's still drawing a small amount of power from the battery — so you could come back to your laptop after a break and find it dead. One solution is to enable "Hybrid sleep", available under "Advanced power options", which will force it to hibernate if your battery runs low.

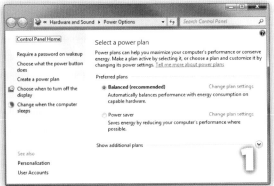

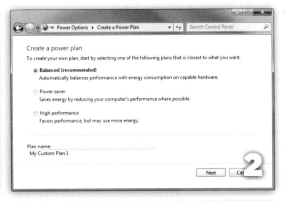

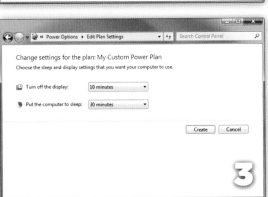

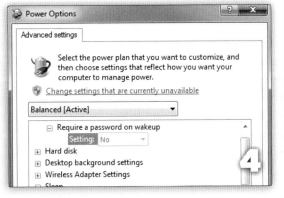

10

Fine-tune Windows 7

Keeping an eye on performance

Windows 7 has tools to help you track your computer's performance and isolate which, if any, of the components in your system are struggling. What's more, with a little know-how you can monitor your applications and see which ones are hogging resources. Using that knowledge, you can make decisions about which applications you might ditch and which parts of your PC might be due for an upgrade.

ARE YOU EXPERIENCED? The Windows Experience Index is effectively an internal benchmark, running a sequence of tests on your PC to assess the key system components. The index breaks these down into five categories – Processor, Memory (RAM), Graphics, Gaming graphics and Primary hard disk – and awards each a score from 1.0 to 7.9. The lowest of these scores, rather meanly, is your Base score.

The Experience Index is of particular interest to gamers. In older versions of Windows, finding out whether a game would run meant checking its requirements against your system, component by component. The Experience Index does all this work for you, as games now list their required Index scores in the Windows Games Explorer, and you can easily compare them with your own results. It's a shame more game publishers don't print these scores where they would be most useful: on the box.

PERFORMANCE ART When you need to dig deeper, click on "Advanced tools" in the Performance Information and Tools dialog box. Performance Monitor helps you analyse system bottlenecks over time. It logs data and presents it on a graph. By default, it tracks just one metric, "% Processor Time" – the percentage of time the processor is busy. This should rarely exceed 70% on most PCs. Press the "+" button above the main graph window to select Counters for other aspects of processor performance plus memory, network and hard disk statistics. The list is long, so the trick is to be sparing. The more Counters you select, the more convoluted and hard to read the graph becomes.

Add the Counters you want, then click on the left-hand pane and go to Action | New | Data Collector Set. Run through the wizard, giving your log a name and a location. Leave the "Run as:" option set to <Default>, then choose "Start this data collection set now". Click Finish. Performance Monitor works in the background, collecting the requested performance data for your log. To check it at a later date, start Performance Monitor, then click the View Log Data icon, second from left above the graph. Browse to your saved log, then open it to check it out.

The second advanced tool is Resource Monitor, which we run through in detail on the opposite page.

Tip

If your computer feels as if it's calculating its way through treacle, don't fret – as we reveal on the following pages, there are plenty of things you can do to boost its performance. A good first step is to install a system clean-up tool such as the free CCleaner utility – see p83.

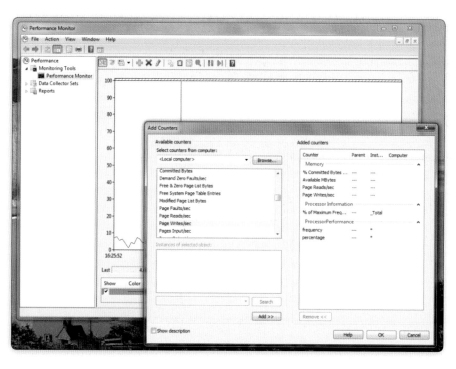

Windows 7's Performance Monitor lets you automatically log a wide variety of system statistics over time, so you can spot where and when problems might be occurring. Interpreting the data it produces can be a rather time-consuming job in itself.

HOW TO...
USE RESOURCE MONITOR

As an everyday tool, Resource Monitor may be more useful than Performance Monitor. Not only does it give you at-a-glance information on how heavily your PC's core components are being utilised, it also shows which applications are hitting them hardest.

1 **GET AN OVERVIEW** The Resource Manager window is split into five tabbed areas. The Overview tab allows you to monitor CPU, disk, memory and network usage at the same time; the small square gauge on each bar provides the most basic data, or you can click on each bar to expand it and get a more detailed view of which processes are using most resources. You'll find the resource hogs at the top of the list, and less demanding apps or processes near the bottom. Meanwhile, the graphs on the right show resource utilisation peaking and dropping as applications load, quit and do whatever you ask them to in between.

2 **DRILL DEEPER** Clicking on a tab drills down to provide even more detailed information. If you want to select a specific process to watch – for example, to see how much CPU power the Google Chrome web browser is using – click on the checkbox next to it in the CPU pane. This will filter out all Services not connected to the processes in question, and give you

a firmer idea of what resources the program as a whole is running. Note, too, the blue line in the CPU total graph and the blue meter in the CPU bar. If you allow Windows to dynamically control CPU speed, usually for power-saving reasons, then the blue bar and line track what percentage of your CPU's processing power is actually available for use at that specific time.

3 **SPOT THE HOGS** The Memory and Disk tabs work along similar lines. The Physical Memory pane in the former tells you exactly how much of the actual RAM installed on your PC is in use at that moment. If most of the bar is green and orange, it might be time to invest in some more RAM. Disk Activity, meanwhile, shows which applications are thrashing the hard disk.

4 **WATCH THE TRAFFIC** Finally, Network Activity allows you to track how much of the available bandwidth between your PC and the network is being used, and which applications are using it. Not only is this a good way to spot if some errant program is tying up your whole connection – even streaming media apps and large downloads should struggle to do that – it's also a good manual check if you suspect dubious programs are streaming large amounts of data upstream. See anything you don't recognise? Google it and find out what it is.

HOW LONG?
The results are instant; understanding them can take a little more time.

HOW HARD?
These aren't tools for beginners, but nor do you have to be a PC genius to fathom how they work.

WINDOWS 7 IS MUCH MORE RESPONSIVE THAN VISTA, BUT WE HAVE A FEW TIPS TO MAXIMISE ITS SPEED AND HELP TO KEEP IT RUNNING SMOOTHLY.

Making Windows 7 faster

We all know the feeling of wishing our PC would run a bit faster. One way to achieve this is with a hardware upgrade – see p160 for our guide to improving performance with new components. But you can often speed up Windows 7 simply by tailoring your software settings. So before you splash out on new hardware, try these free and simple ways to get the best performance out of your existing setup.

COPE WITH LIMITED MEMORY We'd recommend a minimum of 1GB of RAM for Windows 7, and if at all possible 2GB or more. A shortage of RAM is the single biggest factor that will make your PC seem slow – far more so than a slow processor. When Windows runs out of RAM, it uses the hard disk as a fall-back area to store data (known as virtual memory). But the hard disk is much slower to access than memory, leading to a dramatic performance decrease. See p160 for our advice on adding RAM, and switching to a faster hard disk.

If you don't want to open your computer case to add more memory, you could try using Windows 7's ReadyBoost feature instead. This is an option you'll see every time you plug a USB flash memory drive into your system: it tells Windows to use the flash memory as system memory before resorting to the hard disk. In our experience ReadyBoost does very little for performance, but by all means experiment – you've nothing to lose.

If that doesn't help, you can try to make as much RAM as possible available to programs by ensuring it isn't tied up doing unimportant things.

Click the Start orb to show the Start menu, then right-click on Computer and select Properties. The System Properties window will appear, but we want to delve further, so click on "Advanced system settings" in the left pane. The traditional-style System Properties window will appear, with a tab called Advanced. Click on Settings in the Performance area, then choose "Adjust for best performance".

Click OK and prepare for a shock, as Windows 7 turns into a hideous retro monster! The gradients, curves and fripperies of the Aero interface disappear, to be replaced by an old-school angular appearance that predates even XP, looking more like Windows 98. All of Windows 7's advanced features are still available: they're simply now clad in very drab clothes – which take up fewer system resources.

To see how much of a difference is made by this (or any other performance-boosting measure), you can use the Task Manager to monitor system resource usage, as seen on the opposite page. To open Task Manager, right-click on any clear part of the Taskbar and select Start Task Manager.

The bar on the left shows the total **CPU Usage** right now. The graphs show CPU load over time. Since the system here has a dual-core processor, there's one trace for each core.

The more physical memory (RAM) you have free, the better. The **Physical Memory** readout at the foot of the window shows the percentage of RAM that currently remains free.

Processes shows the number of programs running (and potentially competing for CPU time). Click the Processes tab at the top for details.

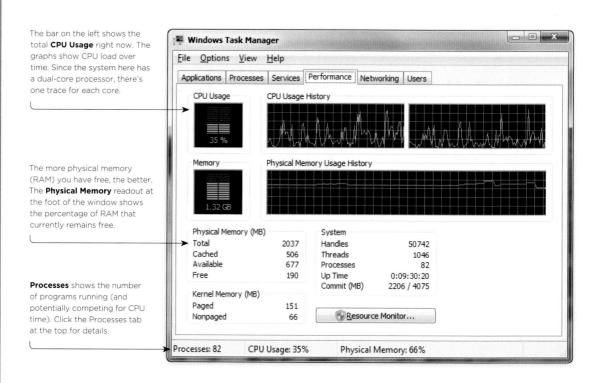

CHECK BACKGROUND TASKS The second way to speed up a PC is to make it spend less time doing things in the background that you didn't know it was doing anyway, and don't care if it doesn't. This can help both to reduce RAM usage and to free up the processor, boosting speed.

In a complex modern operating system there are always dozens of programs running in the background, even on a brand-new PC with a clean installation of Windows 7. If you don't believe us, see for yourself. Click the Start orb, and in the Start menu's Search box type "services", then press Return. After a short pause, you'll be presented with a fearsome-looking list of services.

A service, in this context, is a housekeeping task that runs in the background. On a completely fresh installation of Windows 7 Ultimate edition there are 116 of these, with just under half of them – 52, to be exact – activated and consuming system resources by default.

A note of caution: we're showing you the Services list as an illustration only. Don't alter or disable Services, or your PC may be rendered unbootable. This is under-the-bonnet stuff, and dropping a spanner into an engine is rarely a good way to tune it.

PRUNE STARTUP ENTRIES The best way to get to grips with the programs and services running on your PC is via the System Configuration utility. This handy tool is part of Windows 7, but it's hidden away and doesn't appear in the Start menu. To get to it, you'll have to hit the Start orb and enter "msconfig" into the search box. If User Account Control asks you to confirm your actions, click Continue, and the tool's main window will appear. This is the safest way to prevent unwanted software from running on your PC, but you can still cause problems if you're not careful, so don't fiddle with settings indiscriminately.

What you *can* fiddle with are the program entries you'll see on the Startup tab. On a clean Windows 7 install, there will only be a few items, primarily Windows Defender and a couple of cryptic ones labelled "Microsoft Windows Operating System". The programs listed here are non-critical background tasks – as opposed to Services, which are often critical – that are set to start up when Windows starts. If you come back to this window after a month or two, when you've added some software of your own, you'll probably find there are many more entries here. This is because a lot of third-party software is written by arrogant people who think their program needs to be running whenever Windows is running. But a lot of the time they're wrong.

To get your PC starting up and running faster, uncheck all the program names you recognise but don't want clogging up your system all the time. Or throw caution to the wind, hit Disable All and see what happens. Unlike with Services, you can't mangle your system to the extent that it won't boot. On the other hand, bear in mind that programs such as Windows Defender need to load at startup to be effective, so by turning them off you're opening up your PC to all the internet-borne baddies that Windows 7's security software was put there to guard against in the first place. It

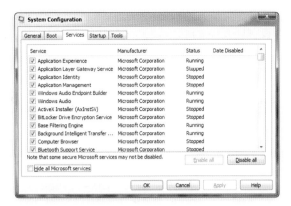

The safe way to eliminate some of the unnecessary chaff that can find its way onto your system is with the System Configuration tool. Any changes you make in the Startup tab are completely reversible – but avoid meddling with the settings in other tabs.

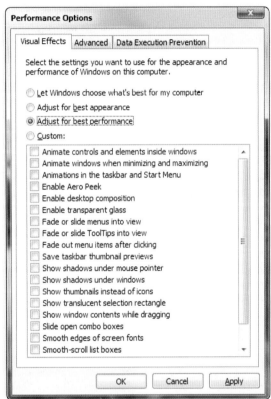

If you're low on memory, you can turn to the Performance Options dialog box. Beware, though, that when you choose "Adjust for best performance" and hit OK, your new operating system will look like Windows 98.

only takes moments for malware to strike.

The beauty of the System Configuration tool is that to reinstate a startup program, you just have to recheck the box next to the program's name; or, if you want to revert to exactly how things were before you started fiddling about, simply click Enable All and then restart the computer.

Tailoring your background tasks in this way can free up your PC's processor and memory subsystems to concentrate on servicing the foreground task – the one you're concentrating on at any given moment, and the one that will make you angry when you have to sit around twiddling your thumbs waiting for. The end result is that your system should seem to work faster, even though the hardware is exactly the same as before. Remember to revisit this technique every couple of months to clear up new detritus that's accumulated.

Boosting speed with new hardware

On p158 we looked at some ways to eke more performance out of your PC by fine-tuning your Windows settings. That can certainly be effective, but if you want a more dramatic speed boost, you'll need to upgrade the hardware. This isn't as hard as it may sound: all you need is a screwdriver and a little understanding of what you're doing. But if you're at all uncomfortable rummaging around inside your PC, we suggest you delegate the task to your local repair shop. The upgrades we discuss on these pages are all simple jobs, and they should be able to do them quickly and cheaply.

THANKS FOR THE MEMORY For Windows 7 to run smoothly your PC needs at least 2GB of RAM, but if you want to run demanding programs such as video-editing tools, or to have lots of windows open at once, adding 4GB will make a big difference. That's the maximum you can install in a 32-bit operating system: 64-bit Windows can go higher (see p13), but for everyday use more than 4GB is probably overkill.

Upgrading your PC's memory is as easy as buying some new memory modules – commonly called called DIMMs (short for dual inline memory modules) – and inserting them in your computer's memory slots. If you have a laptop or an all-in-one these slots can normally be found on the underside or rear of your PC, behind a trap-door secured with a couple of screws. On desktop systems, you'll have to open up the case, which in some cases may invalidate your warranty: check before you dive in. If all your slots are already full, you'll have to remove some existing modules in order to replace them with higher capacity ones.

Modules are normally sold in pairs, so if you want to buy 4GB of memory, look for a pair of 2GB modules. There are lots of different types of module, so make sure you buy the right sort. It's safest to confirm the precise model of your PC with the retailer, or buy from a website that lets you do this, such as that of memory manufacturer Kingston (www.kingston.com).

When you install your new modules, make sure your PC is completely disconnected from the mains. If it's a laptop you should take out the battery too. There's no danger to you from the low voltages inside a PC, but you could damage the computer if you start tinkering inside while there's still power going around the system.

Make sure the modules are installed firmly and correctly into the slots – they have notches to make sure you haven't installed them the wrong way round, and clips to hold them in place. Then replace the cover or case, and power on your PC. The new memory will be automatically detected, and Windows should feel distinctly smoother.

Tip

Memory modules come rated at different speeds: you might, for example, see some modules rated at 1,066MHz while more expensive models are rated at 1,333MHz. This sounds like a significant leap, but the speed of your RAM only has a tiny effect on the overall speed of your system. It's fine to buy the slowest modules that are compatible with your PC: what's important is how much RAM you have, not how fast it runs.

Installing more RAM or a new graphics card into a desktop PC means opening up the case and getting friendly with the motherboard – the backbone of your computer, which joins all the components together. It may look daunting, but the various sockets and connectors are quite distinctive, and they're often helpfully colour coded. If you refer to your manual and take care it's not hard to perform your own upgrades.

A FASTER DISK Upgrading your hard disk won't have such a dramatic effect on performance as upgrading the RAM, but it can make programs start up more quickly, and it can make Windows feel more responsive – especially if you invest in a solid-state drive (SSD for short) that uses memory chips instead of spinning platters.

Replacing the hard disk in a laptop is awkward, though: there's normally only a connector for one hard disk (of the compact 2.5in type), so if you want to replace it you'll have to back up all your data to an external device, then install the new disk in your laptop, install Windows 7 onto it, then recover your data.

On a desktop PC, there are normally connectors for several disks, in either the 2.5in or 3.5in format. All you need to do is mount your new disk in the case and hook up two cables: one comes from the power supply, while the other cable (known as a SATA cable) connects the disk to the motherboard. You can use a free tool such as Macrium Reflect (www.macrium.com) to copy the contents of your old hard disk onto the new one, and either remove the old disk or format it and use it as additional storage.

A NEW PROCESSOR A faster processor can make a big difference if your computer is slow at number-crunching tasks such as creating video files or working with large spreadsheets. Ordinarily, it's not possible to upgrade the processor in a laptop, but in desktop PCs it's a fairly simple operation. To access the CPU socket, first open the case and remove the heatsink, which will be held onto the motherboard by either a lever or a set of rotating clips. The CPU can be popped out by releasing a lever.

Be warned, motherboards generally only support CPUs from a particular family. So, for example, if you currently have a Core 2 Duo processor, you may only be able to replace it with another Core 2 Duo. You can check the motherboard manufacturer's website for a list of CPUs your board supports. If you want to upgrade to a CPU that isn't supported, you'll have to replace the motherboard, which introduces all sorts of complications: at that stage it normally makes more sense just to buy a whole new PC.

If you do replace your CPU, it's worth investing in a tube of thermal paste to squirt between the CPU and the heatsink, to help conduct the heat away. And make sure the heatsink is put back on properly before you reassemble your PC and start using your new processor. Otherwise your system may overheat and become unstable.

OTHER UPGRADES If you're using a desktop PC, you can upgrade many other parts of your system too. Installing a new graphics card, for example, should make the graphics in 3D games smoother. A beefed-up sound card might let you attach multiple speakers for more immersive gaming and movie-watching. With a faster optical drive you can burn data to disc more quickly. Desktop and laptop users alike can invest in a big monitor to gain some more screen space. None of these upgrades will directly improve the performance of your applications; but they can nevertheless make your PC more versatile and more pleasant to use.

CHECK YOUR SPEED

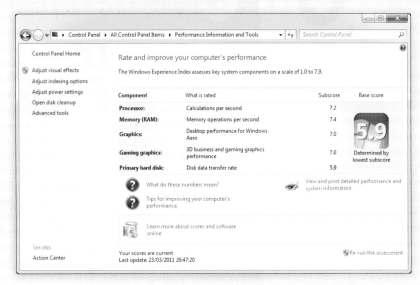

Once you've installed a swanky new hardware component, you'll want to know just how much faster your PC is. A simple measure of this is the Windows Experience Index, which we mentioned on p156. You'll find it in the Control Panel within the System and Security category, under the System heading. It gives a series of performance scores from 1.0 to (strangely) 7.9 in various categories. Click "Re-run the assessment" to update it after a hardware upgrade and see how your performance has changed.

Comparing your PC's performance to other systems is a dangerous game – no matter how much you spend, you'll never catch up with the state of the art. But if you want to do it there are plenty of tools that can help. The free system analysis application SiSoftware Sandra (see p85) comes with a series of built-in benchmarking modules that can reveal the technical capabilities of your hardware. But these "synthetic" performance figures don't always tell the whole story when it comes to what you'll see in the real world.

The best way to quantify the benefit of a hardware is to time how long it takes your PC to perform a given task before carrying out the upgrade – then time it again afterwards. This is what technology magazines such as *PC Pro* and *Computer Shopper* do to measure overall PC performance, using real-world applications such as Word and Photoshop to perform common tasks. Find yourself a stopwatch and a set of your most commonly used applications and you can subject your own system to a similar real-world test.

WINDOWS 7'S ENHANCED ACCESSIBILITY SETTINGS AIM TO MAKE THE NEW
OPERATING SYSTEM A BETTER EXPERIENCE FOR EVERYONE.

Introducing Accessibility Settings

As Windows has developed, so Microsoft has laboured to make it more accessible and easier to use. Anyone with visual impairments, hearing problems or conditions affecting our manual dexterity can have a hard time using a computer in the conventional way, as can those with conditions that affect writing ability or cognitive functions.

Windows 7 builds on the features provided in previous versions to overcome these difficulties, while providing enhanced versions of some core accessibility tools. With these, even people with severe impairments can work, communicate, learn and be entertained using their PC.

These tools and features can be found in the Ease of Access Center in the Control Panel. This provides almost instant access to the main accessibility features, while offering guidance to users who may not know which tools and options can help them.

For newcomers, the best place to start is Recommendations. You're asked five questions relating to your eyesight, dexterity, hearing, speech and reasoning (for example, whether you find it difficult to concentrate or remember). The program responds with a sequence of actions that you can opt in or out of by clicking a checkbox.

Alternatively, a series of "Explore all settings"

options below offer tasks described in plain English, phrased to achieve precise goals such as "Make the computer easier to see" or "Make the keyboard easier to use".

VISION ON For those with visual impairments, Windows 7 offers several useful options. Some are small but effective, such as enlarging the size of text and icons. Others include switching to the simplified white-on-black High Contrast theme and turning on the Narrator and the Magnifier.

The former gives an audio description of the active window, menu items and key presses, although in practice its approach can be confusing, and the American voice slips into such unnatural practices as describing our full stop as a period. Use the settings to control what announcements it makes, however, and the Narrator can be a useful tool.

The Magnifier is more useful to those with less severe vision defects, and has been improved since the version seen in Vista. There's just one spot of bad news: the High Contrast theme won't work with Aero Glass graphics effects – and without Aero Glass you lose not only many of Windows 7's more exciting visual flourishes, but also the Magnifier, which is now powered by Aero Glass. Irritatingly, this means that you can't use two of the operating system's most useful accessibility features at the same time.

Windows 7's accessibility tools include enhanced speech control. If your command isn't immediately recognised, you can have user interface elements automatically labelled with numbers, so that you can quickly select the one you want.

The High Contrast mode is still available, but it doesn't work with the Magnifier – frustrating, if you need both features.

Both speech recognition (dictating text) and speech control (telling the PC what to do) are now easier to use and more accurate, with sensible workarounds to ensure you can make yourself understood.

IN TOUCH Users with hearing difficulties lose out on audio alarms and any other audio feedback used by Windows 7. Luckily, the "Get visual indications for sound" option replaces all those beeps and sirens with graphical equivalents, such as a flashing caption bar or window. There's also an option to get text captions for spoken dialogue, although this works only in programs that support it.

Finally, there's help for those who have trouble using a keyboard or a mouse. Along with options such as Sticky Keys – where you can press keystroke combinations in sequence rather than simultaneously – Windows 7 offers keyboard and mouse filters designed to intelligently assist your movements and weed out rogue clicks and presses. There's also a revised onscreen keyboard for users who work only with a mouse or other pointing device, plus improved speech control and recognition. The onscreen keyboard has a basic predictive text feature, with likely words appearing in easy-to-see slots above the virtual keypad.

Meanwhile, speech recognition goes beyond mere dictation – good as this is – with a speech control system that works on the principle of "say what you see". Speak the name of a button or menu item, for instance, and it should be selected. If that fails, just say "show numbers", and Windows covers active areas of the current window with numbers by which you can then refer to them.

Mention the number of your chosen option, and Windows clicks on that button or link. Such systems used to take hours to train and configure, but Windows 7 makes the process relatively quick and easy, and – cleverly – a series of tutorial and training exercises help you learn the system at the same time as training it to recognise your voice.

HOW TO...
USE THE MAGNIFIER

The Magnifier is a useful tool for anyone who has difficulty reading text on screen. It enlarges the specific area that you need to see so that it becomes easily legible, without reducing your screen resolution.

 ZOOM FOR IMPROVEMENT If you run through the Ease of Access recommendations or pick an option such as "Make the computer easier to see", starting up the Magnifier is one of the suggested actions. You can also switch it on by visiting the Ease of Access Center and clicking the Start Magnifier button in the Quick Access box at the top of the window.

THE BIGGER PICTURE By default the Magnifier works in full-screen mode, enlarging the whole of the current section of the display, with the view shifting as you move the pointer towards the edge of the screen. Clicking on the magnifying glass icon on the screen opens up the streamlined toolbar. The plus and minus keys adjust the level of zoom.

THROUGH THE LENS Click on the Views dropdown menu to change how the Magnifier operates. In Lens mode, illustrated below,

it will behave like a traditional magnifying glass, enlarging the area under the lens, which moves along with the mouse pointer. If you click on the Options button in the toolbar you can increase or decrease the height or width of the lens according to your needs. Making it shorter but wider can help, for instance, when you're reading or writing a long text document.

 ENJOY THE VIEW Switching to Dock mode moves the Lens to a specific area of the screen, although by default it will still magnify the area surrounding the pointer. If you want to change this, click on the Options button and you can command the Lens to track the current keyboard focus or the text insertion point in, say, a Word or Excel document. The Dock mode gives you all the advantages of large screen real-estate, while ensuring you can still see exactly what you're typing.

The Magnifier supports a few keyboard shortcuts which can make your life easier. If you hold down the Windows key and hit the plus or minus keys, your view will zoom in and ou. Hold down <Ctrl+Alt> and press F, L or D to switch between full screen, Lens and Dock modes respectively.

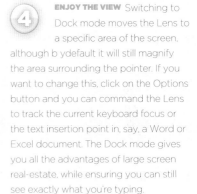

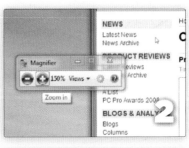

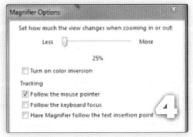

IN THIS CHAPTER

11

Solving problems

SOLVING SYSTEM

By now you'll appreciate that there's lots of great stuff in Windows 7 – not least improvements to stability and security that make it the most hassle-free version of Windows yet. Unfortunately, even in such an advanced operating system, things can go wrong from time to time. The good news is that Windows 7 includes several tools that can help if your PC runs into difficulties. In

PROBLEMS

this chapter, we point out the essential Control Panel settings; show how to fix a compromised PC with System Restore; and explain how to make a System Repair Disc that can help rescue your computer when all else fails. You'll also see how Remote Desktop lets you control your PC from anywhere on the internet, just as if you were sitting in front of it.

WINDOWS 7 IS (PROBABLY) THE MOST DEPENDABLE VERSION EVER – BUT FROM TIME TO TIME, THINGS CAN STILL GO WRONG. HERE'S HOW TO FIX THEM.

Troubleshooting Windows 7

Windows 7 makes it easy to install and configure software and hardware – and to remove it again if necessary. All the same, every so often things just don't work as they're supposed to. We can't give you specific help with the millions of software packages available, but we can show you some basic tools built into Windows that could save the day when a program – or Windows itself – starts misbehaving.

We'll start with the Troubleshooting section of the Control Panel. To open it, look under the System and Security heading in Control Panel and click "Find and fix problems". The first entry in the list that appears (pictured below), Programs, is specifically concerned with software compatibility. Windows 7 largely supports applications written for older versions of Windows, but it does bring new security features and upgraded components, so occasionally older programs may not work as expected. If you've come across one, click "Run programs made for previous versions of Windows", then choose your app from the list. Windows will try to apply the right settings to make it work, and in our experience it usually succeeds – see p56 for more details.

Below this, the Hardware and Sound options scan your hardware and drivers and try to repair anything that isn't working, be it an internal device, a printer or an audio component. Even if Windows can't get a recalcitrant device going, it can often tell you what you need to do to fix it.

You'll also find troubleshooting wizards to help you with networking problems and Windows 7's Aero desktop effects. And finally, under System and Security, there are a few general tools to help you keep Windows running as it should.

SYSTEM RESTORE Control Panel can help with the day-to-day running of your PC, but what if something goes badly wrong when you're installing new software or making a major change to your system settings? The good news is that Windows automatically takes a snapshot of your system before applying such changes, so if you later find that the new program or configuration is causing problems, you can easily roll back your system to its previous state. See the panel on the opposite page for more information about System Restore.

ADVANCED BOOT OPTIONS If the Control Panel can't help you, and System Restore doesn't do the trick, you could try a more advanced approach. Reboot your computer and then quickly, just before the Starting Windows screen appears, press the F8 key on your keyboard. You'll see a menu listing Advanced Boot Options. Some of these options demand technical expertise, so don't select anything you're not sure about. To get out of this menu, use the down cursor key to

FAQ

Q: I want to run System Restore, but if I roll back my computer to last week, won't I lose the files I've created and edited in the meantime?

A: No. System Restore is designed to roll back the operating system, not your files. It won't touch anything in your personal Libraries, nor anything it recognises as a personal data file (such as word processing documents or MP3 files). If you're anxious, back up your files onto an external hard disk or USB flash drive before running System Restore.

In the **Control Panel**, click the link labelled "Find and fix problems" to open this collection of system troubleshooting options.

If you're having trouble with **older programs** after upgrading to Windows 7, click here to fix them.

Make sure this box is ticked to **update your troubleshooting options** on an ongoing basis with the latest advice.

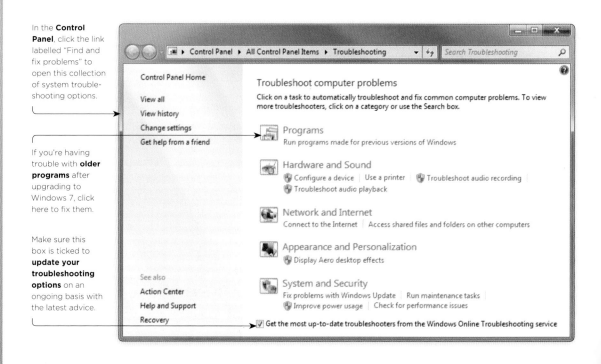

The Hardware and Sound section of Control Panel lets you check the settings and drivers for each of the hardware components of your system, including built-in and external multimedia accessories.

scroll down to Start Windows Normally at the bottom of the screen, then press Return.

If you're having trouble with your display settings, for example, choose "Enable low-resolution video (640x480)". This will launch Windows with basic screen settings, ensuring you can see what you're doing while you make any adjustments you need to. When you next reboot, the settings you've chosen will take effect.

Another useful option is Safe Mode, which loads Windows with a minimum of hardware support and system components. This gets you into the system if a rogue driver is preventing startup, for example, and lets you configure and uninstall software and drivers that are inaccessible in normal use. Again, reboot and the system goes back to normal, with the changes you made while in Safe Mode.

Another way to help deal with situations where the PC won't boot up is to create a system repair disc, as explained in our guide on p155.

PROBLEM STEPS RECORDER If none of these approaches can solve your problem, the maker of your PC or software should be able to offer technical support. But how do you tell them exactly what the problem is? In the past you simply had to describe it as best you could, but with Windows 7's Problem Steps Recorder you can show them.

The tool itself is hidden away in the depths of the Control Panel: the easiest way to find it is to open the Start menu and type "record steps". Press Return to launch it.

Once the recorder is running, just click Start Record, then do whatever you need to do to reproduce the problem. The recorder will start recording the activity on your screen, along with any mouse clicks; if you want to comment on something you're doing, simply click on Add Comment to drop in a note at the appropriate point. Optionally, you can also highlight an area of the screen to illustrate your comment.

When you hit Stop Record, your actions will be saved in an archive, with pictures and a full technical description, which you can easily send to a support engineer to help them diagnose your problem.

USING SYSTEM RESTORE

Whenever something makes a significant change to your system, Windows creates a restore point, saving the state of your PC so that the change can be rolled back if necessary. For example, a restore point is made when you install a new application, or when the system is updated via Windows Update. You can also create your own restore points: to do this, simply select "Create a restore point" from the Control Panel.

By default, restore points are kept for 90 days before being deleted, although if they start to take up too much hard disk space the oldest ones are erased to free up space as needed. You can change how much space is permitted from the System Protection tab of System Properties: click the Configure button to access these settings. If you're very low on hard disk space, you can also disable System Restore altogether from here, but we certainly don't recommend that – it's far too useful to give up.

In System Properties, choose where restore points are stored (if you have more than one hard disk) and how much disk space they're allowed to consume.

POINTS OF VIEW When you launch System Restore, Windows will suggest you roll back to the most recent restore point. It will show you when that point was created, and provide a description of the action that triggered its creation (for example, "Installed Microsoft Office"). This is the action that will be undone if you proceed, along with any other changes you may have made since. If you want to know in more detail what changes will be reversed, click "Scan for affected programs" and you'll see a list of drivers and software packages that will be removed. If you need to go further back in time, you can click the link labelled "Show more restore points" to choose an earlier state. When you're ready, click Next to apply the changes. Windows needs to restart to apply a System Restore, so first save your work in any open programs. When the PC reboots, it's as if your last installation or system change never happened (but see FAQ, opposite).

RECOVERY POSITION Don't confuse Windows 7's System Restore with the "recovery" software that may have been provided with your PC. Such software typically reverts your machine to exactly the state it was in when you bought it – wiping out all your files and settings. This is a last resort if your PC goes haywire, or a way to prepare it before passing it on to a new owner.

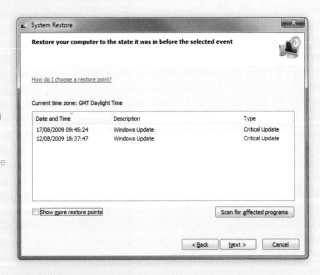

System Restore lists each available restore point along with a brief description of the action that prompted its creation. To go further back, click "Show more restore points". The maximum number of restore points depends on the amount of disk space allocated to System Restore.

WHEN YOU NEED TO USE A PC THAT'S ELSEWHERE, REMOTE DESKTOP IS THE ANSWER – SO LONG AS YOU HAVE THE RIGHT VERSION OF WINDOWS 7.

Introducing Remote Desktop

In chapter 5 we discussed the remote access feature of Windows Live Mesh. It's a great tool for accessing the files and programs installed on a different PC without having to physically go there – a potential godsend for anyone who travels or works from home. However, going through Live Mesh means you can only connect to other PCs that have Live Mesh installed.

If the computer you want to access is running Windows 7 Professional, Enterprise or Ultimate, you have another option. These editions come with Remote Desktop built directly into the operating system.

WHAT IT DOES Remote Desktop works just like Live Mesh remote access: it shows you the desktop of a different Windows PC, and lets you control that computer just as if you were sitting in front of it. You can use it to connect to any other Windows 7 computer in the world – it doesn't need any special software so long as it's running an appropriate edition of Windows, and is configured to allow Remote Desktop connections (see box, opposite).

The only other requirement is that the PC naturally needs to be accessible over the internet. If you're connecting to a home PC, you may need to configure your router to permit this: the site http://portforward.com offers guides to doing this on a wide range of routers. If the PC you want to connect to is at your office, you may need to request access from the network administrator, and get them to confirm the computer's internet address.

Although the remote PC must be running Windows 7 Professional, Enterprise or Ultimate in order to accept connections, the one you connect *from* can be running any edition of Windows 7.

WHAT IT DOESN'T DO If someone else is sitting in front of the remote PC while you're using it, they won't see what you're doing – they'll just see a logon screen showing that you're using the PC. This means you can't use Remote Desktop to demonstrate a procedure to someone. If that's what you want to do, you can use Windows Remote Assistance, which is in the Start menu under Maintenance.

With Remote Assistance, you generate an "invitation", either in the form of an email code or a 12-character password, and pass it on to a friend or colleague. With this code, they can then connect to your desktop, see what you're doing and take control of the system (with your permission). It's very helpful for troubleshooting and collaboration, but both computers need somebody present to send and receive the invitation.

Tip

If you have the option, it's easier to use Live Mesh for your remote connections rather than Remote Desktop. Live Mesh requires no network configuration, it works through most firewalls and routers and supports all editions of Windows 7. If you want to connect to a range of PCs without adding them to your Live Mesh account, try a third-party remote access service such as www.logmein.com or www.gotomypc.com

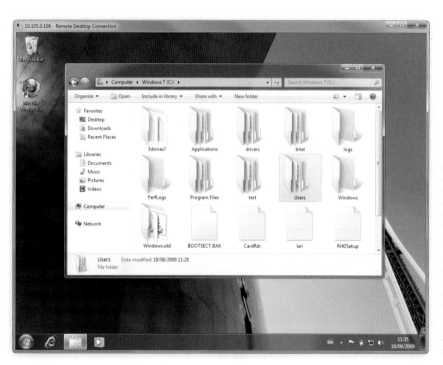

With Remote Desktop you can operate one PC from another, whether it's on the same network or elsewhere on the internet. You can do this from a PC running any version of Windows 7, including Home Premium, but the PC you're going to control must have the Professional, Enterprise or Ultimate edition, and you (or someone with Administrator access to it) must set it up first to accept Remote Desktop connections.

HOW TO...
GET REMOTE DESKTOP WORKING

① ENABLE CONNECTIONS In order to control a PC remotely, you need to configure it to accept Remote Desktop connections. Search for "Advanced system settings". In the Remote tab at the top right, you'll see settings for both Remote Assistance and Remote Desktop. (If you don't, your edition of Windows 7 doesn't support incoming Remote Desktop connections). By default, Remote Desktop won't allow connections. If you want to connect from a PC running Vista or Windows 7, select the bottom option. If you want to connect from Windows XP, choose the middle option.

② SELECT USERS To connect, you'll need to provide the username and password for a user with an account on this PC (blank passwords aren't allowed). Type in the name and password for an Administrator account and you'll be allowed straight in; but Standard users need permission to connect remotely. To grant this, click Select Users, and in the next window that opens click Add. In the dialog box that appears, type in the name of a Standard user to grant them remote access.

③ CONNECT Now try to connect from your other PC. The icon for opening a Remote Desktop Connection can be found in the Start menu under Accessories. If the remote computer you want to connect to

is on the same network as the one you're connecting from, you can just type its name, such as BEDROOM-PC. If it's on a different network you may need to provide an IP address, such as 212.100.242.151. If you want to connect to a home PC in this way, you might need to configure port forwarding on your router – the site http://portforward.com offers help on doing this. To connect to a work PC, you may need to engage the assistance of your IT support staff.

Hit Connect to open the connection and, if everything works as it should, you'll be asked for your remote username and password. Windows might complain that no "trusted certifying authority" has confirmed the identity of your remote PC; click Yes to proceed. Finally, the remote desktop will appear in full-screen view. Click in the bar along the top of the screen to shrink it into a window if you prefer.

④ OPTIONS If you click the Options dropdown menu before hitting Connect, you'll see all sorts of settings you can change, including what the screen looks like and how the keyboard behaves. You can also configure which hardware on your own PC will be available to the remote PC when you're connected. By default, sounds are routed out of your speakers rather than through those connected to the remote PC (which would be pointless in most circumstances), and you can print from the remote PC directly to your local printer.

HOW LONG?
Allow ten minutes to configure user accounts and settings on both PCs.

HOW HARD?
Once you understand what you're doing, and if your two PCs can communicate across the network, it isn't difficult.

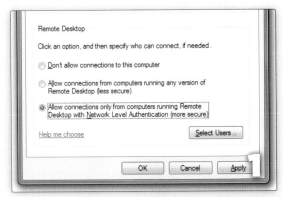

11

Solving problems

Repairing a broken system

It doesn't happen often, but a PC that won't start is a real pain. If you do end up in this situation, there are several steps you can try that may resolve the situation.

If your computer used to work and is suddenly refusing to boot, the question is: what's changed? If you've added (or removed) a piece of hardware, try removing or replacing it to see if that cures the problem. If so, it could be physically faulty, or there may be a problem with its driver.

BOOT OPTIONS If that doesn't help, your first port of call should be the Advanced Boot Options menu. As we mentioned on p166, you get here by pressing F8 before the Starting Windows prompt appears. If there's a problem with your graphics card, you may be able to get into Windows by using the cursor keys to move down to the option labelled "Enable low-resolution video (640x480)". If the problem is with another driver, Safe Mode may work. If you can get into Windows this way, you can use System Restore to roll back your PC to a working state, or try updating hardware drivers or software to see if this helps.

If none of these methods gets you into Windows, another possible approach is to select Last Known Good Configuration from the Advanced Boot Options. This is similar to System Restore, but much cruder: it simply tries to boot the computer using the same drivers and settings that were used last time Windows started up successfully. That means there's a chance it will get you into Windows, from where you can perform more sophisticated troubleshooting.

STARTUP REPAIR If you still can't boot up, your next step is to try Windows' built-in Startup Repair tools. If you can get to the Advanced Boot Options, you can run this directly from the menu; if not, you can boot from the Windows 7 installation DVD and, from the title screen, select "Repair your computer". If you bought a PC with Windows 7 preinstalled, you may not have an installation DVD; in that case, you'll need to create a recovery disc to run Startup Repair. Obviously, you can't do this if you can't get into Windows, so it's a good idea to plan ahead and create the disc now, as explained opposite. (You may, at a pinch, be able to start up from a Vista install disc, although tools such as System Image Recovery may not work properly.)

If none of this works, as a last resort you may have to reinstall Windows 7. If you do this from an original Windows 7 installation disc, your personal files will be preserved in a folder called Windows.old. If you reinstall from a PC manufacturer's recovery partition, your entire hard disk will be overwritten and your files will be gone.

Tip

Before delving into Windows' startup repair options, make sure the problem really is with your hard disk. If there's a DVD in your optical drive, or if you've left a USB flash drive or external hard disk connected, the problem could simply be that your PC is trying to boot from that drive instead, and naturally failing to find your Windows installation on it. Remove any such items and try again.

Even when all seems lost, Windows 7 provides emergency tools that may be able to bring your system back to life.

HOW TO...
USE A SYSTEM REPAIR DISC

① MAKE A REPAIR DISC Creating a recovery disc is easy. You'll find an icon labelled "Create a system repair disc" in the Start menu under Maintenance. Click this and you'll be prompted to select your CD or DVD drive. Insert a blank CD or DVD and click Create; the files will be written, and within a few minutes you'll have a disc you can boot from in case of emergency.

② REPAIR ON STARTUP When you need to use Startup Repair, boot from your new disc by inserting it into the drive before starting the PC. Alternatively, launch the process via the Advanced Boot Options menu or from the Windows 7 installation DVD, as described opposite. You may need to choose a username and type its password before your main options appear.

The menu offers five options. The first is Startup Repair: choose this and Windows will automatically scan your hard disk for operating system installations that might have become inaccessible (this can happen if, for example, you've used maintenance software that's changed the way your computer starts up). Once the Startup Repair process finds Windows 7 on your hard disk, it will try to rebuild the startup sequence so as to make Windows accessible again. In many cases, this is all that's required: hit Restart once it's finished and you may well find Windows is restored to perfect working order.

③ SYSTEM RESTORE From this window you can also launch System Restore or System Image Recovery. We've already covered System Restore on p167: this tool may allow you to revert your PC to a working condition by undoing the changes associated with installing software or drivers. System Image Recovery takes a rather more drastic approach: run it and your PC will be completely restored to an earlier state, obliterating any changes or new files created since then. To use this, you must previously have created a system image within Windows. You can do this from the Control Panel, under System and Security. Images can be saved to an external hard disk, a DVD or a network drive.

④ MEMORY DIAGNOSTICS If your system suddenly stops working without your making any changes, it's possible there's a problem with your PC's memory. The fourth Startup Repair option, Memory Diagnostics, will test your RAM for errors. If any are found, it's best to remove or replace the faulty module.

Finally, you can open a command prompt from which you can run advanced tools with full access to your hard disk. If all else fails, try opening this and entering **bootrec /fixmbr** followed by **bootrec /rebuildbcd**. These commands write new Windows startup code to your hard disk and just might get your PC working again.

HOW LONG?
Creating a recovery disc takes only a few minutes, but saving a system image or testing your RAM could take hours.

HOW HARD?
These procedures aren't difficult, but there are quite a few options to work your way through.

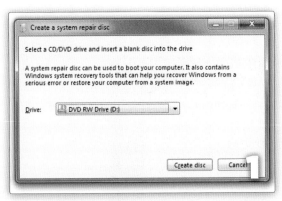

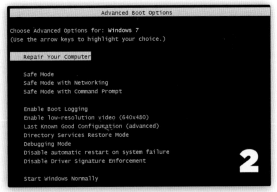

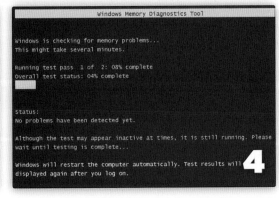

WHETHER YOU DON'T KNOW YOUR UAC FROM YOUR AERO OR YOU JUST NEED TO POLISH UP YOUR PC TERMINOLOGY, YOU'LL FIND THE ANSWERS HERE.

Windows jargon explained

32-BIT/64-BIT Refers to either the processor or the operating system. See p13 for more information.

802.11 The name of the official standard that governs aspects of wireless networking and hardware. 802.11b, 802.11g and 802.11n denote the three types of consumer wireless connections. 802.11b is the oldest and slowest, 802.11g is faster, and 802.11n is the latest and fastest type, now becoming the norm for all new equipment. 802.11n was only recently ratified, so you may see some devices refer to it as "draft-n" wireless.

A

AERO The new look of Windows originally introduced in Vista and enhanced in Windows 7, including transparent window frames (see Aero Glass), live previews of windows (Aero Peek), a 3D carousel of your open windows (Flip 3D), the ability to snap windows to positions within your desktop (Aero Snap), and the option to minimise all windows apart from the active one by giving it a good old shake (Aero Shake). See p52 for full details.

ADSL (ASYMMETRIC DIGITAL SUBSCRIBER LINE) The most common form of broadband internet connection, working over traditional phone lines. Regular ADSL offers maximum speeds of up to 8Mbits/sec; where ISPs have installed new equipment at the local exchange this may increase to 20Mbits/sec. The major alternatives are cable or fibre-optic broadband, which can offer speeds of up to 50Mbits/sec in neighbourhoods served by cable or fibre.

AERO GLASS A subset of the Windows Aero theme, Glass is the effect that makes windows translucent. Not included in Windows 7 Starter edition, and may be disabled in other editions when the PC's processing power is insufficient.

APPLOCKER Unique to Windows 7 Ultimate/Enterprise, AppLocker is a feature aimed at large businesses that want to control exactly what applications can be installed and run by users on its PCs.

B

BIOS The Basic Input/Output System configures your motherboard at startup and boots your PC. It's stored on a flash memory chip on the motherboard; its settings can be accessed by holding a specified key during startup.

BITLOCKER / BITLOCKER TO GO BitLocker and BitLocker To Go are only found in the Ultimate and Enterprise editions of Windows. BitLocker was first introduced in Windows Vista as a way to encrypt an entire hard disk, making it virtually impossible for laptop thieves to access the owner's data. BitLocker To Go is new to Windows 7 and applies the same principle to external disks, such as USB flash drives. See p148.

BLU-RAY The successor to DVD, storing up to nine hours of high-definition video or 50GB of data on a disc.

BREADCRUMB BAR (OR BREADCRUMB TRAIL) A navigation aid in Windows Explorer; each "crumb" shows a folder you've clicked through to reach your present location, and clicking on one takes you directly back to that folder.

C

CPU (CENTRAL PROCESSING UNIT) Also known simply as a processor, the CPU is the component that interprets and executes computer programs. Common CPUs in personal computers include Intel's Core i3 and i5 series and AMD's Athlon II and Phenom II ranges.

D

DESKTOP The primary working area of Windows, visible whenever your screen isn't covered by application windows, and home to Gadgets and shortcut icons.

DEVICE STAGE A new feature of Windows 7, Device Stage is intended to make managing devices such as printers and MP3 players easier. The Device Stage for each device shows a picture and shortcuts to settings and controls, such as a scanner's settings. Theoretically, manufacturers could also provide shopping links here for consumables such as printer inks. See p58.

DIRECTX A set of Windows extensions from Microsoft to accelerate games and other performance-hungry software by allowing them to use your PC's graphics hardware to the full. DirectX 11 is introduced in Windows 7.

DUAL BOOT It's entirely possible to run two operating systems on one computer, for example if you wish to keep Windows XP to run ageing games but use Windows 7 as your main environment. As we explain on p26, you don't even need two hard disks to make this work.

DVB-T (DIGITAL VIDEO BROADCASTING – TERRESTRIAL)
A standard used by Freeview digital TV in the UK, enabling digital TV tuner cards and USB sticks to receive digital programmes through a regular rooftop aerial. DVB-T2 tuners can also receive Freeview HD (high-definition) channels.

F

FAT32 A hard disk format used by older operating systems such as Windows 98 and also devices such as USB flash drives. Windows 7 can happily read and write FAT32 drives, but the more advanced NTFS format is more reliable and is now the standard for hard disks.

FIREWALL Software or hardware designed to protect networks and PCs from hackers, or from malicious software that they control.

FIREWIRE Also known as IEEE-1394 or iLink, this is a high-speed method of connecting external devices such as MiniDV camcorders. It's an alternative to USB, but more popular on the Apple Macintosh than in the PC world.

FLASH MEMORY A type of RAM used in USB memory drives and the memory cards for digital cameras. Flash memory retains its data even when power is removed.

FULL-DISK ENCRYPTION A system that encypts all of the data on a disk, making it impossible for a potential hacker to gain access to the information on it without the password. The encryption may be enforced by a dedicated processor embedded on a PC's motherboard (called a Trusted Platform Module or TPM chip). BitLocker, included with the Ultimate/Enterprise edition of Windows 7, is the brand name of Microsoft's full-disk encryption technology (see p148).

G

GADGETS Small, usually single-purpose programs that live on the Windows 7 desktop. See p40.

GIGABYTE (GB) 1,024 megabytes when referred to in the context of RAM; 1,000 megabytes in the context of hard disks. No one said this would be easy.

GPU (GRAPHICS PROCESSING UNIT) The chip in your PC, either built into your motherboard or onto a graphics card, that handles 3D games, as well as driving your screen display.

H

HARD DISK A form of storage that usually holds all of the data stored permanently within your PC. Usually these are based on spinning magnetic disks inside a metal case, but the newest and fastest drives use memory chips instead: these are known as solid-state drives, or SSDs (see p160).

HDCP (HIGH DEFINITION CONTENT PROTECTION) A form of DRM (digital rights management) used to ensure that PCs and related equipment can play, but not copy high definition (HD) media such as Blu-ray movies.

HDMI (HIGH DEFINITION MULTIMEDIA INTERFACE) A connector designed to carry video and audio signals between high-definition devices.

HDTV 720P, 1080I, 1080P High Definition film and television standards, specifying how much information is encoded in a movie clip or TV show. The numbers refer to the number of horizontal lines in a picture, and whether those lines are interlaced (i) or progressive (p). Higher numbers are better, and "p" is better than "i".

HOMEGROUP New in Windows 7, HomeGroup is Microsoft's name for a technology that allows you to quickly and easily share files and devices between all the PCs and laptops on your home network, even if the printer (for example) is connected to a different PC. See p98.

I

INTERNET EXPLORER Microsoft's web browser. Windows 7 comes with Internet Explorer 8, but this has now been superseded by Internet Explorer 9, which faces strong competition from Mozilla Firefox and others (see chapter 6).

ISP (INTERNET SERVICE PROVIDER) A company that provides internet access to end users.

IP ADDRESS A number assigned to a PC on a network to allow it to be identified, so that incoming data can find its way to the correct computer.

J

JUMP LISTS One of the neatest new features introduced in Windows 7, Jump Lists is Microsoft's term for the dozen or so documents that spring to life when you right-click on a program icon on the Taskbar. Software makers can add extra features to Jump Lists too; for instance, Microsoft's Media Player lets you access playback controls straight from its Jump List. See p38.

L

LIBRARIES A new concept introduced with Windows 7, there are four different types of Library: Documents, Music, Pictures and Video. Even if you store your music in several different places on your PC or network, you can access all of it from the Music Library. See p42.

LIVE MESH A free Microsoft service for synchronising documents across the net and remotely accessing different computers over the internet. See p80.

LIVE PREVIEWS An element of Windows Aero, these allow you to see what's happening in a window or application by hovering the mouse pointer over its icon in the Taskbar.

LOCAL Describes a folder, file or resource that's stored within or connected directly to the PC you're using, rather than on a network or another computer.

M

MEDIA CENTER Microsoft's simple-to-use program for viewing photos, video and TV (and for listening to music). Designed to work with a remote control, but can also be controlled via the mouse and keyboard. At its most powerful in a PC with a TV tuner. See p108.

MEDIA CENTER EXTENDER A device, such as the Xbox 360, that can connect to your Windows 7 PC over a network and output all the music, video and TV stored on it directly to a television or hi-fi. See p114-119.

MEDIA STREAMING See streaming.

MULTITOUCH The capability for a computer or another interactive device (most famously, Apple's iPhone) to translate two or more finger touches into a command. For example, pinch two fingers together on a Windows 7 touchscreen PC running Photo Gallery and the picture will zoom out. Keep one finger down and rotate the other, and the image will rotate with you. See p60.

N

NTFS (NEW TECHNOLOGY FILE SYSTEM) A hard disk format used in Windows NT, 2000, XP, Vista and Windows 7. The successor to FAT.

O

OEM (ORIGINAL EQUIPMENT MANUFACTURER) The manufacturer of an entire PC or an individual component. You can buy so-called OEM versions of equipment and software, including Windows, which are cheaper but will come without manuals or technical support. See p12.

OPTICAL DRIVE A catch-all term for CD, DVD and Blu-ray disc drives.

P

PARENTAL CONTROLS A software system that monitors and controls how your children use your computer. Typically parental controls will restrict internet access to specified times and websites, and limit which applications can be run. Windows 7 has basic parental controls built in, and you can download more advanced controls via Windows Live Family Safety. See p122-125.

PARTITIONS Artificially segregated areas of a hard disk. If you create two partitions, it's possible to install two different versions of Windows (or any other operating system), one on each partition. See p26.

R

RAM (RANDOM ACCESS MEMORY) A high-speed form of memory holding the data and documents that you're currently using. The contents of RAM is lost when the PC is switched off (except in the case of flash RAM).

S

SAVED SEARCHES Folders that contain a set of user-defined search results, which update dynamically as files matching the criteria are added. See p46.

SECURITY ESSENTIALS Microsoft's antivirus tool, not built into Windows 7 but available as a free download via Windows Update. See p130.

SKYDRIVE Not to be confused with Live Mesh, Windows Live SkyDrive is a free Microsoft service that gives you 25GB of online storage. See p78.

START MENU/ORB Pressing the Windows key on your keyboard will launch the Start menu. It's a simple way to access programs installed on your PC, and settings via the Control Panel. You can also click the "Start orb", the circular shape containing the Windows logo that sits at the bottom left of your desktop by default.

STREAMING If you want to listen to a piece of music stored on one computer on another, the simplest method is to "stream" it. Rather than copy the file and save it on the new PC, this process sends the music bit by bit; when you've finished listening, any information is automatically deleted from the receiving PC. If you ever use services such as BBC iPlayer, this uses a similar technology.

SYSTEM RESTORE A way to "roll back" Windows to a previously saved set of settings. By default, Windows 7 takes a snapshot of settings each time a major change occurs, such as the addition of a new piece of hardware. See p167.

SYSTEM TRAY A small area at the right of the Taskbar that's used to show volume settings, network status, and other applications that are running in the background. See p35.

T

TABLET PC A slate-style mobile computer – such as Apple's iPad – that doesn't include a keyboard, instead relying on a touchscreen for navigation and data input. Can also refer to a laptop that includes a touchscreen in addition to a keyboard. See p146.

TASKBAR Arranged by default along the bottom of the screen, the Taskbar is home to the System Tray and Start orb, as well as the Taskbar buttons of programs that are currently running. In Windows 7, you can also pin favourite applications here. See p34.

TCP/IP (TRANSMISSION CONTROL PROTOCOL/INTERNET PROTOCOL) A set of protocols used to transmit data over networks; the fundamental protocols at the heart of the internet. Happily, Windows 7 can normally configure TCP/IP settings automatically, so you don't need to worry about it.

U

UAC (USER ACCOUNT CONTROL) A security feature of Windows 7 that prevents software from making major changes to your programs and settings without your explicit authorisation. See p128.

USB (UNIVERSAL SERIAL BUS) A "plug and play" interface which is used to connect the vast majority of peripherals to a PC. Comes in three versions: the original USB 1 connector runs at 12Mbits/sec, while the upgraded USB 2 can carry a much faster 480Mbits/sec over the same cables. The latest version of the standard, USB 3, supports transfers of 4,800Mbits/sec using new "SuperSpeed" cables.

W

WAN (WIDE AREA NETWORK) A network that extends over a large geographical area, as opposed to a LAN (local area network). A broadband modem's external connection (to the internet) is referred to as a WAN.

WEP (WIRED EQUIVALENT PRIVACY) A common, but flawed, method of encrypting the data sent over a Wi-Fi connection. It gives fair protection but can be broken by a determined eavesdropper. See WPA.

WI-FI The generic term for wireless networks and connections based on the 802.11a, 802.11b, 802.11g and 802.11n standards.

WINDOWS EXPLORER The built-in way to browse your files (and your network) in Windows. Not to be confused with Internet Explorer, which is used for web browsing.

WINDOWS LIVE ESSENTIALS A collection of downloadable software that Microsoft offers free to all Windows 7 users. Highlights include Windows Live Mail, Live Messenger, Live Photo Gallery, Live Mesh, Family Safety and Movie Maker. See chapter 5.

WPA (WI-FI PROTECTED ACCESS) A very secure method of encrypting the data transmitted on a wireless network – you should use this in preference to WEP wherever possible. The WPA2 standard is even tougher again.

The Ultimate Guide to Windows 7

EDITORIAL

Editor
Tim Danton tim_danton@dennis.co.uk

Managing Editor
Priti Patel

Designer
Sarah Ratcliffe

Sub Editors
Gareth Beach, Steve Haines

Original design and layout
Adam Banks adam@adambanks.com

Contributors
Stuart Andrews, David Bayon, Jon Bray, Barry Collins, Darien Graham-Smith, Mike Jennings, Sasha Muller, Dave Stevenson.

Stuart Turton entirely failed to make the tea.

LICENSING & SYNDICATION

International Licensing & Syndication
Dharmesh Mistry +44 20 7907 6100

ADVERTISING & MARKETING

Advertising Manager
Ben Topp +44 20 7907 6625

Digital Production Manager
Nicky Baker +44 20 7907 6056

MagBook Manager
Dharmesh Mistry +44 20 7907 6100

Marketing Manager
Claire Scrase +44 20 7907 6113

MANAGEMENT +44 20 7907 6000

Publishing Director
Ian Westwood

MD of Advertising
Julian Lloyd-Evans

Production Director
Julian Lloyd-Evans

Newstrade Director
David Barker

Chief Operating Officer
Brett Reynolds

Group Finance Director
Ian Leggett

Chief Executive
James Tye

Chairman
Felix Dennis

Index